To R...
The sky is Free*

Dandelion

DANDELION, Vol. I. First printing. June 2024. Published by Image Comics, Inc. Office of publication: PO BOX 14457, Portland, OR 97293. Copyright © 2024 Sabir Pirzada. All rights reserved. "Dandelion," its logos, and the likenesses of all characters herein are trademarks of Sabir Pirzada, unless otherwise noted. "Image" and the Image Comics logos are registered trademarks of Image Comics, Inc. No part of this publication may be reproduced or transmitted, in any form or by any means (except for short excerpts for journalistic or review purposes), without the express written permission of Sabir Pirzada, or Image Comics, Inc. All names, characters, events, and locales in this publication are entirely fictional. Any resemblance to actual persons (living or dead), events, or places, without satirical intent, is coincidental. Printed in the USA. For international rights, contact: foreignlicensing@imagecomics.com. ISBN: 978-1-5343-9754-5

CREATOR AND WRITER — SABIR **PIRZADA**

ARTISTS — MARTÍN **MORAZZO** · VANESA **DEL REY** · ERIC **KODA** · ROY ALLAN **MARTINEZ**
GEGÊ **SCHALL** · THOMAS **CAMPI** · ADRIAN **RIVERO** · JUHA **VELTTI** · MARQUIS **ROGERS**

COLORISTS — JUHA **VELTTI**
JACOB **PHILLIPS**
LEE **LOUGHRIDGE**

LETTERERS — ADITYA **BIDIKAR**
TAYLOR **ESPOSITO**

DANDELION CONCEPT ARTIST — CORWIN **HERSE WOO**

LOGO AND BOOK DESIGNER — BEN **DIDIER**

PIN-UP ARTIST — DAVID **MACK**

COVER ARTIST — TULA **LOTAY**

BACK COVER ARTIST — MARK S. **BRUNNER**

IMAGE COMICS, INC. **Robert Kirkman:** Chief Operating Officer · **Erik Larsen:** Chief Financial Officer · **Todd McFarlane:** President · **Marc Silvestri:** Chief Executive Officer · **Jim Valentino:** Vice President · **Eric Stephenson:** Publisher/Chief Creative Officer · **Nicole Lapalme:** Vice President of Finance · **Leanna Caunter:** Accounting Analyst · **Sue Korpela:** Accounting & HR Manager · **Matt Parkinson:** Vice President of Sales & Publishing Planning · **Kat Salazar:** Director of PR & Marketing · **Drew Gill:** Cover Editor · **Heather Doornink:** Production Director · **Nicole Lapalme:** Controller · **Lorelei Bunjes:** Vice President of Digital Strategy · **Dirk Wood:** Vice President of International Sales & Licensing **Ryan Brewer:** International Sales & Licensing Manager · **Alex Cox:** Director of Direct Market Sales · **Chloe Ramos:** Book Market & Library Sales Manager · **Emilio Bautista:** Digital Sales Coordinator · **Jon Schlaffman:** Specialty Sales Coordinator · **Kat Salazar:** Vice President of PR & Marketing · **Deanna Phelps:** Marketing Design Manager · **Drew Fitzgerald:** Marketing Content Associate · **Heather Doornink:** Vice President of Production · **Drew Gill:** Art Director · **Hilary DiLoreto:** Print Manager · **Tricia Ramos:** Traffic Manager · **Melissa Gifford:** Content Manager · **Erika Schnatz:** Senior Production Artist · **Wesley Griffith:** Production Artist · **Rich Fowlks:** Production Artist · IMAGECOMICS.COM

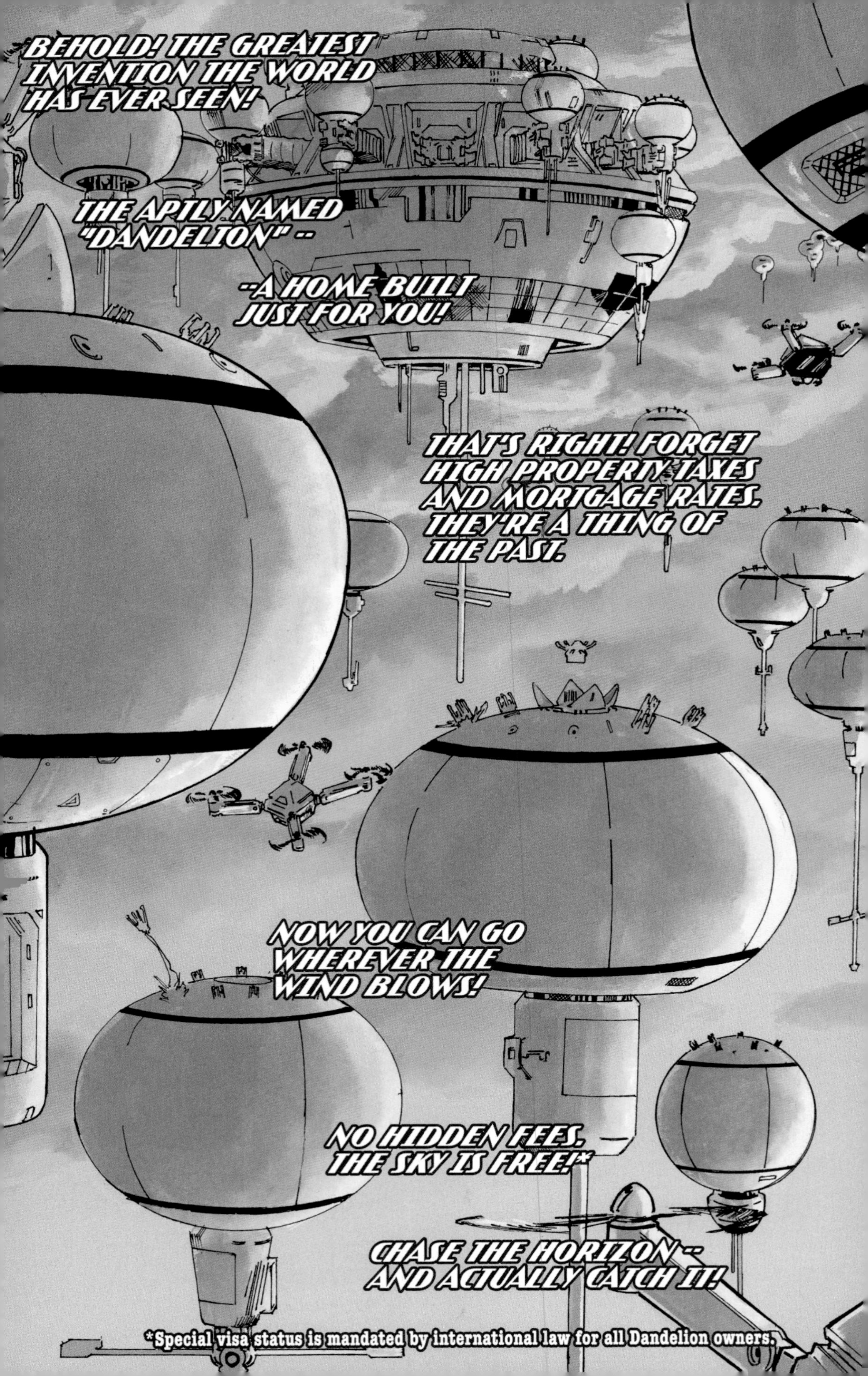
BEHOLD! THE GREATEST INVENTION THE WORLD HAS EVER SEEN!
THE APTLY NAMED "DANDELION" --
--A HOME BUILT JUST FOR YOU!
THAT'S RIGHT! FORGET HIGH PROPERTY TAXES AND MORTGAGE RATES. THEY'RE A THING OF THE PAST.
NOW YOU CAN GO WHEREVER THE WIND BLOWS!
NO HIDDEN FEES. THE SKY IS FREE!*
CHASE THE HORIZON -- AND ACTUALLY CATCH IT!
*Special visa status is mandated by international law for all Dandelion owners.

ONE-WAY TICKET

ART

MARTÍN **MORAZZO**

COLORS

JUHA **VELTTI**

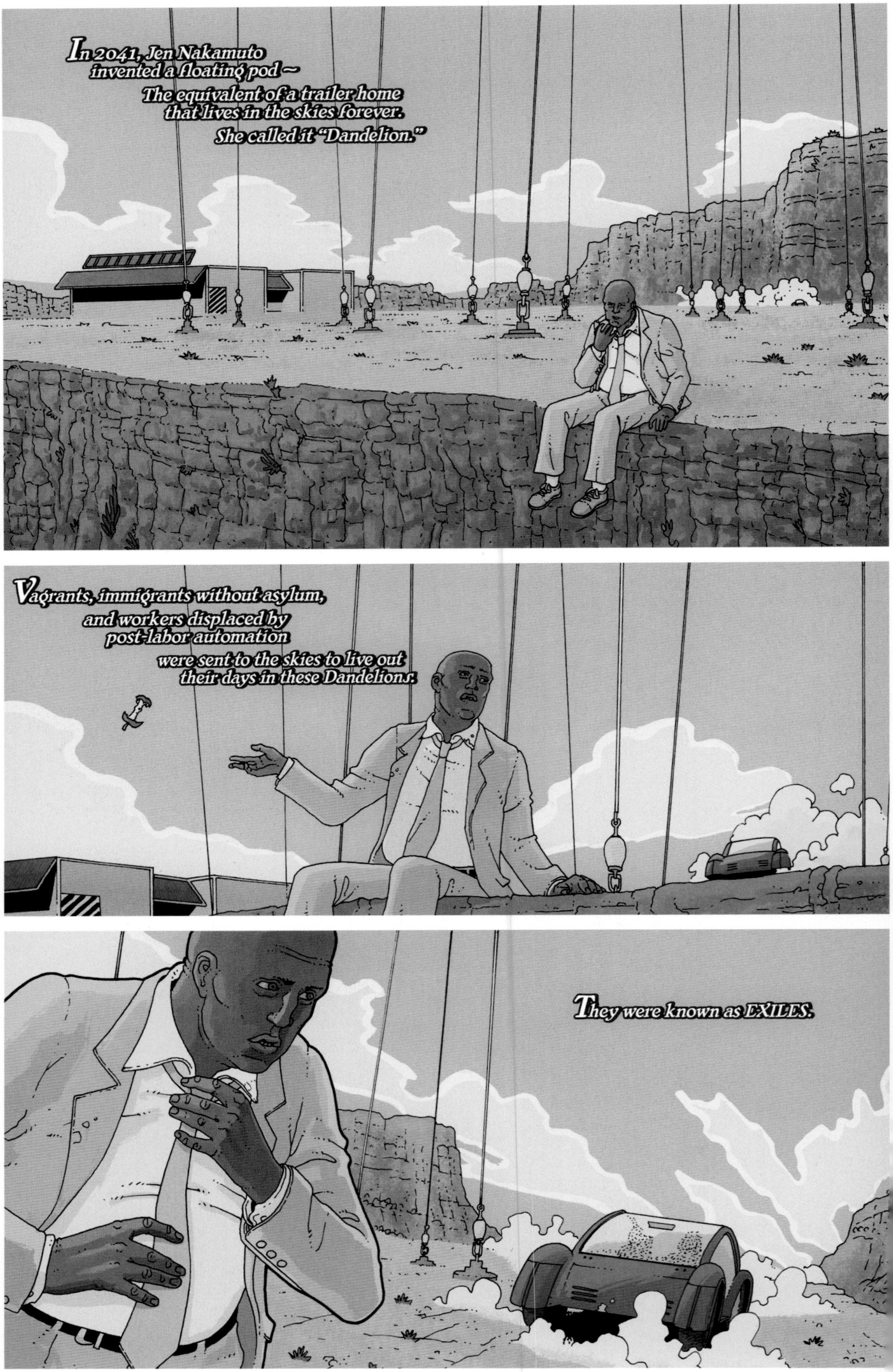
In 2041, Jen Nakamuto invented a floating pod ~
The equivalent of a trailer home that lives in the skies forever.
She called it "Dandelion."
Vagrants, immigrants without asylum, and workers displaced by post-labor automation
were sent to the skies to live out their days in these Dandelions.
They were known as EXILES.

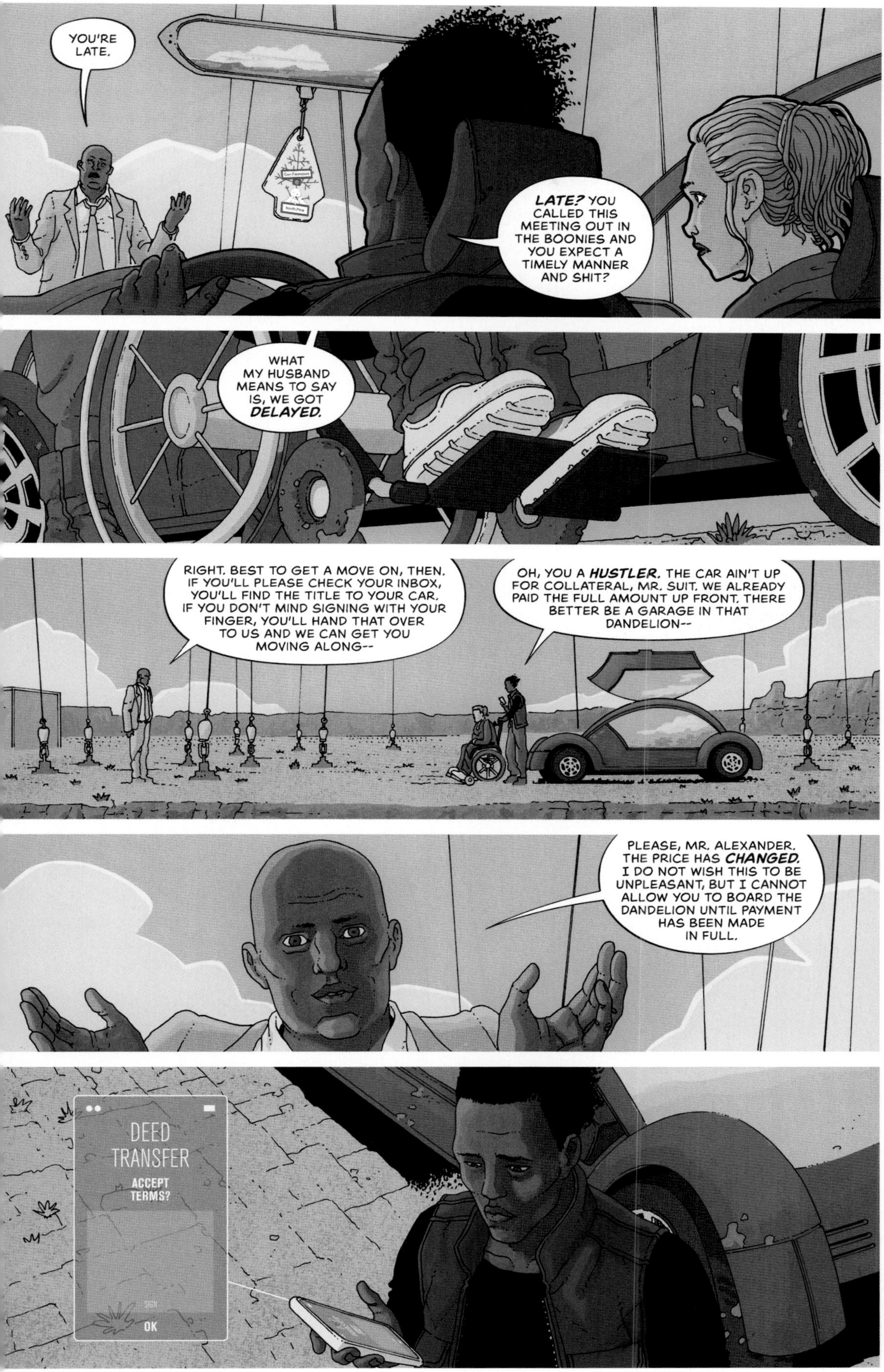
YOU'RE LATE.
LATE? YOU CALLED THIS MEETING OUT IN THE BOONIES AND YOU EXPECT A TIMELY MANNER AND SHIT?
WHAT MY HUSBAND MEANS TO SAY IS, WE GOT DELAYED.
RIGHT. BEST TO GET A MOVE ON, THEN. IF YOU'LL PLEASE CHECK YOUR INBOX, YOU'LL FIND THE TITLE TO YOUR CAR. IF YOU DON'T MIND SIGNING WITH YOUR FINGER, YOU'LL HAND THAT OVER TO US AND WE CAN GET YOU MOVING ALONG--
OH, YOU A HUSTLER. THE CAR AIN'T UP FOR COLLATERAL, MR. SUIT. WE ALREADY PAID THE FULL AMOUNT UP FRONT. THERE BETTER BE A GARAGE IN THAT DANDELION--
PLEASE, MR. ALEXANDER. THE PRICE HAS CHANGED. I DO NOT WISH THIS TO BE UNPLEASANT, BUT I CANNOT ALLOW YOU TO BOARD THE DANDELION UNTIL PAYMENT HAS BEEN MADE IN FULL.
DEED TRANSFER
ACCEPT TERMS?
SIGN
OK

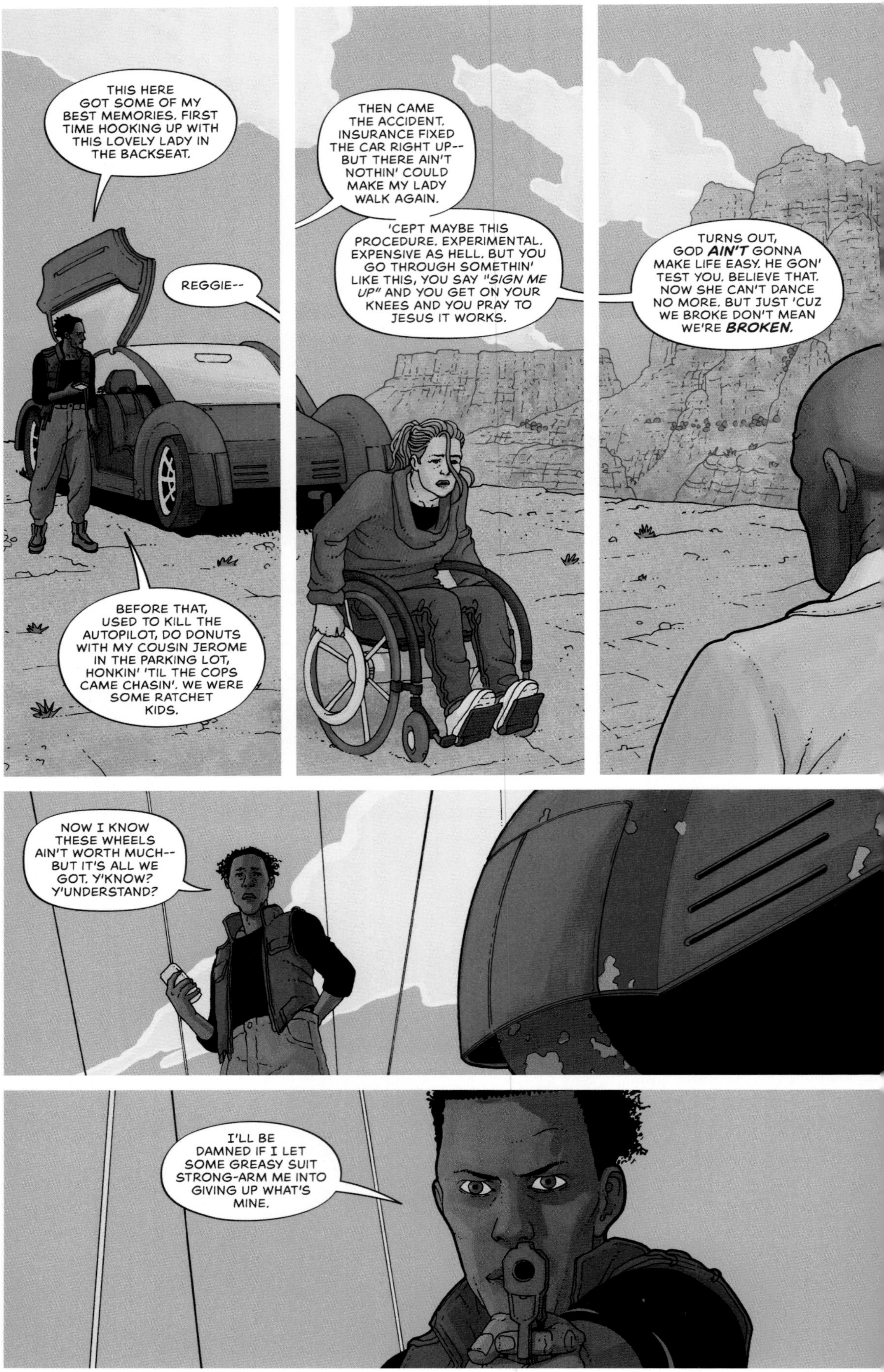
THIS HERE GOT SOME OF MY BEST MEMORIES. FIRST TIME HOOKING UP WITH THIS LOVELY LADY IN THE BACKSEAT.
REGGIE--
BEFORE THAT, USED TO KILL THE AUTOPILOT, DO DONUTS WITH MY COUSIN JEROME IN THE PARKING LOT, HONKIN' 'TIL THE COPS CAME CHASIN'. WE WERE SOME RATCHET KIDS.
THEN CAME THE ACCIDENT. INSURANCE FIXED THE CAR RIGHT UP-- BUT THERE AIN'T NOTHIN' COULD MAKE MY LADY WALK AGAIN.
'CEPT MAYBE THIS PROCEDURE. EXPERIMENTAL. EXPENSIVE AS HELL. BUT YOU GO THROUGH SOMETHIN' LIKE THIS, YOU SAY *"SIGN ME UP"* AND YOU GET ON YOUR KNEES AND YOU PRAY TO JESUS IT WORKS.
TURNS OUT, GOD ***AIN'T*** GONNA MAKE LIFE EASY. HE GON' TEST YOU. BELIEVE THAT. NOW SHE CAN'T DANCE NO MORE, BUT JUST 'CUZ WE BROKE DON'T MEAN WE'RE ***BROKEN.***
NOW I KNOW THESE WHEELS AIN'T WORTH MUCH-- BUT IT'S ALL WE GOT. Y'KNOW? Y'UNDERSTAND?
I'LL BE DAMNED IF I LET SOME GREASY SUIT STRONG-ARM ME INTO GIVING UP WHAT'S MINE.

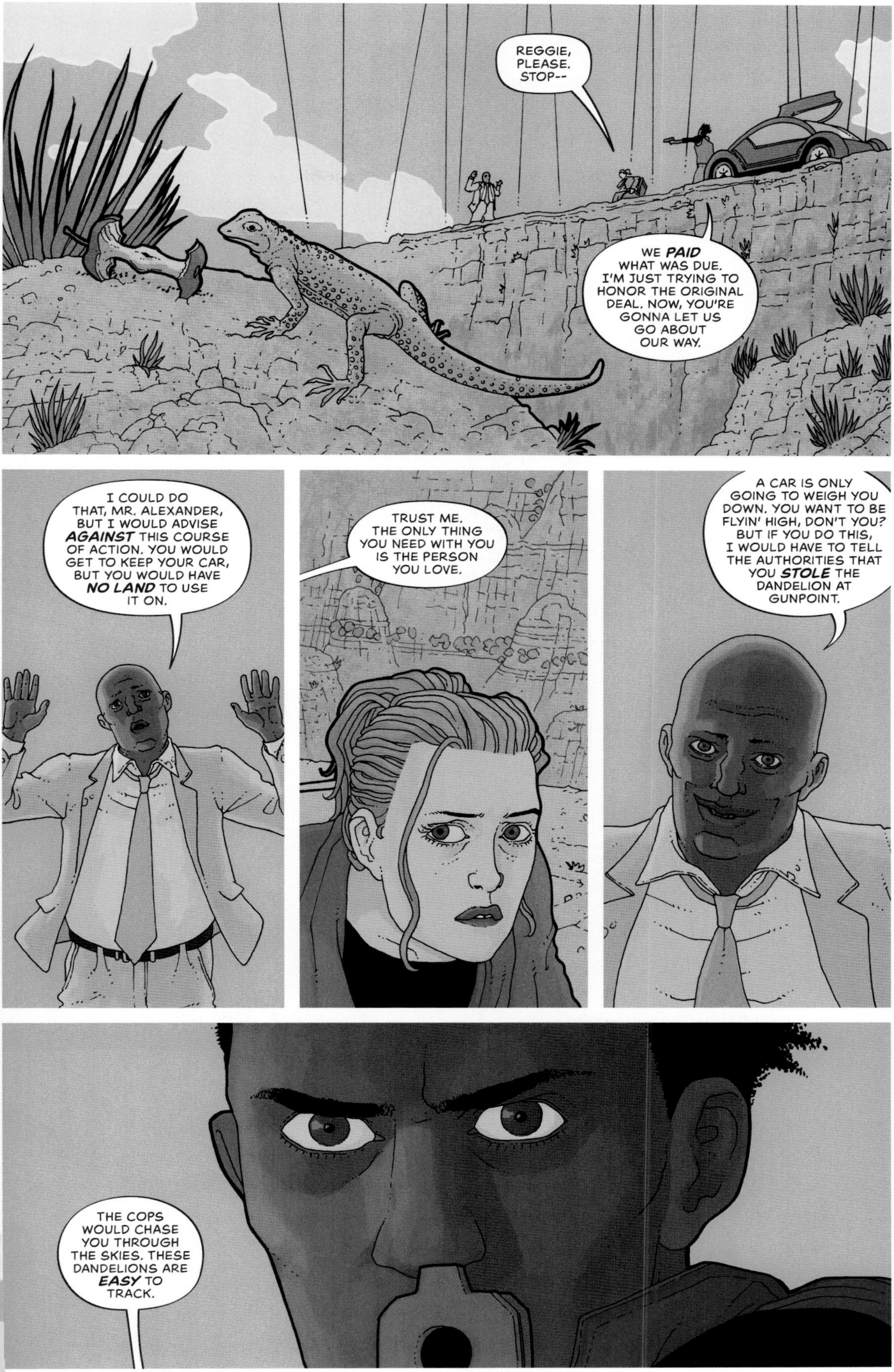
REGGIE, PLEASE. STOP--
WE PAID WHAT WAS DUE. I'M JUST TRYING TO HONOR THE ORIGINAL DEAL. NOW, YOU'RE GONNA LET US GO ABOUT OUR WAY.
I COULD DO THAT, MR. ALEXANDER, BUT I WOULD ADVISE AGAINST THIS COURSE OF ACTION. YOU WOULD GET TO KEEP YOUR CAR, BUT YOU WOULD HAVE NO LAND TO USE IT ON.
TRUST ME. THE ONLY THING YOU NEED WITH YOU IS THE PERSON YOU LOVE.
A CAR IS ONLY GOING TO WEIGH YOU DOWN. YOU WANT TO BE FLYIN' HIGH, DON'T YOU? BUT IF YOU DO THIS, I WOULD HAVE TO TELL THE AUTHORITIES THAT YOU STOLE THE DANDELION AT GUNPOINT.
THE COPS WOULD CHASE YOU THROUGH THE SKIES. THESE DANDELIONS ARE EASY TO TRACK.

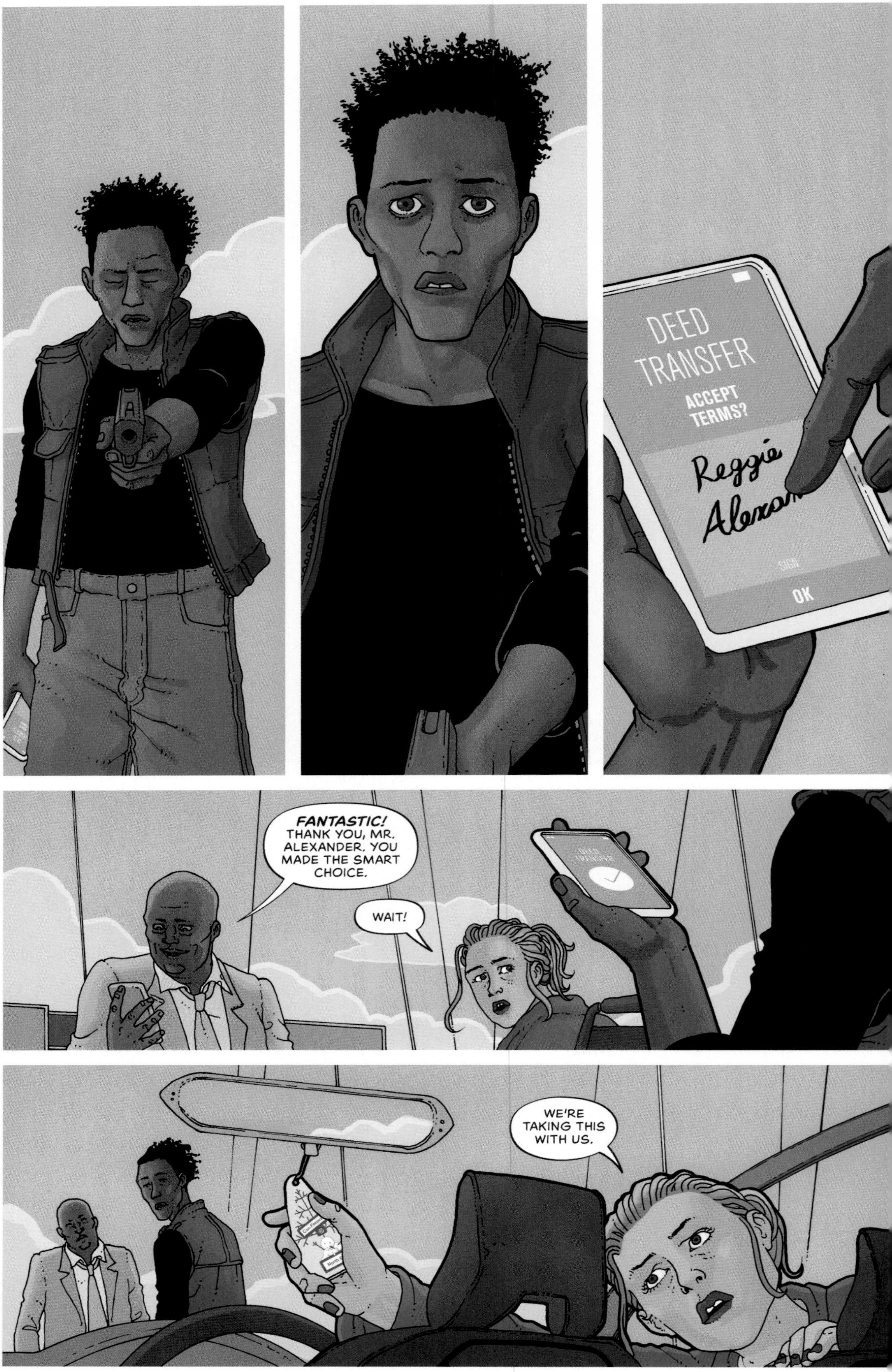
DEED TRANSFER
ACCEPT TERMS?
Reggie
SIGN
OK
FANTASTIC! THANK YOU, MR. ALEXANDER. YOU MADE THE SMART CHOICE.
WAIT!
DEED TRANSFER
WE'RE TAKING THIS WITH US.

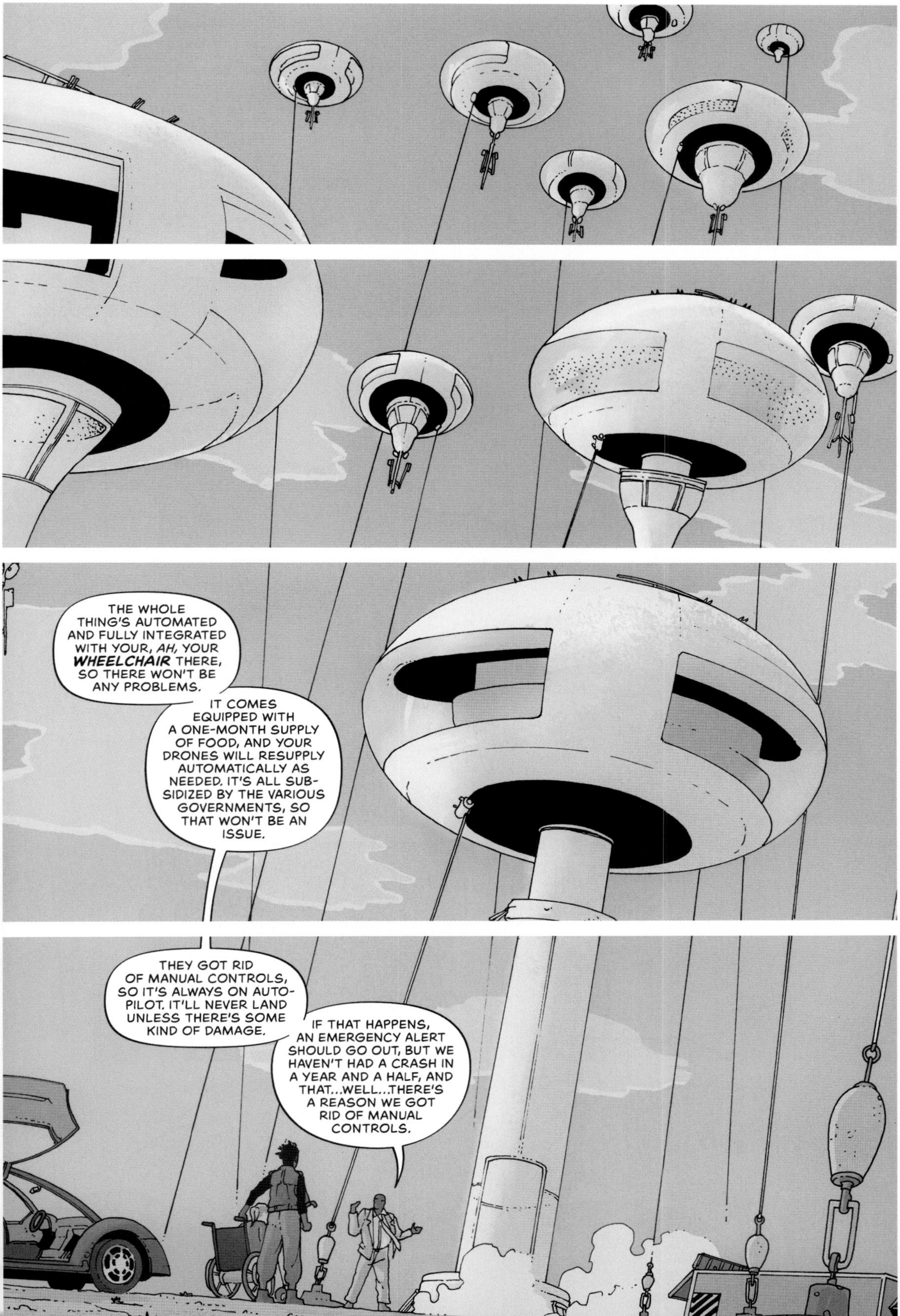
THE WHOLE THING'S AUTOMATED AND FULLY INTEGRATED WITH YOUR, *AH,* YOUR ***WHEELCHAIR*** THERE, SO THERE WON'T BE ANY PROBLEMS.
IT COMES EQUIPPED WITH A ONE-MONTH SUPPLY OF FOOD, AND YOUR DRONES WILL RESUPPLY AUTOMATICALLY AS NEEDED. IT'S ALL SUB-SIDIZED BY THE VARIOUS GOVERNMENTS, SO THAT WON'T BE AN ISSUE.
THEY GOT RID OF MANUAL CONTROLS, SO IT'S ALWAYS ON AUTO-PILOT. IT'LL NEVER LAND UNLESS THERE'S SOME KIND OF DAMAGE.
IF THAT HAPPENS, AN EMERGENCY ALERT SHOULD GO OUT, BUT WE HAVEN'T HAD A CRASH IN A YEAR AND A HALF, AND THAT...WELL...THERE'S A REASON WE GOT RID OF MANUAL CONTROLS.

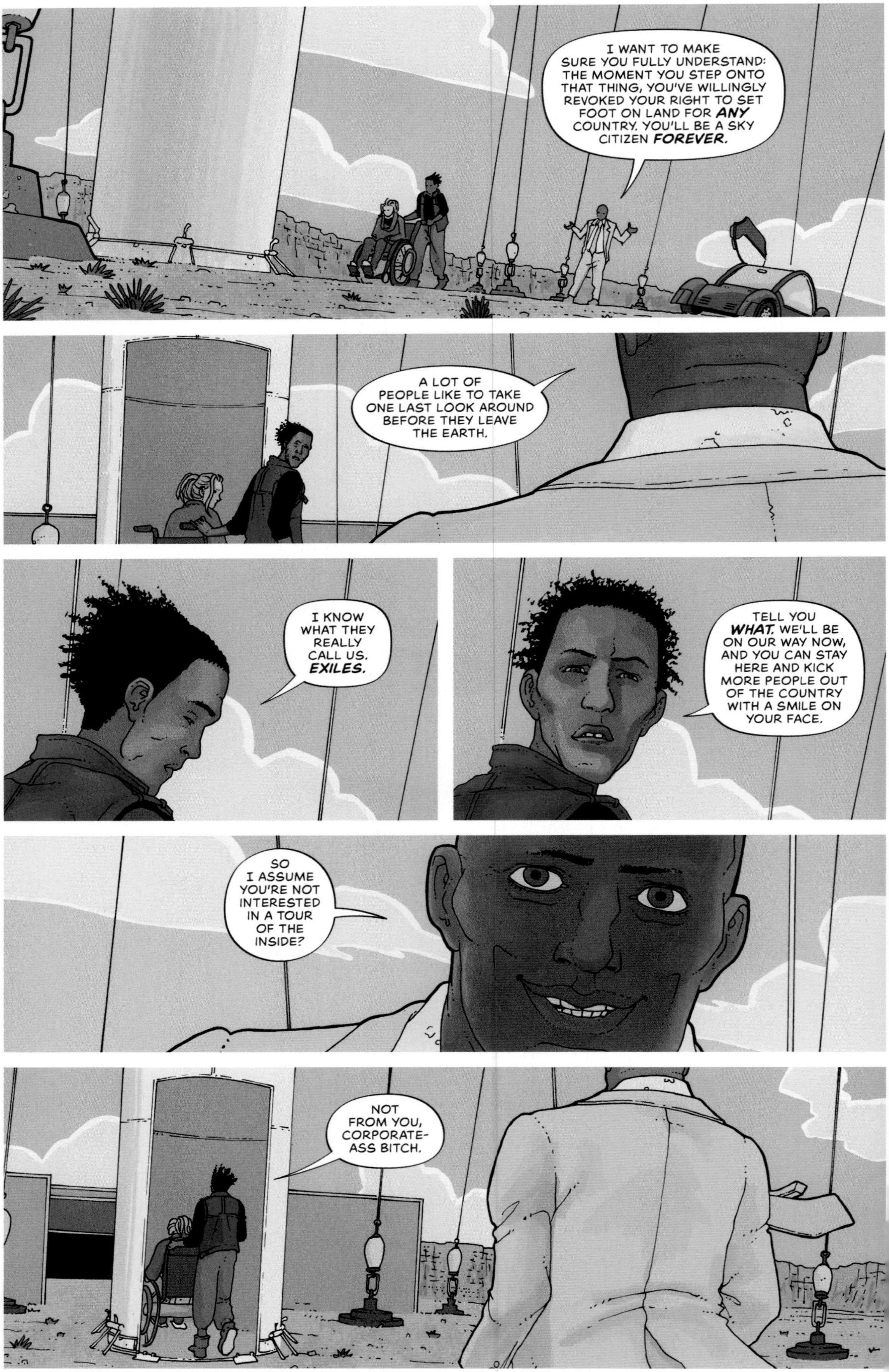
I WANT TO MAKE SURE YOU FULLY UNDERSTAND: THE MOMENT YOU STEP ONTO THAT THING, YOU'VE WILLINGLY REVOKED YOUR RIGHT TO SET FOOT ON LAND FOR ***ANY*** COUNTRY. YOU'LL BE A SKY CITIZEN ***FOREVER.***
A LOT OF PEOPLE LIKE TO TAKE ONE LAST LOOK AROUND BEFORE THEY LEAVE THE EARTH.
I KNOW WHAT THEY REALLY CALL US. ***EXILES.***
TELL YOU ***WHAT.*** WE'LL BE ON OUR WAY NOW, AND YOU CAN STAY HERE AND KICK MORE PEOPLE OUT OF THE COUNTRY WITH A SMILE ON YOUR FACE.
SO I ASSUME YOU'RE NOT INTERESTED IN A TOUR OF THE INSIDE?
NOT FROM YOU, CORPORATE-ASS BITCH.

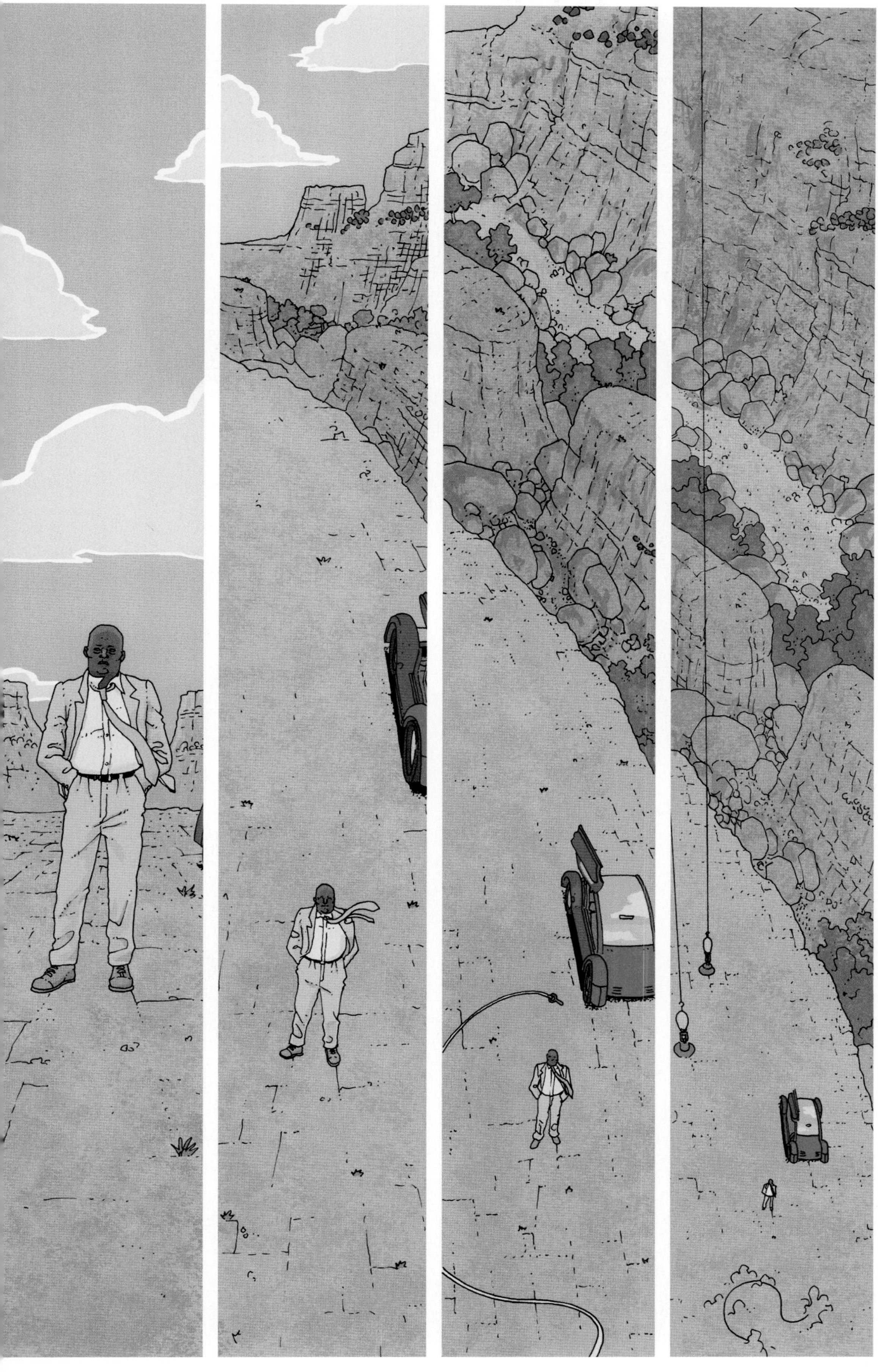

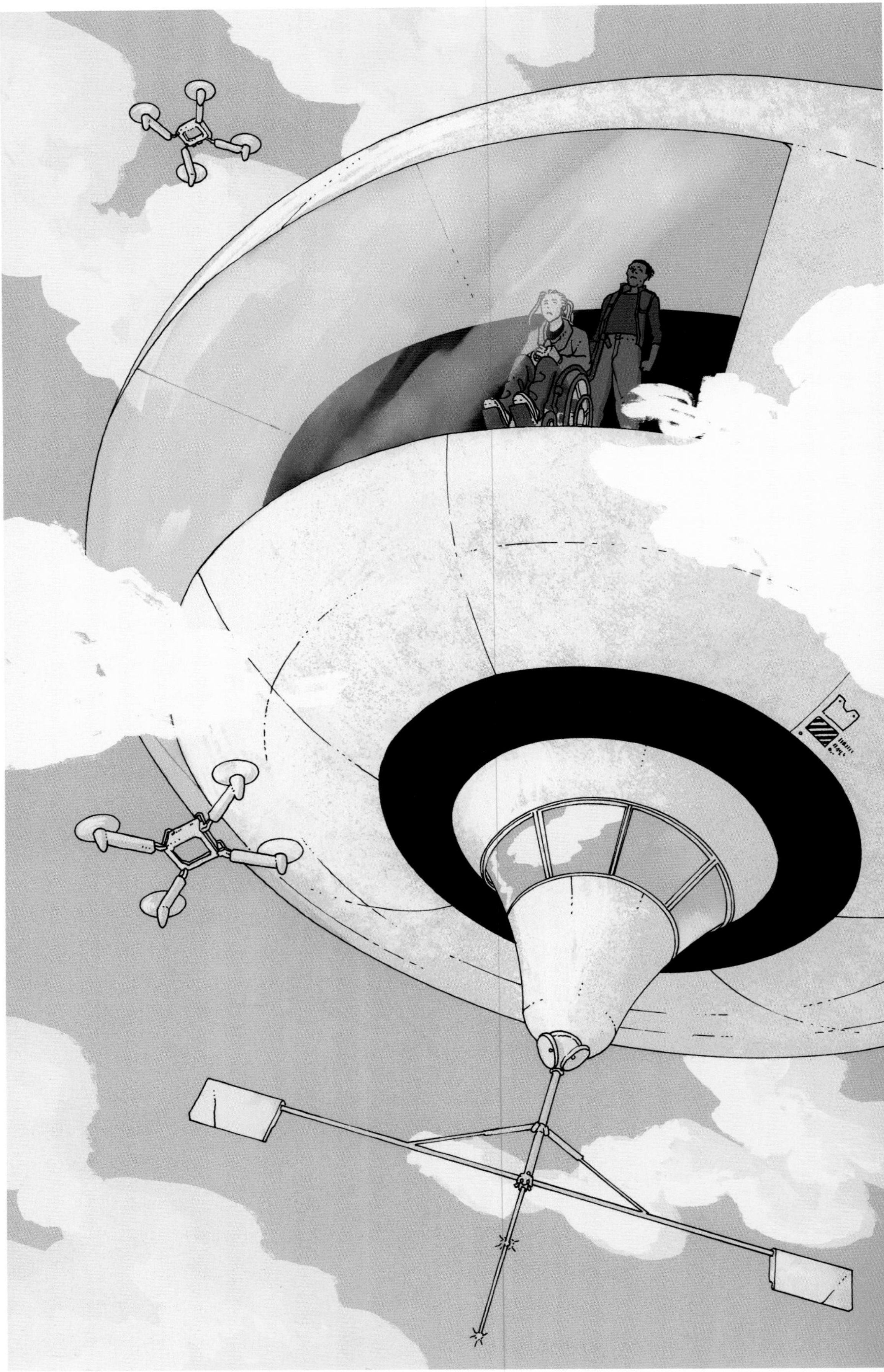

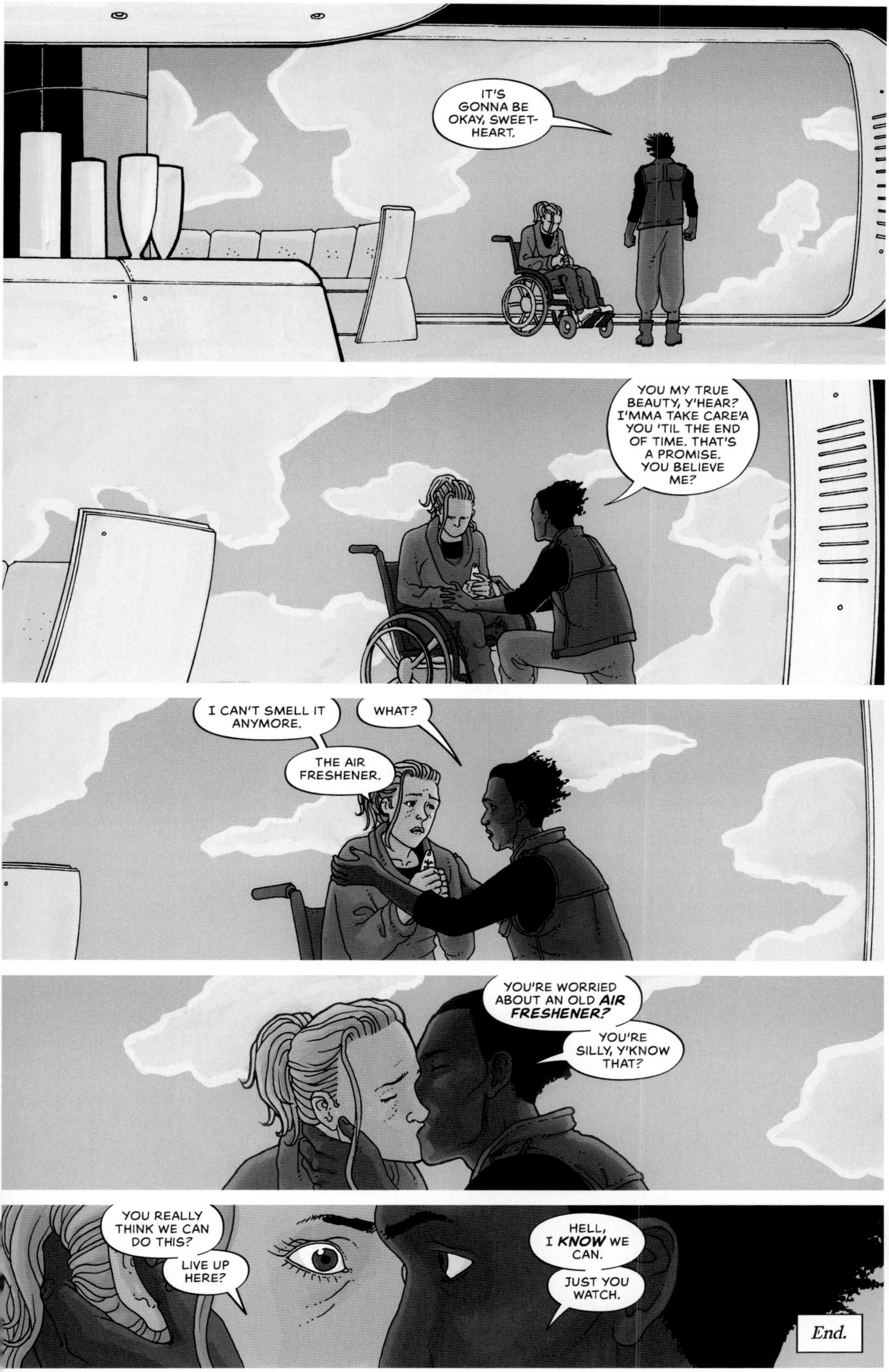
IT'S GONNA BE OKAY, SWEET-HEART.
YOU MY TRUE BEAUTY, Y'HEAR? I'MMA TAKE CARE'A YOU 'TIL THE END OF TIME. THAT'S A PROMISE. YOU BELIEVE ME?
I CAN'T SMELL IT ANYMORE.
WHAT?
THE AIR FRESHENER.
YOU'RE WORRIED ABOUT AN OLD **AIR FRESHENER?**
YOU'RE SILLY, Y'KNOW THAT?
YOU REALLY THINK WE CAN DO THIS?
LIVE UP HERE?
HELL, I **KNOW** WE CAN.
JUST YOU WATCH.
End.

**Excerpt from the Stratosphere podcast:
Interview with Jen Nakamuto, inventor of the Dandelion.
Recorded on April 12th, 2047.**

Here's the thing. If you look at the history of innovation, it's somewhat linear. There was a time when we kept imagining that flying cars and interstellar space travel were going to become commonplace.

That's not what linear innovation did. Things didn't get bigger and fly above us. Things got smaller and zoomed below us. And I don't just mean transportation. I mean everything.

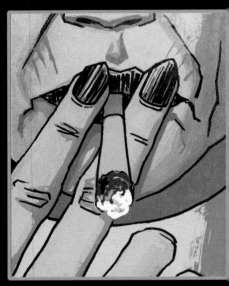

Phones could summon a cab with your fingerprint and voice ID. Your wristwatch could check your blood pressure and tip off an ambulance if you were having a heart attack. For a dollar, you could hop on an electric-powered scooter and zip over to the beach.

Everyone was looking down. I wanted to change that. I wanted people to look **up** again. To dare to dream of bigger things. I wanted humanity to aim higher. That's why the Dandelion had to be big, obnoxious, hard to ignore. It needed to put our heads back in the clouds.

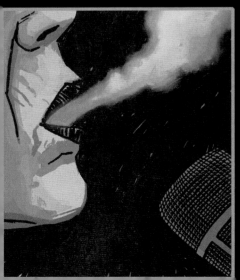

SMILE

ART

ROY ALLAN **MARTINEZ**

COLORS

JUHA **VELTTI**

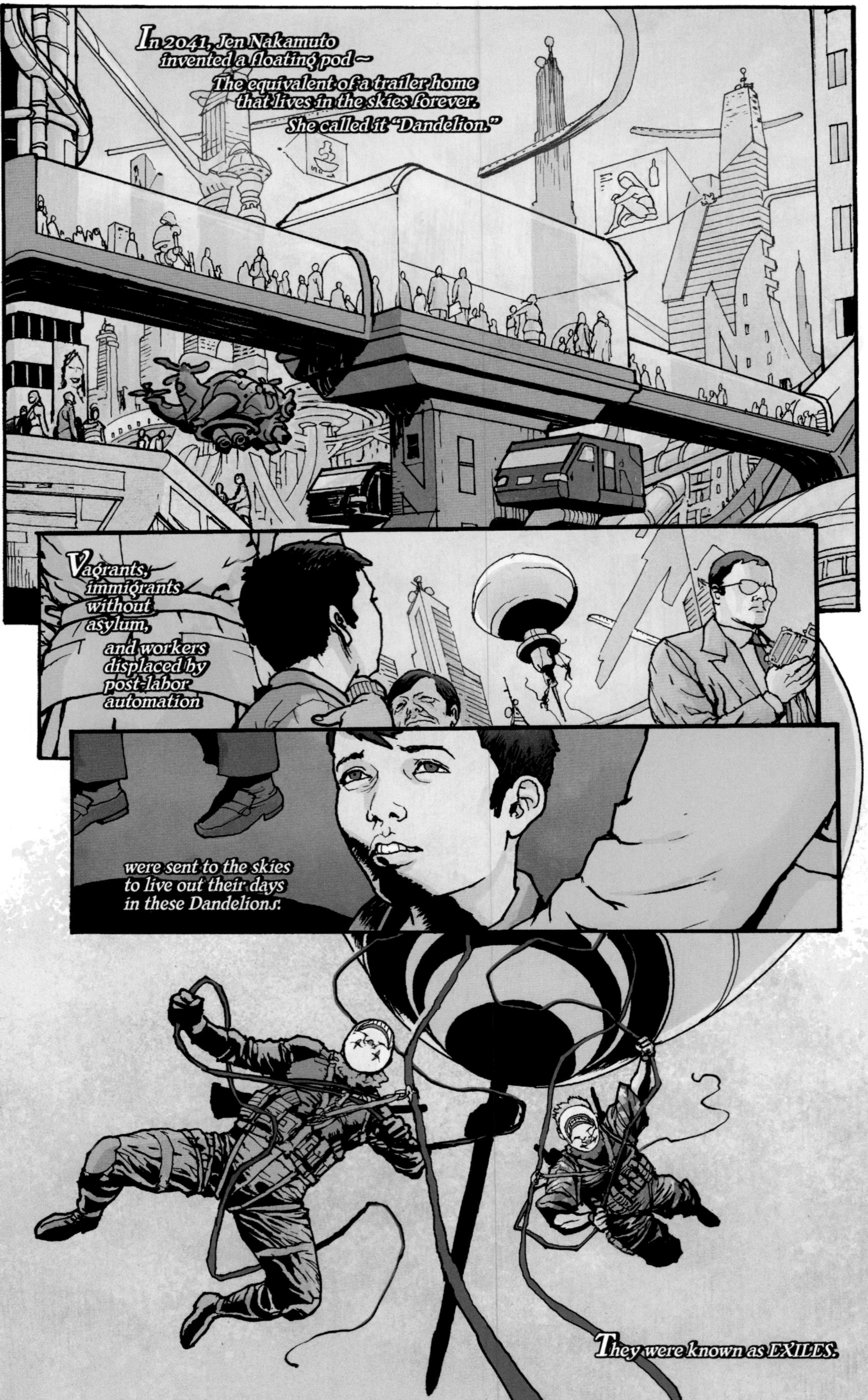
In 2041, Jen Nakamuto invented a floating pod ~
The equivalent of a trailer home that lives in the skies forever.
She called it "Dandelion."
Vagrants, immigrants without asylum,
and workers displaced by post-labor automation
were sent to the skies to live out their days in these Dandelions.
They were known as EXILES.

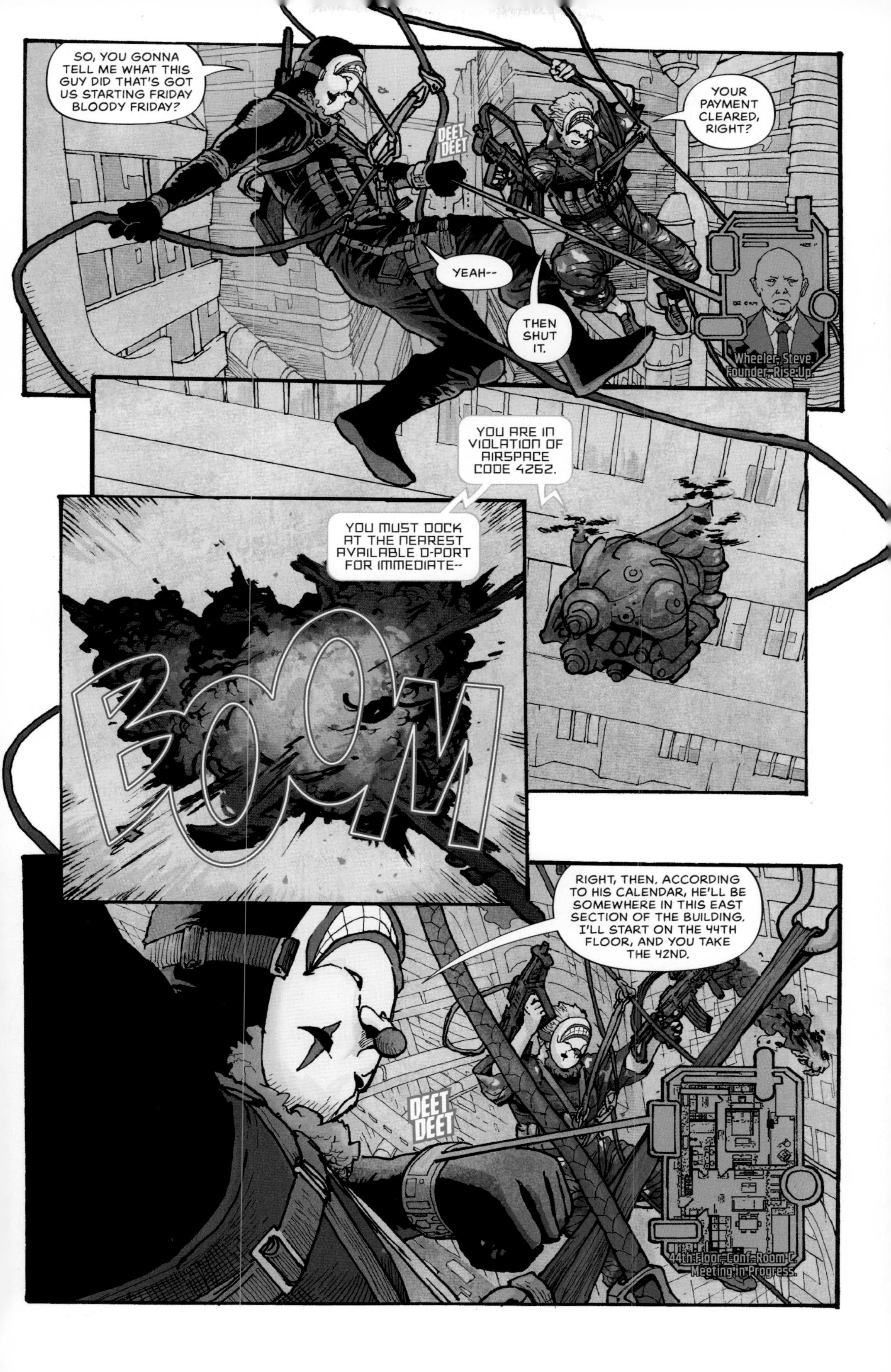
SO, YOU GONNA TELL ME WHAT THIS GUY DID THAT'S GOT US STARTING FRIDAY BLOODY FRIDAY?
DEET DEET
YOUR PAYMENT CLEARED, RIGHT?
YEAH--
THEN SHUT IT.
Wheeler, Steve.
Founder, Rise Up.
YOU ARE IN VIOLATION OF AIRSPACE CODE 4262.
YOU MUST DOCK AT THE NEAREST AVAILABLE D-PORT FOR IMMEDIATE--
BOOM
RIGHT, THEN. ACCORDING TO HIS CALENDAR, HE'LL BE SOMEWHERE IN THIS EAST SECTION OF THE BUILDING. I'LL START ON THE 44TH FLOOR, AND YOU TAKE THE 42ND.
DEET DEET
44th Floor, Conf. Room C.
Meeting in Progress.

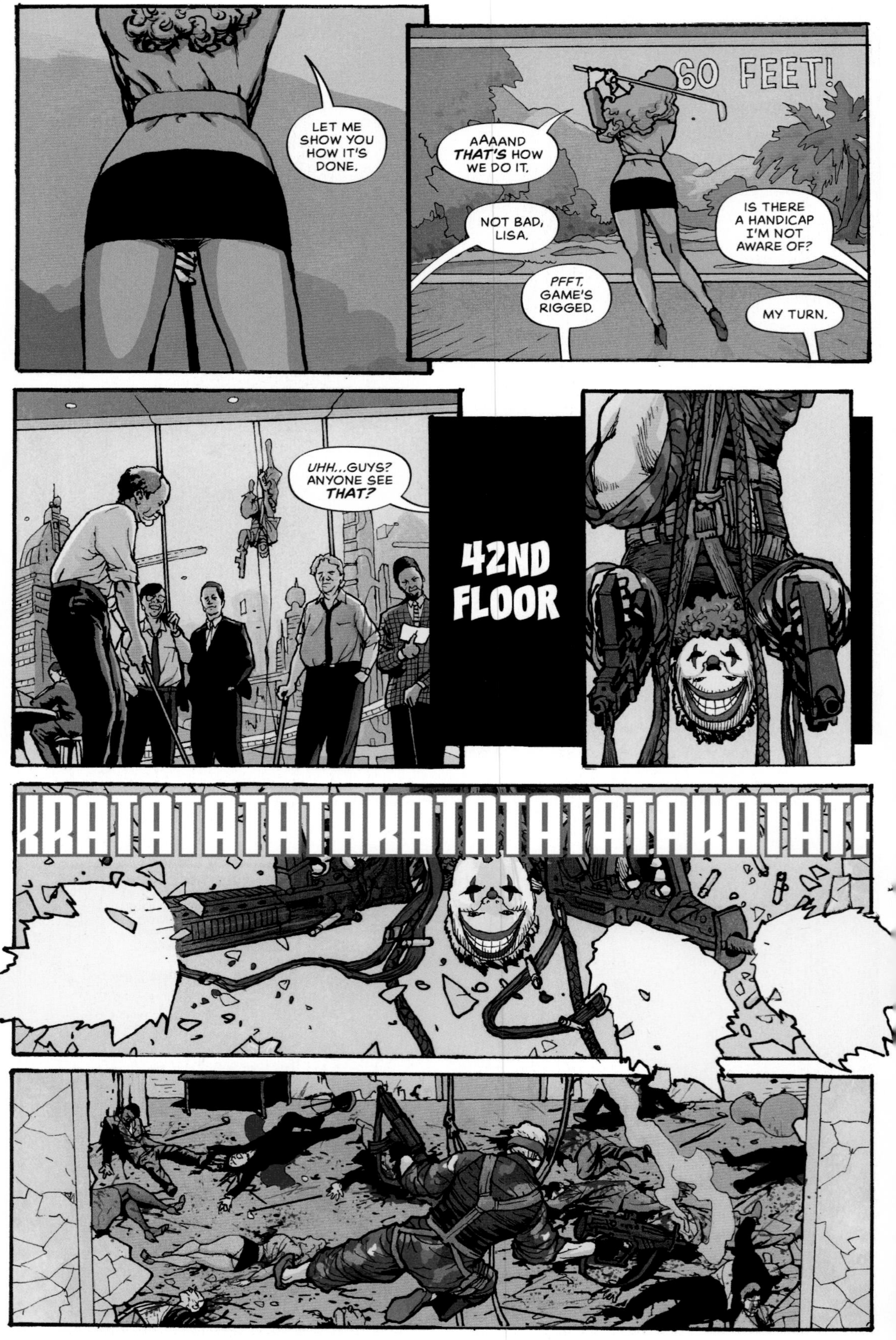
LET ME SHOW YOU HOW IT'S DONE.
60 FEET!
AAAAND THAT'S HOW WE DO IT.
NOT BAD, LISA.
PFFT. GAME'S RIGGED.
IS THERE A HANDICAP I'M NOT AWARE OF?
MY TURN.
UHH...GUYS? ANYONE SEE THAT?
42ND FLOOR
KRATATATATAKATATATATAKATATA

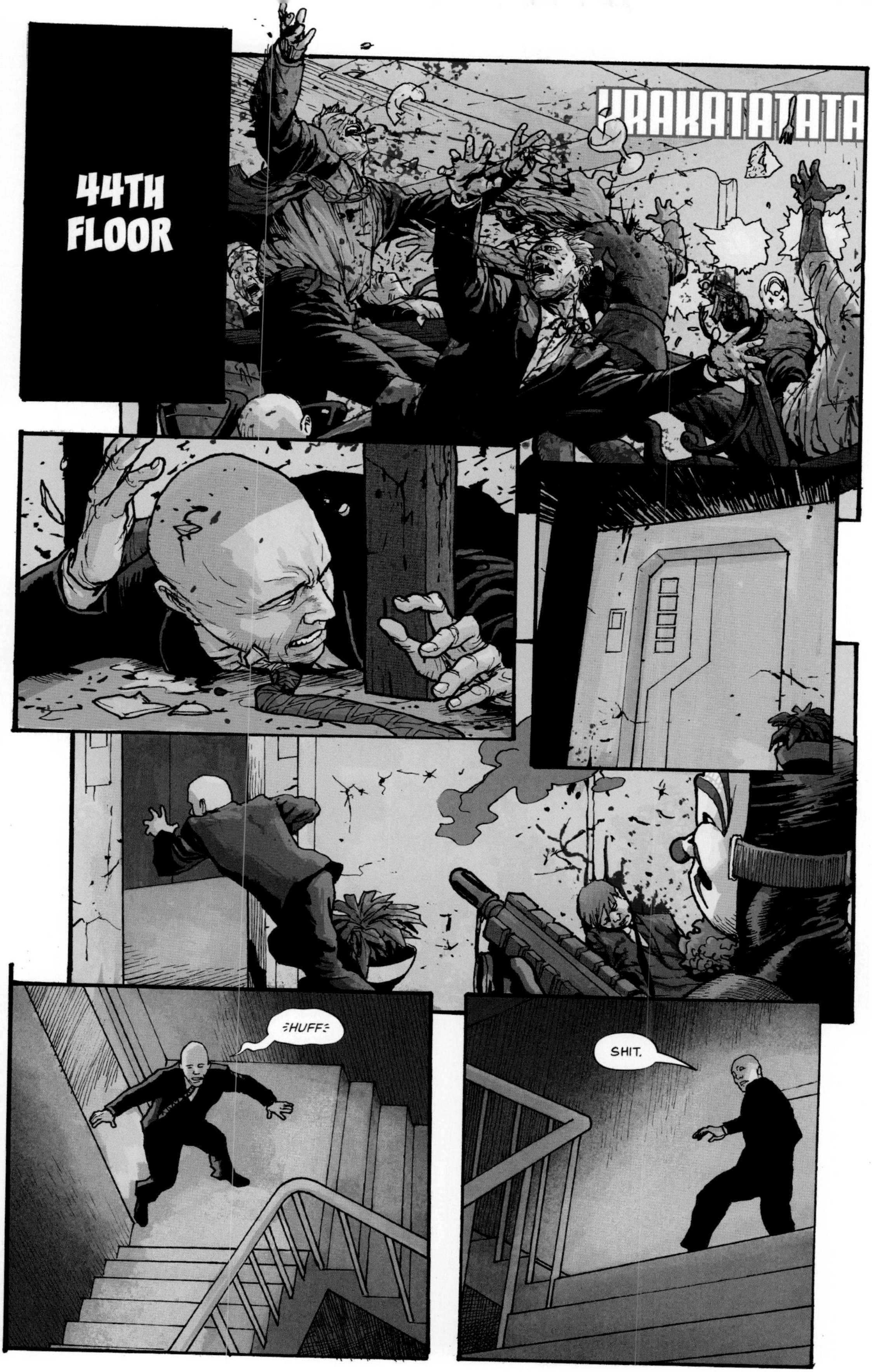
44TH FLOOR
KRAKATATATA
HUFF
SHIT.

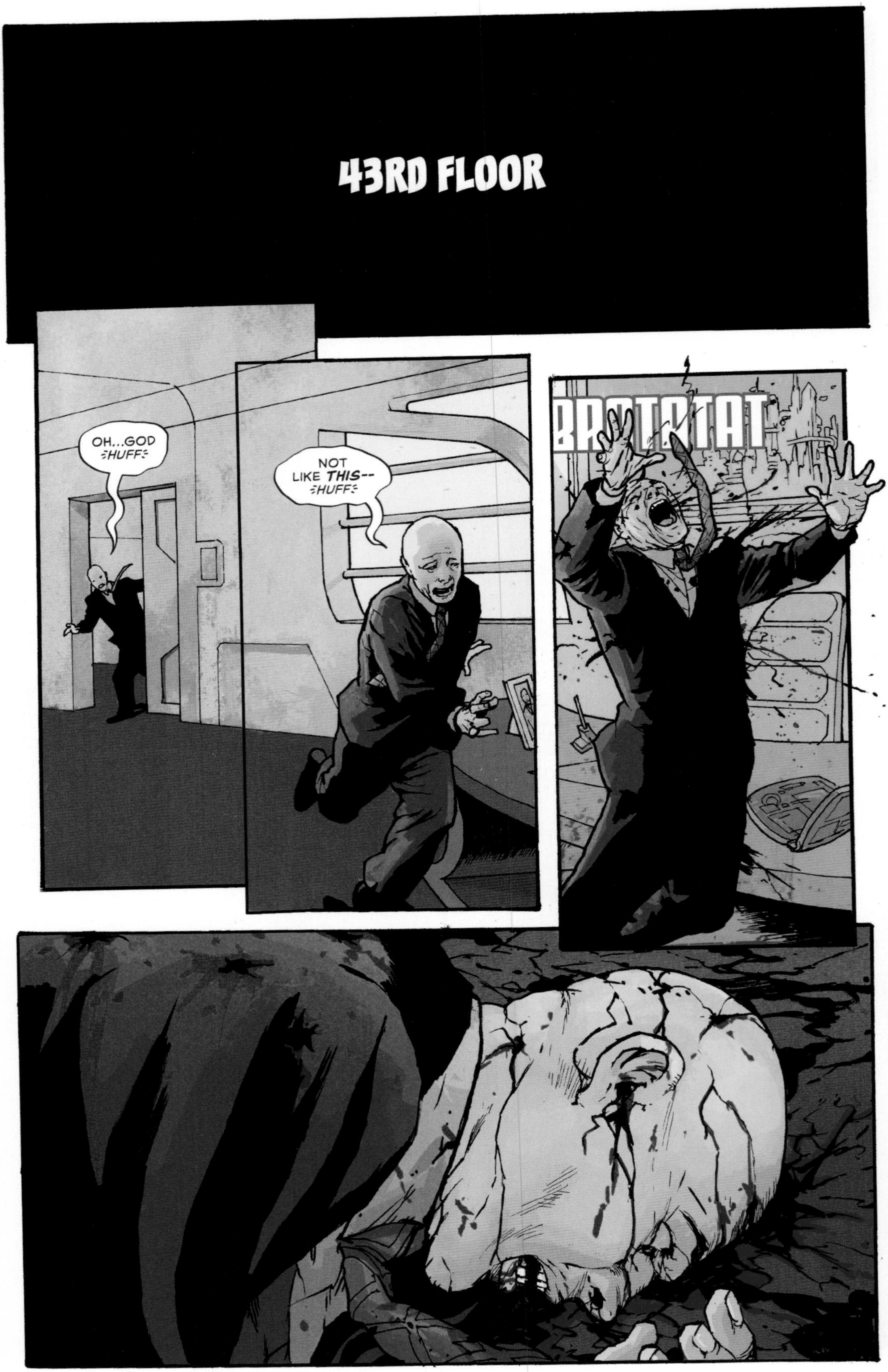
43RD FLOOR
OH...GOD *HUFF*
NOT LIKE *THIS*-- *HUFF*
BRATATAT

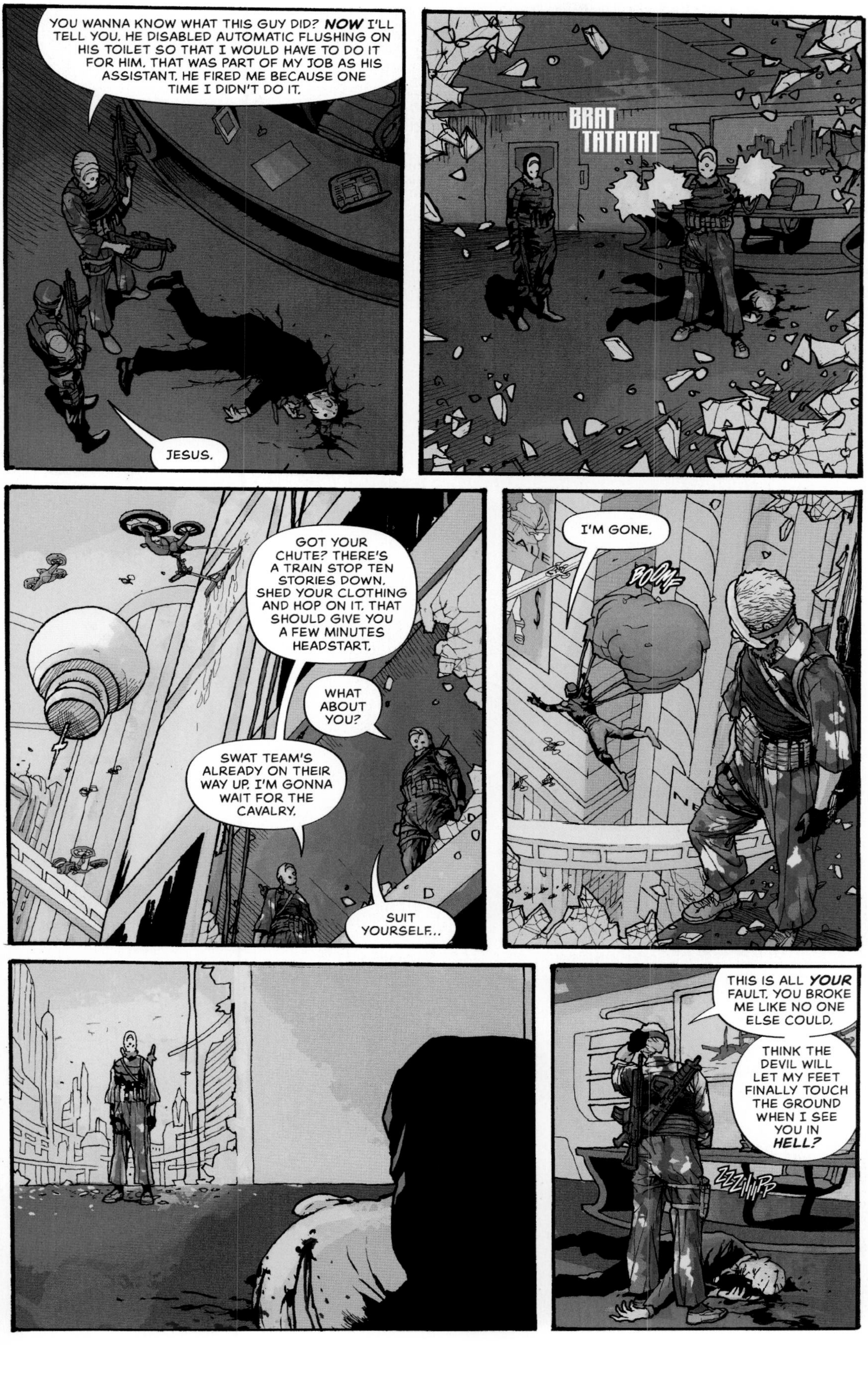
YOU WANNA KNOW WHAT THIS GUY DID? **NOW** I'LL TELL YOU. HE DISABLED AUTOMATIC FLUSHING ON HIS TOILET SO THAT I WOULD HAVE TO DO IT FOR HIM. THAT WAS PART OF MY JOB AS HIS ASSISTANT. HE FIRED ME BECAUSE ONE TIME I DIDN'T DO IT.
JESUS.
BRAT TATATAT
GOT YOUR CHUTE? THERE'S A TRAIN STOP TEN STORIES DOWN. SHED YOUR CLOTHING AND HOP ON IT. THAT SHOULD GIVE YOU A FEW MINUTES HEADSTART.
WHAT ABOUT YOU?
SWAT TEAM'S ALREADY ON THEIR WAY UP. I'M GONNA WAIT FOR THE CAVALRY.
SUIT YOURSELF...
I'M GONE.
BOOMF
THIS IS ALL **YOUR** FAULT. YOU BROKE ME LIKE NO ONE ELSE COULD.
THINK THE DEVIL WILL LET MY FEET FINALLY TOUCH THE GROUND WHEN I SEE YOU IN **HELL?**
ZZZIIIPP

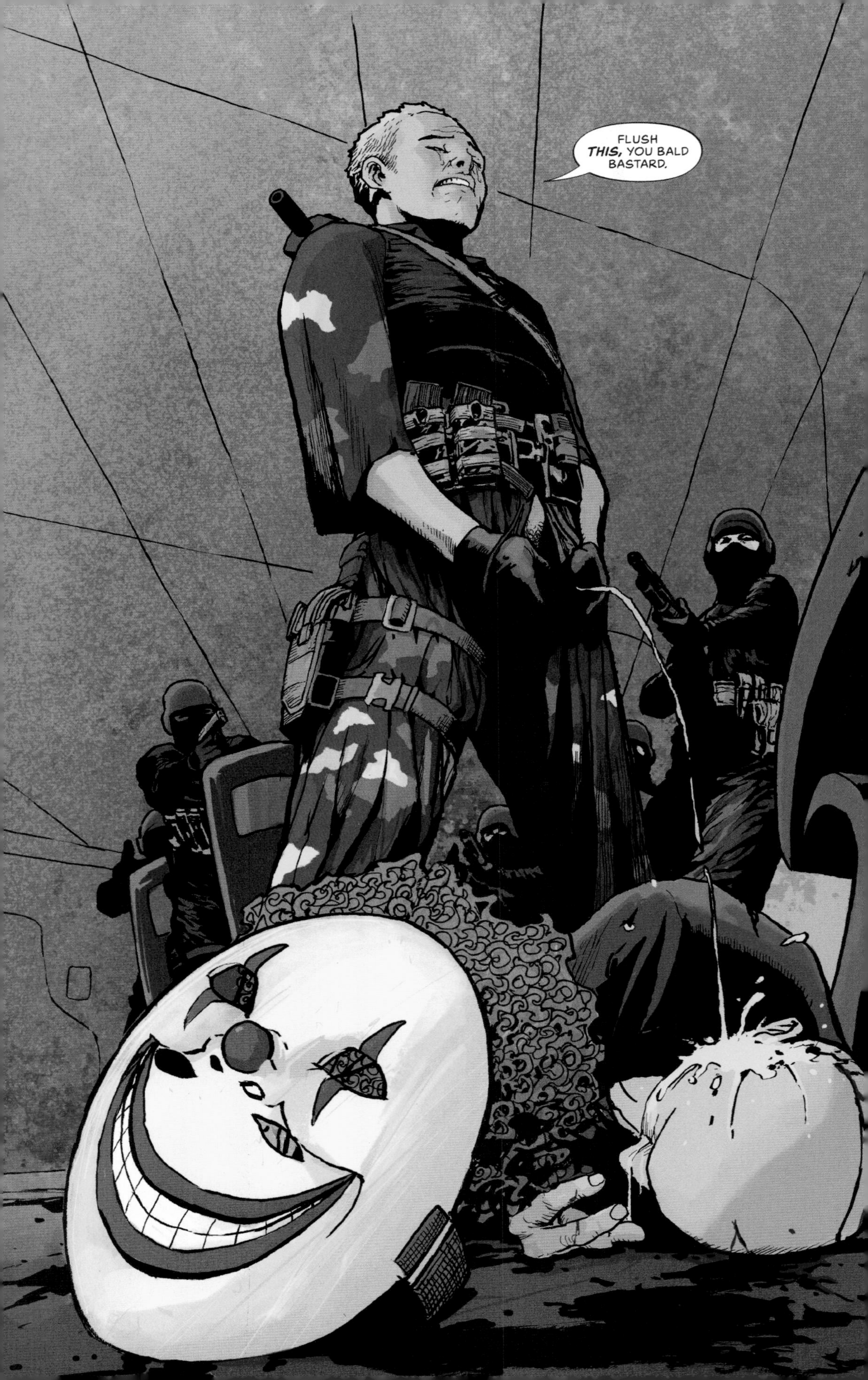
FLUSH THIS, YOU BALD BASTARD.

Excerpt from the Stratosphere podcast: Interview with Jen Nakamuto, inventor of the Dandelion. Recorded on April 12th, 2047.

…Sora was his name. He must have been in his 90s by the time we started having lunch together at the commissary. Mind you, this was maybe a "once a week" thing if that. He was quite reclusive, and so was I.

We had this system. Every day, I would look up at Sora's window on the third floor of our retirement community. I don't know how it is in other countries, but we have lots of retirement communities in Japan. Long lives. Don't ask me why.

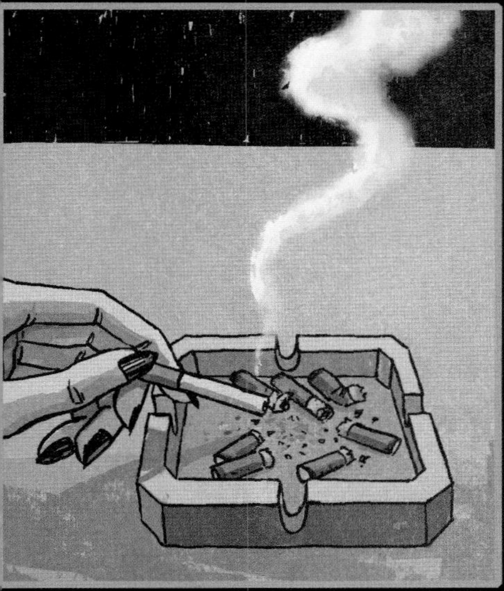

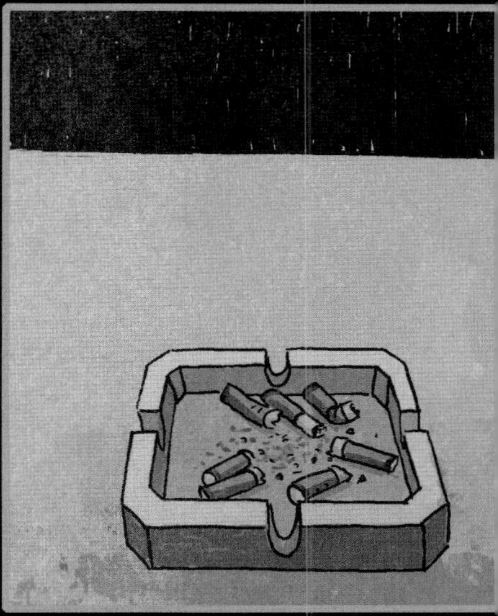

So the system was, I'd look up at Sora's window. If the blinds were down, he was alive. If they were up, he was dead and I should call the medics. If you didn't have a buddy, then your body would just rot for two weeks until the smell of your corpse wafted into other units.

One day, Sora's blinds were up. That's when I knew I didn't want do die on this land. I wanted to float away. I wanted to live and die in the skies.

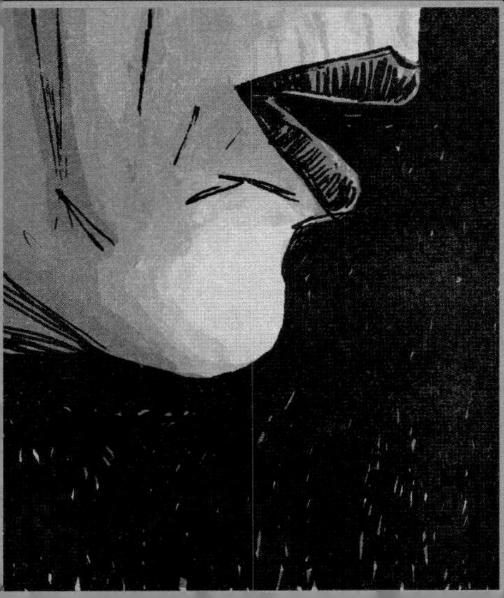

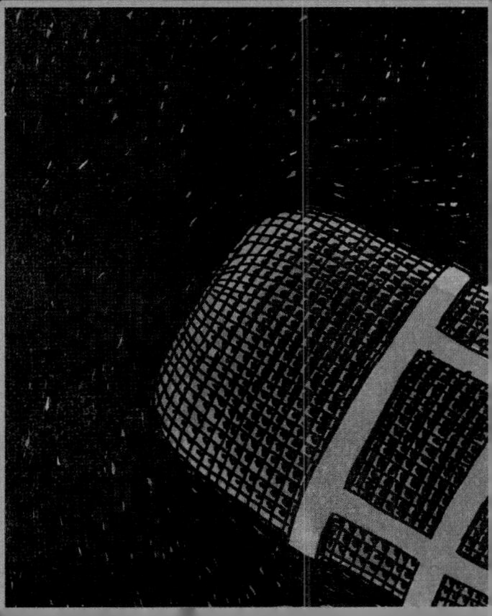

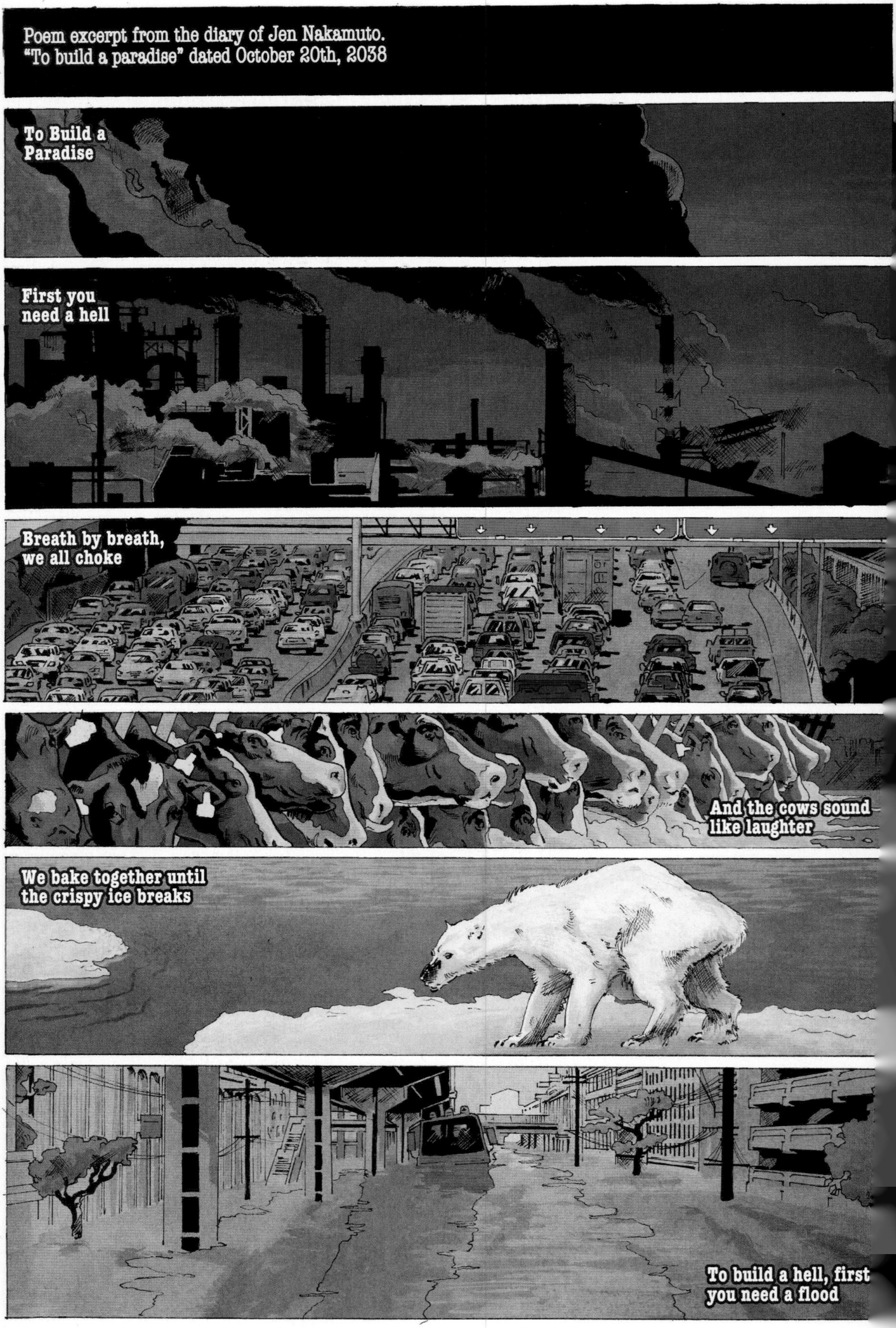
Poem excerpt from the diary of Jen Nakamuto.
"To build a paradise" dated October 20th, 2038
To Build a Paradise
First you need a hell
Breath by breath, we all choke
And the cows sound like laughter
We bake together until the crispy ice breaks
To build a hell, first you need a flood

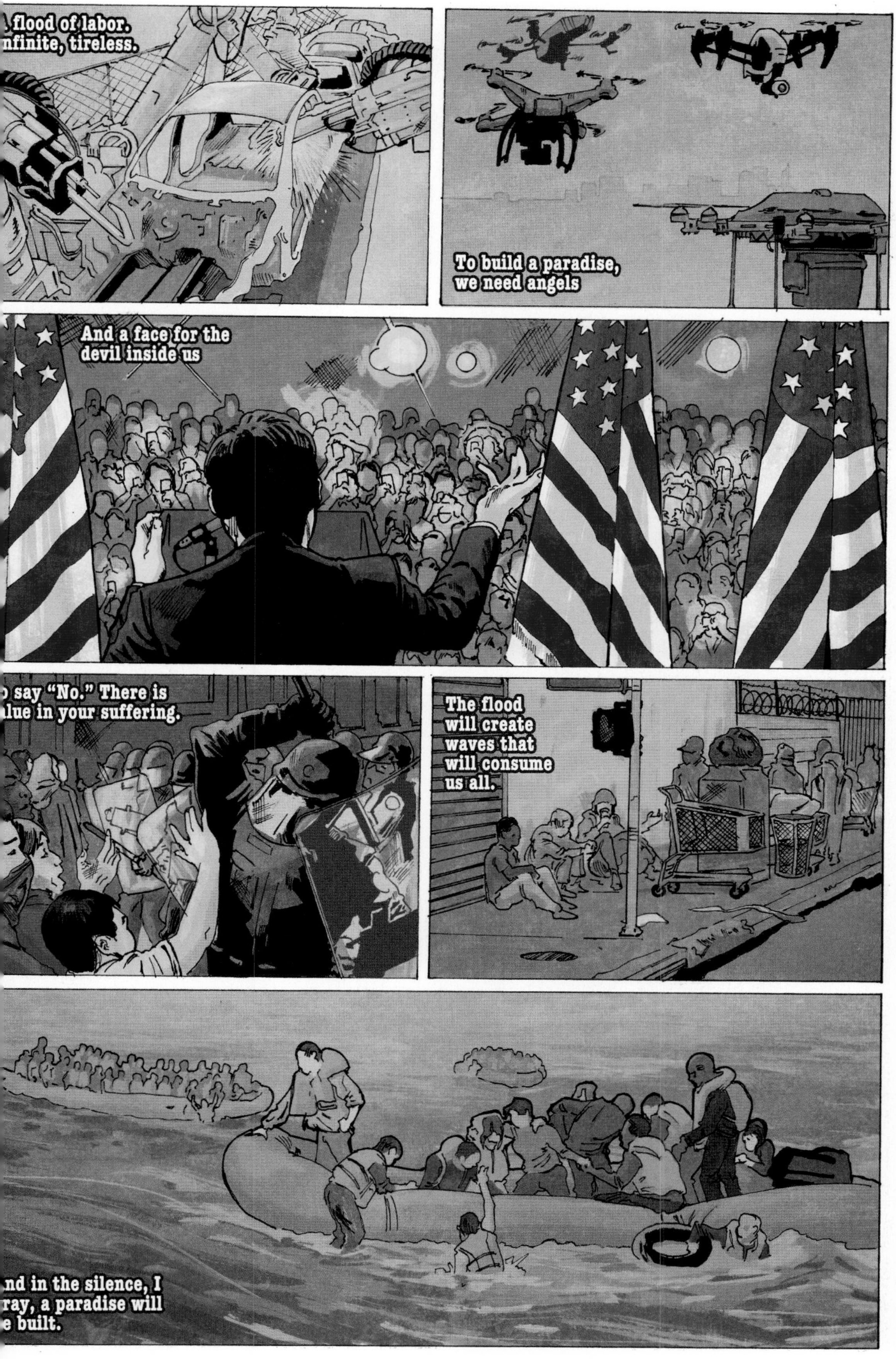
flood of labor.
nfinite, tireless.
To build a paradise,
we need angels
And a face for the
devil inside us
say "No." There is
lue in your suffering.
The flood
will create
waves that
will consume
us all.
nd in the silence, I
ray, a paradise will
e built.

THE FIRE

ART

ADRIAN **RIVERO**

COLORS

LEE **LOUGHRIDGE**

Bay of Bengal.

18:45.

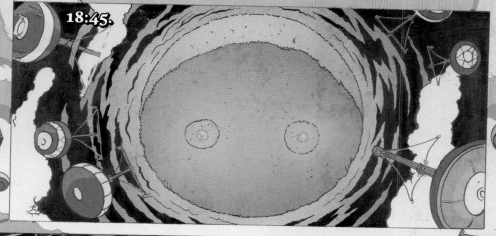

Low Tide.

--THESE TWO GUYS, THEY DROP DOWN FROM A DANDELION AND START GUNNING DOWN EVERYONE AT THIS HEDGE FUND.

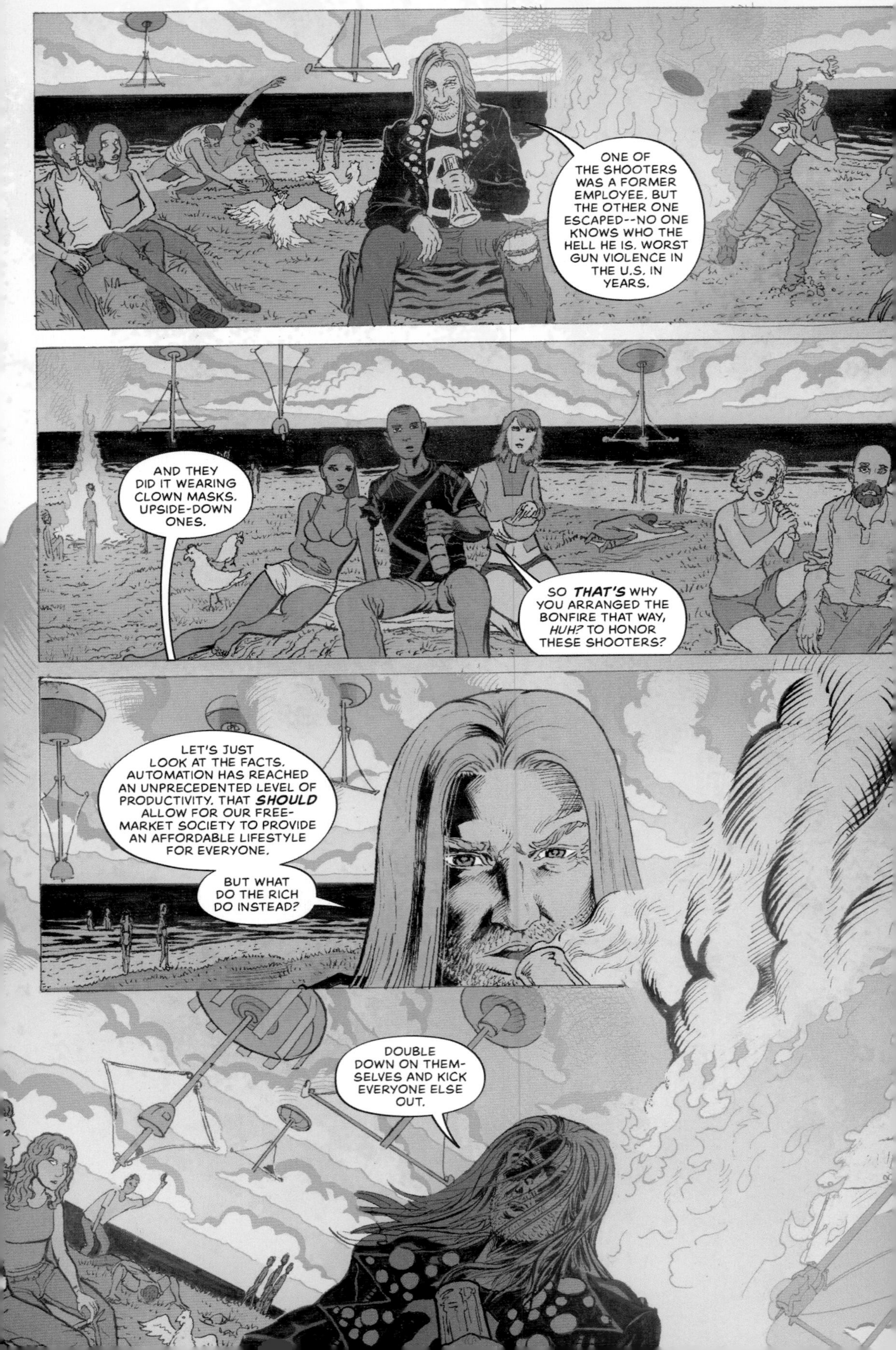
ONE OF THE SHOOTERS WAS A FORMER EMPLOYEE. BUT THE OTHER ONE ESCAPED--NO ONE KNOWS WHO THE HELL HE IS. WORST GUN VIOLENCE IN THE U.S. IN YEARS.
AND THEY DID IT WEARING CLOWN MASKS. UPSIDE-DOWN ONES.
SO THAT'S WHY YOU ARRANGED THE BONFIRE THAT WAY, HUH? TO HONOR THESE SHOOTERS?
LET'S JUST LOOK AT THE FACTS. AUTOMATION HAS REACHED AN UNPRECEDENTED LEVEL OF PRODUCTIVITY. THAT SHOULD ALLOW FOR OUR FREE-MARKET SOCIETY TO PROVIDE AN AFFORDABLE LIFESTYLE FOR EVERYONE.
BUT WHAT DO THE RICH DO INSTEAD?
DOUBLE DOWN ON THEMSELVES AND KICK EVERYONE ELSE OUT.

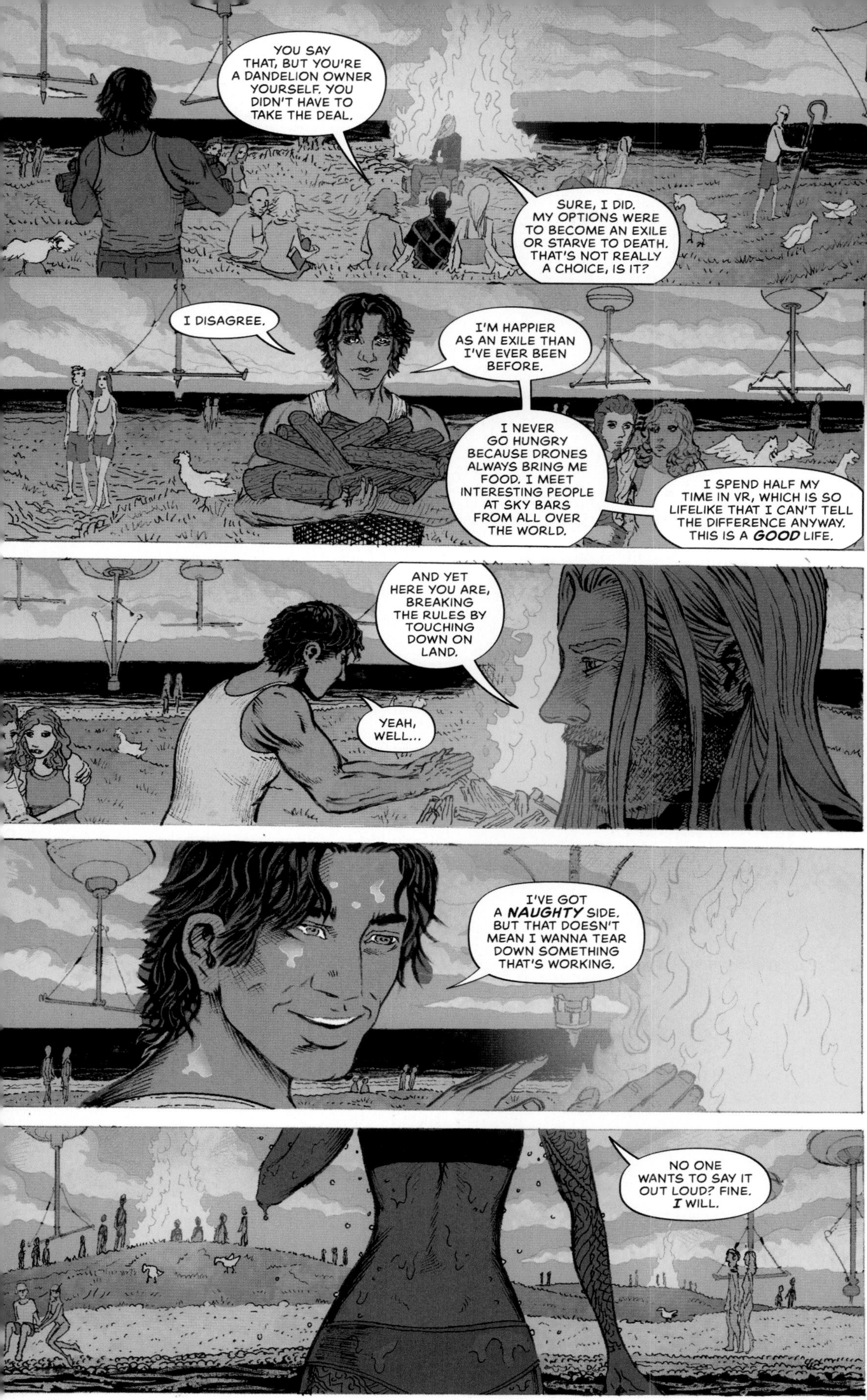
YOU SAY THAT, BUT YOU'RE A DANDELION OWNER YOURSELF. YOU DIDN'T HAVE TO TAKE THE DEAL.
SURE, I DID. MY OPTIONS WERE TO BECOME AN EXILE OR STARVE TO DEATH. THAT'S NOT REALLY A CHOICE, IS IT?
I DISAGREE.
I'M HAPPIER AS AN EXILE THAN I'VE EVER BEEN BEFORE.
I NEVER GO HUNGRY BECAUSE DRONES ALWAYS BRING ME FOOD. I MEET INTERESTING PEOPLE AT SKY BARS FROM ALL OVER THE WORLD.
I SPEND HALF MY TIME IN VR, WHICH IS SO LIFELIKE THAT I CAN'T TELL THE DIFFERENCE ANYWAY. THIS IS A **GOOD** LIFE.
AND YET HERE YOU ARE, BREAKING THE RULES BY TOUCHING DOWN ON LAND.
YEAH, WELL...
I'VE GOT A **NAUGHTY** SIDE. BUT THAT DOESN'T MEAN I WANNA TEAR DOWN SOMETHING THAT'S WORKING.
NO ONE WANTS TO SAY IT OUT LOUD? FINE. **I** WILL.

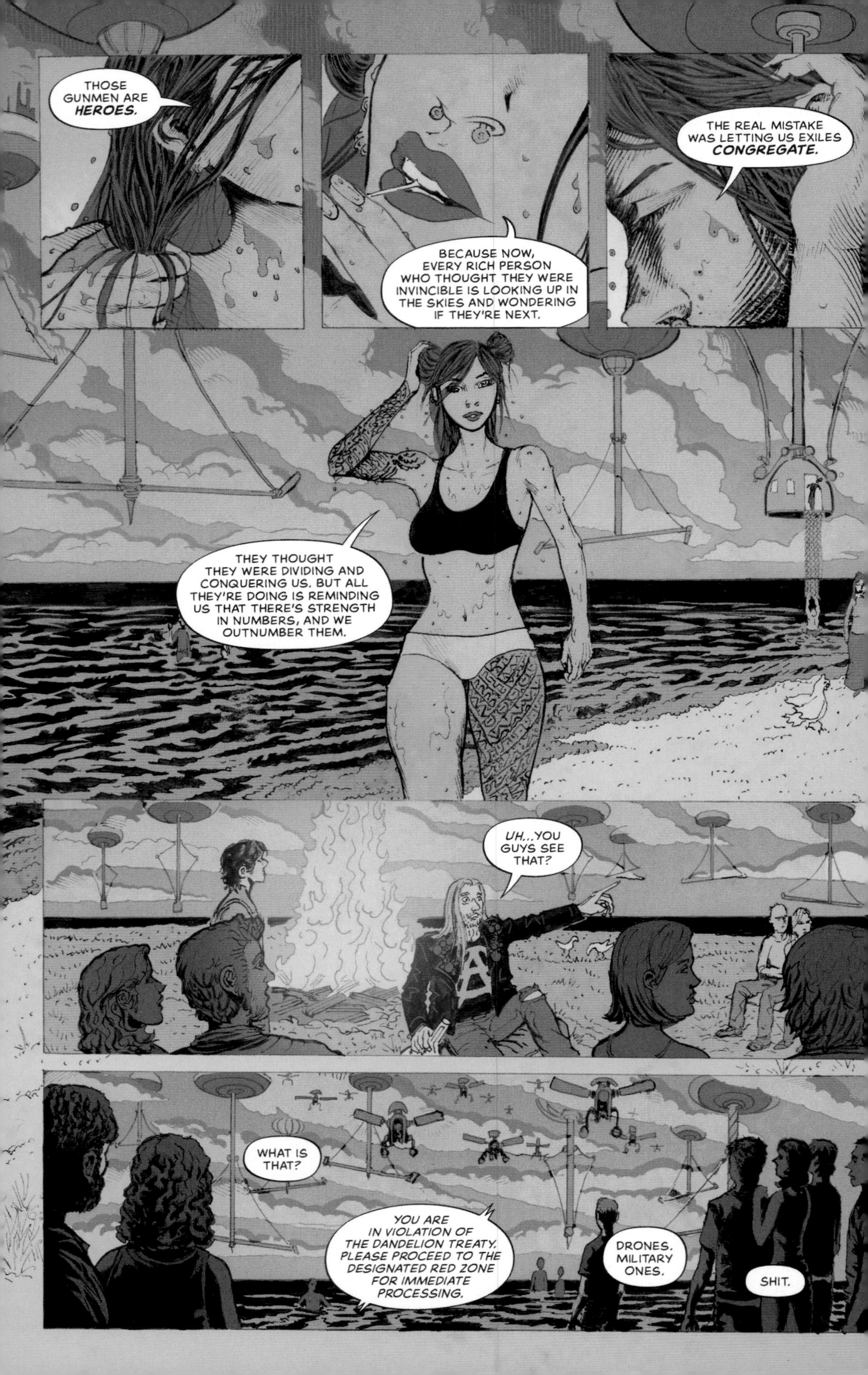
THOSE GUNMEN ARE **HEROES.**
BECAUSE NOW, EVERY RICH PERSON WHO THOUGHT THEY WERE INVINCIBLE IS LOOKING UP IN THE SKIES AND WONDERING IF THEY'RE NEXT.
THE REAL MISTAKE WAS LETTING US EXILES **CONGREGATE.**
THEY THOUGHT THEY WERE DIVIDING AND CONQUERING US. BUT ALL THEY'RE DOING IS REMINDING US THAT THERE'S STRENGTH IN NUMBERS, AND WE OUTNUMBER THEM.
UH...YOU GUYS SEE THAT?
WHAT IS THAT?
YOU ARE IN VIOLATION OF THE DANDELION TREATY. PLEASE PROCEED TO THE DESIGNATED RED ZONE FOR IMMEDIATE PROCESSING.
DRONES. MILITARY ONES.
SHIT.

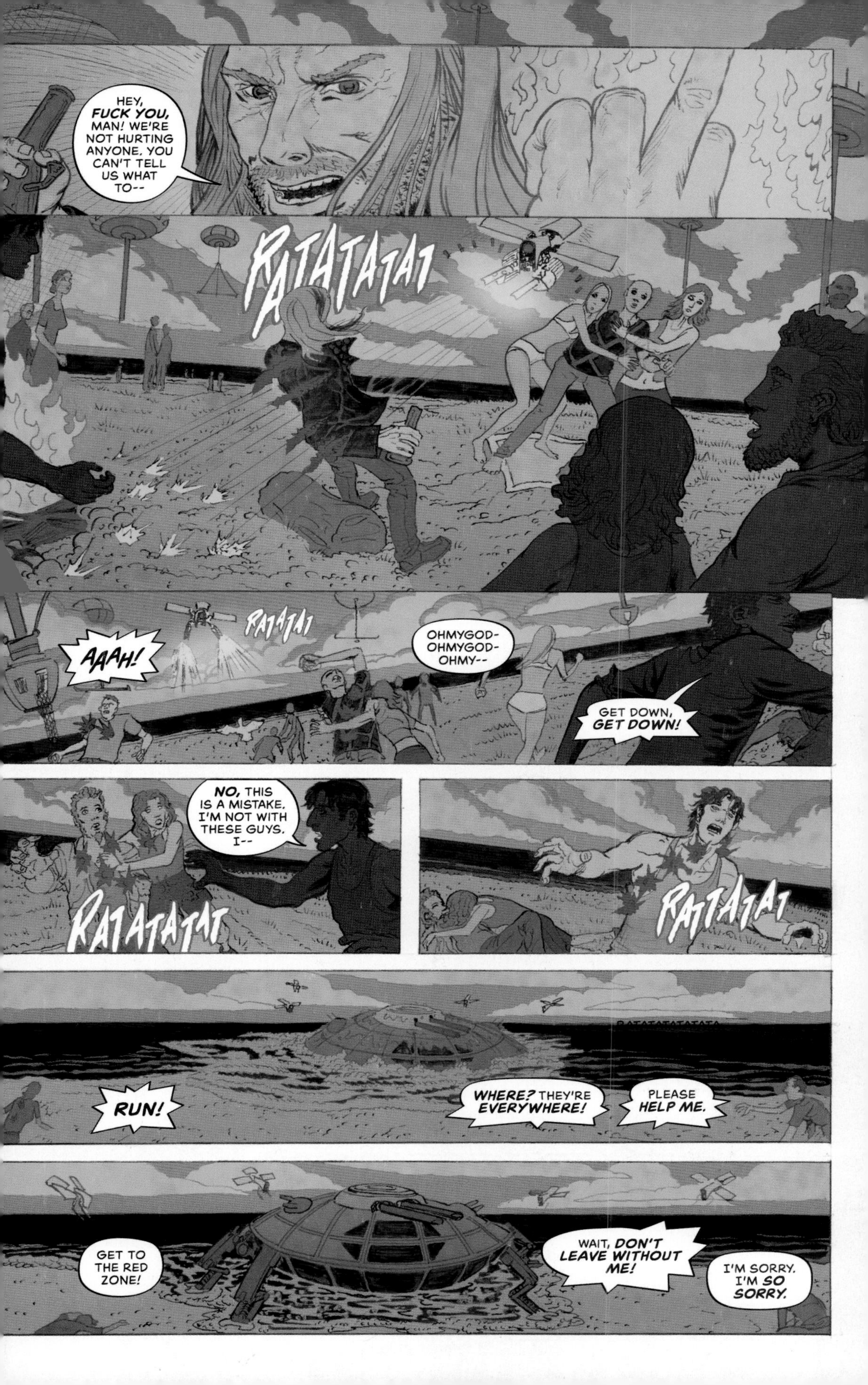
HEY, FUCK YOU, MAN! WE'RE NOT HURTING ANYONE. YOU CAN'T TELL US WHAT TO--
RATATATAT
AAAH!
RATATAT
OHMYGOD-OHMYGOD-OHMY--
GET DOWN, GET DOWN!
NO, THIS IS A MISTAKE. I'M NOT WITH THESE GUYS. I--
RATATATAT
RATATAT
RATATATATATATA
RUN!
WHERE? THEY'RE EVERYWHERE!
PLEASE HELP ME.
GET TO THE RED ZONE!
WAIT, DON'T LEAVE WITHOUT ME!
I'M SORRY. I'M SO SORRY.

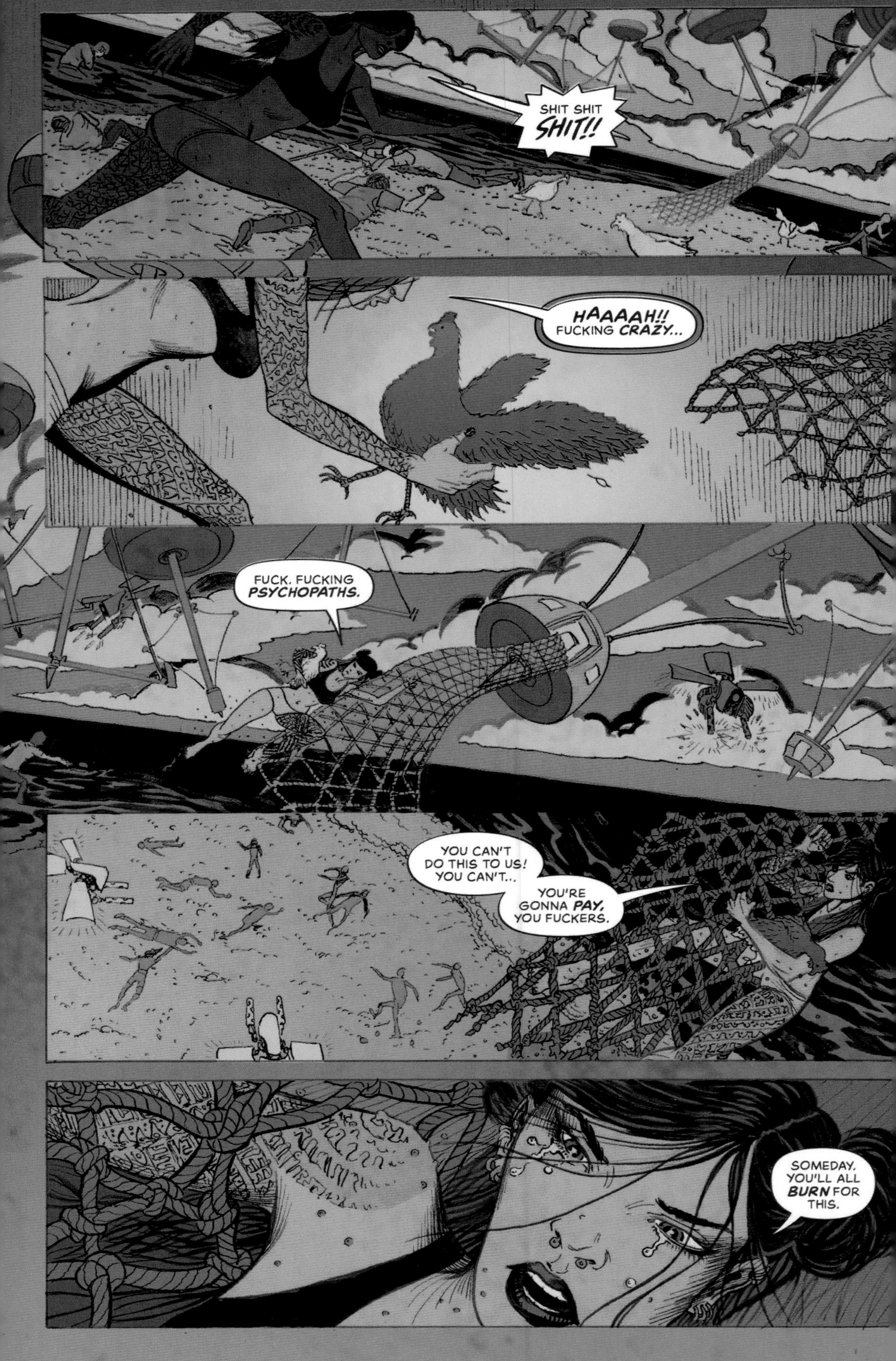
SHIT SHIT SHIT!!
HAAAAH!! FUCKING CRAZY...
FUCK. FUCKING PSYCHOPATHS.
YOU CAN'T DO THIS TO US! YOU CAN'T...
YOU'RE GONNA PAY, YOU FUCKERS.
SOMEDAY, YOU'LL ALL BURN FOR THIS.

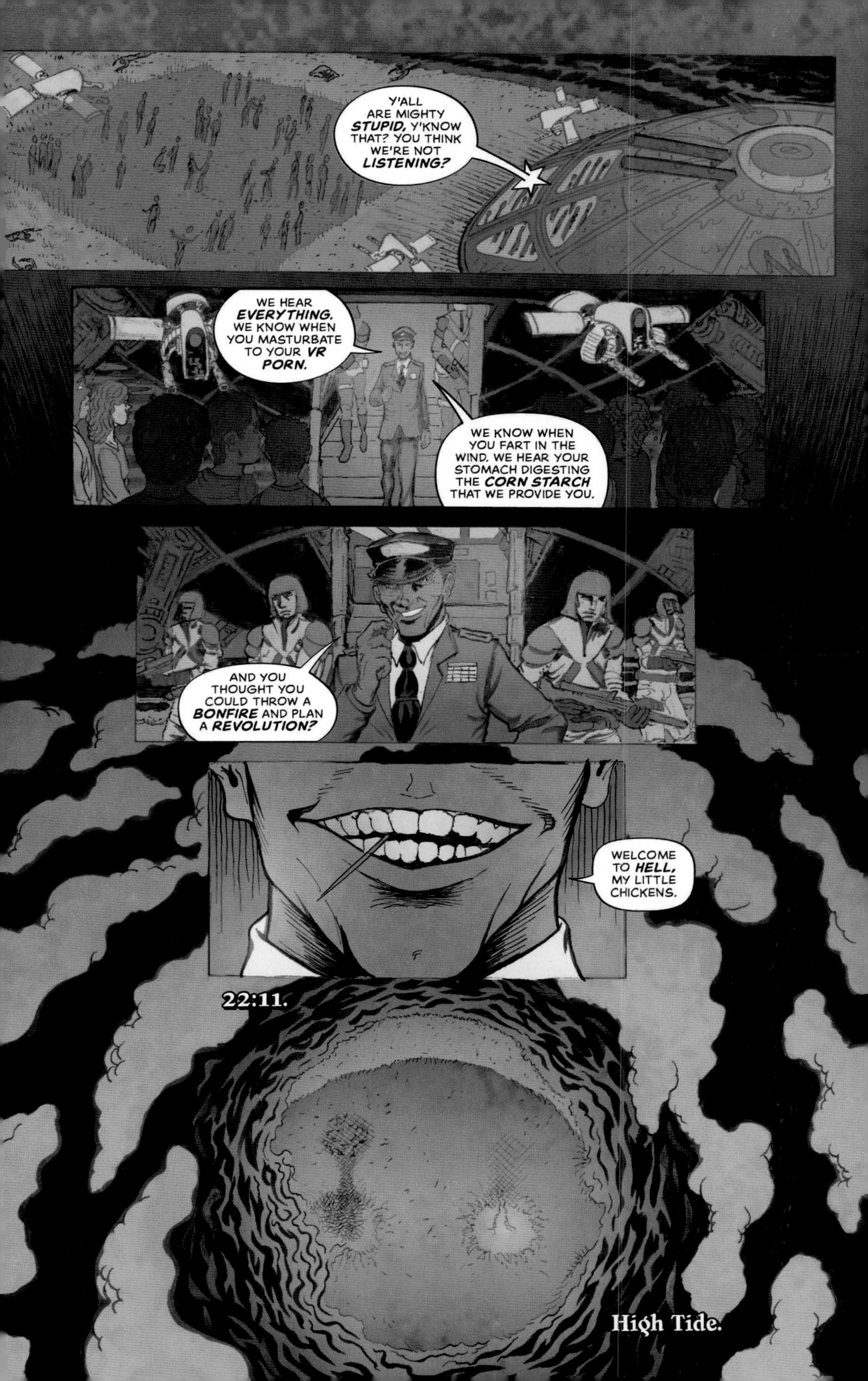
Y'ALL ARE MIGHTY STUPID, Y'KNOW THAT? YOU THINK WE'RE NOT LISTENING?
WE HEAR EVERYTHING. WE KNOW WHEN YOU MASTURBATE TO YOUR VR PORN.
WE KNOW WHEN YOU FART IN THE WIND. WE HEAR YOUR STOMACH DIGESTING THE CORN STARCH THAT WE PROVIDE YOU.
AND YOU THOUGHT YOU COULD THROW A BONFIRE AND PLAN A REVOLUTION?
WELCOME TO HELL, MY LITTLE CHICKENS.
22:11.
High Tide.

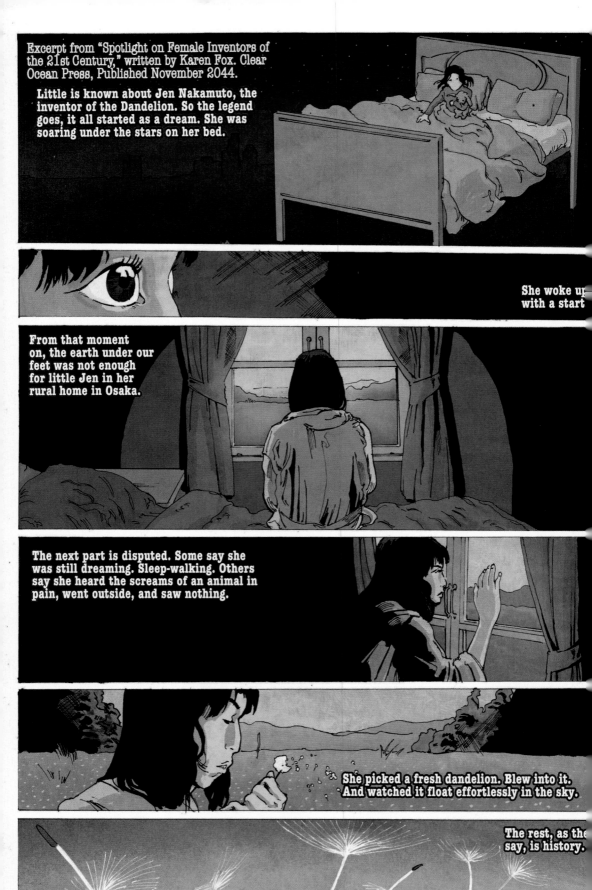

Excerpt from "Spotlight on Female Inventors of the 21st Century," written by Karen Fox. Clear Ocean Press, Published November 2044.

Little is known about Jen Nakamuto, the inventor of the Dandelion. So the legend goes, it all started as a dream. She was soaring under the stars on her bed.

She woke up with a start.

From that moment on, the earth under our feet was not enough for little Jen in her rural home in Osaka.

The next part is disputed. Some say she was still dreaming. Sleep-walking. Others say she heard the screams of an animal in pain, went outside, and saw nothing.

She picked a fresh dandelion. Blew into it. And watched it float effortlessly in the sky.

The rest, as they say, is history.

STAR-CROSSED

ART

VANESA **DEL REY**

COLORS

JUHA **VELTTI**

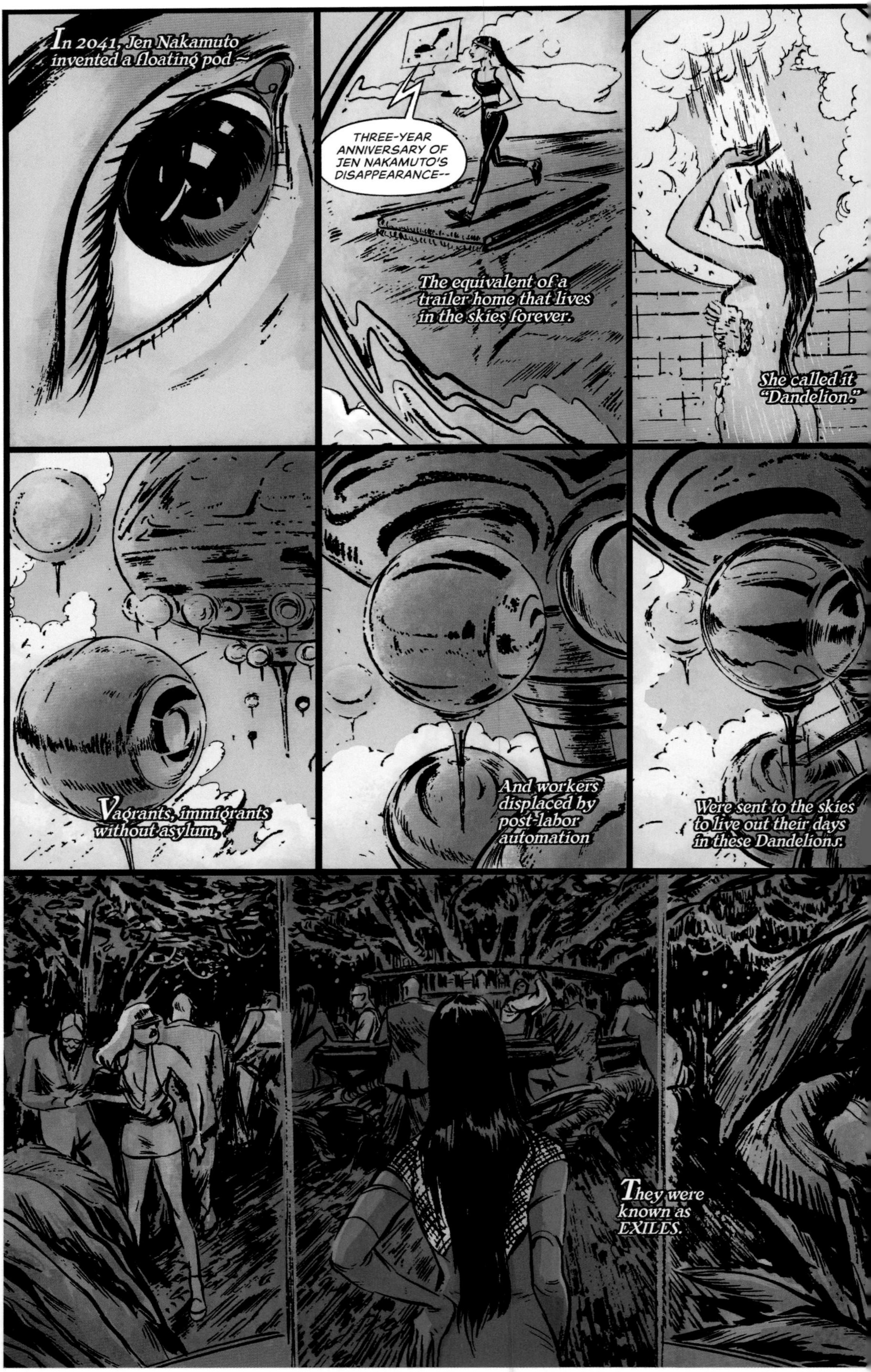
In 2041, Jen Nakamuto invented a floating pod ~
THREE-YEAR ANNIVERSARY OF JEN NAKAMUTO'S DISAPPEARANCE--
The equivalent of a trailer home that lives in the skies forever.
She called it "Dandelion."
Vagrants, immigrants without asylum,
And workers displaced by post-labor automation
Were sent to the skies to live out their days in these Dandelions.
They were known as EXILES.

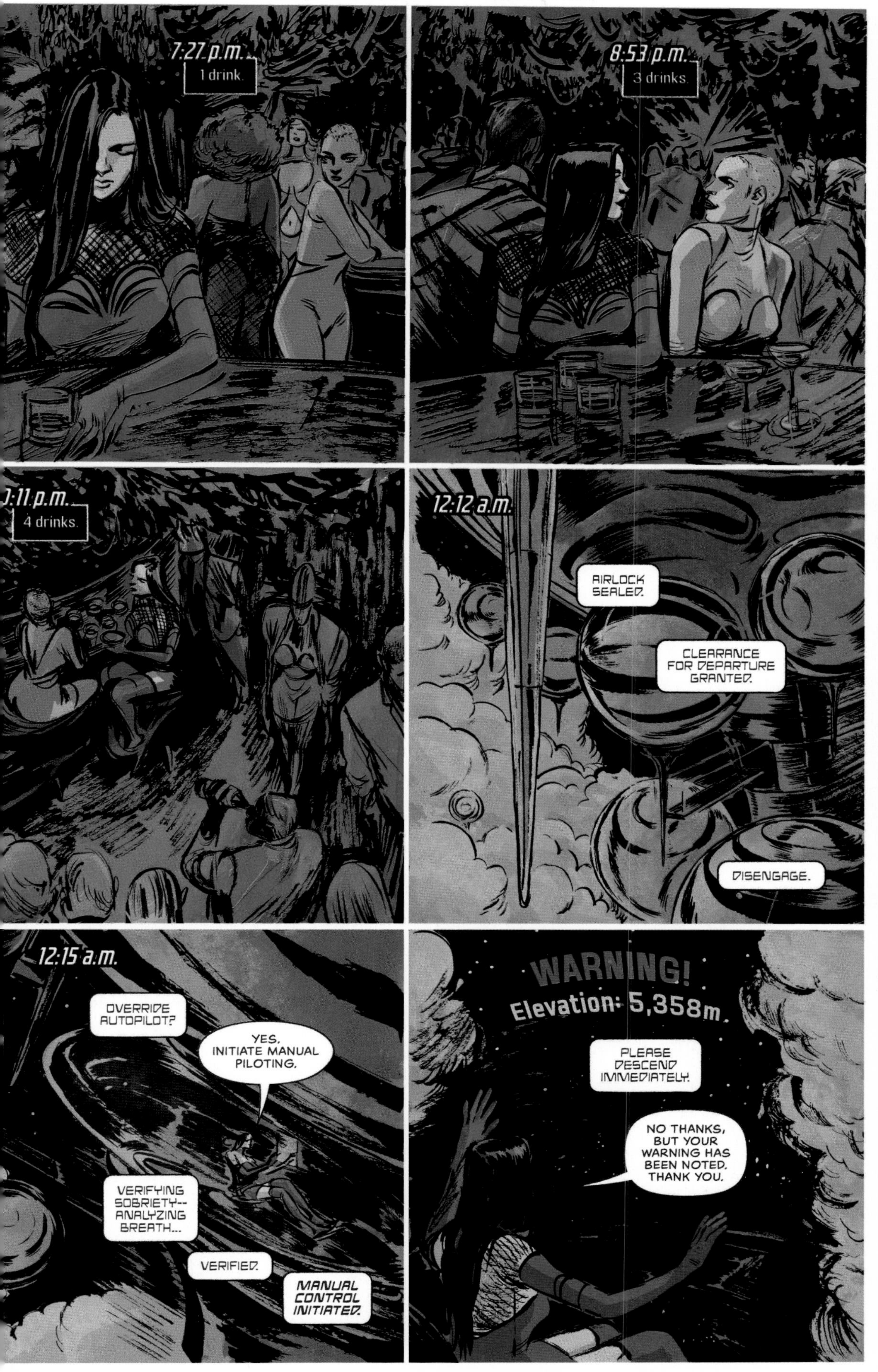
7:27 p.m.
1 drink.
8:53 p.m.
3 drinks.
:11 p.m.
4 drinks.
12:12 a.m.
AIRLOCK SEALED.
CLEARANCE FOR DEPARTURE GRANTED.
DISENGAGE.
12:15 a.m.
OVERRIDE AUTOPILOT?
YES. INITIATE MANUAL PILOTING.
VERIFYING SOBRIETY-- ANALYZING BREATH...
VERIFIED.
MANUAL CONTROL INITIATED.
WARNING!
Elevation: 5,358m
PLEASE DESCEND IMMEDIATELY.
NO THANKS, BUT YOUR WARNING HAS BEEN NOTED. THANK YOU.

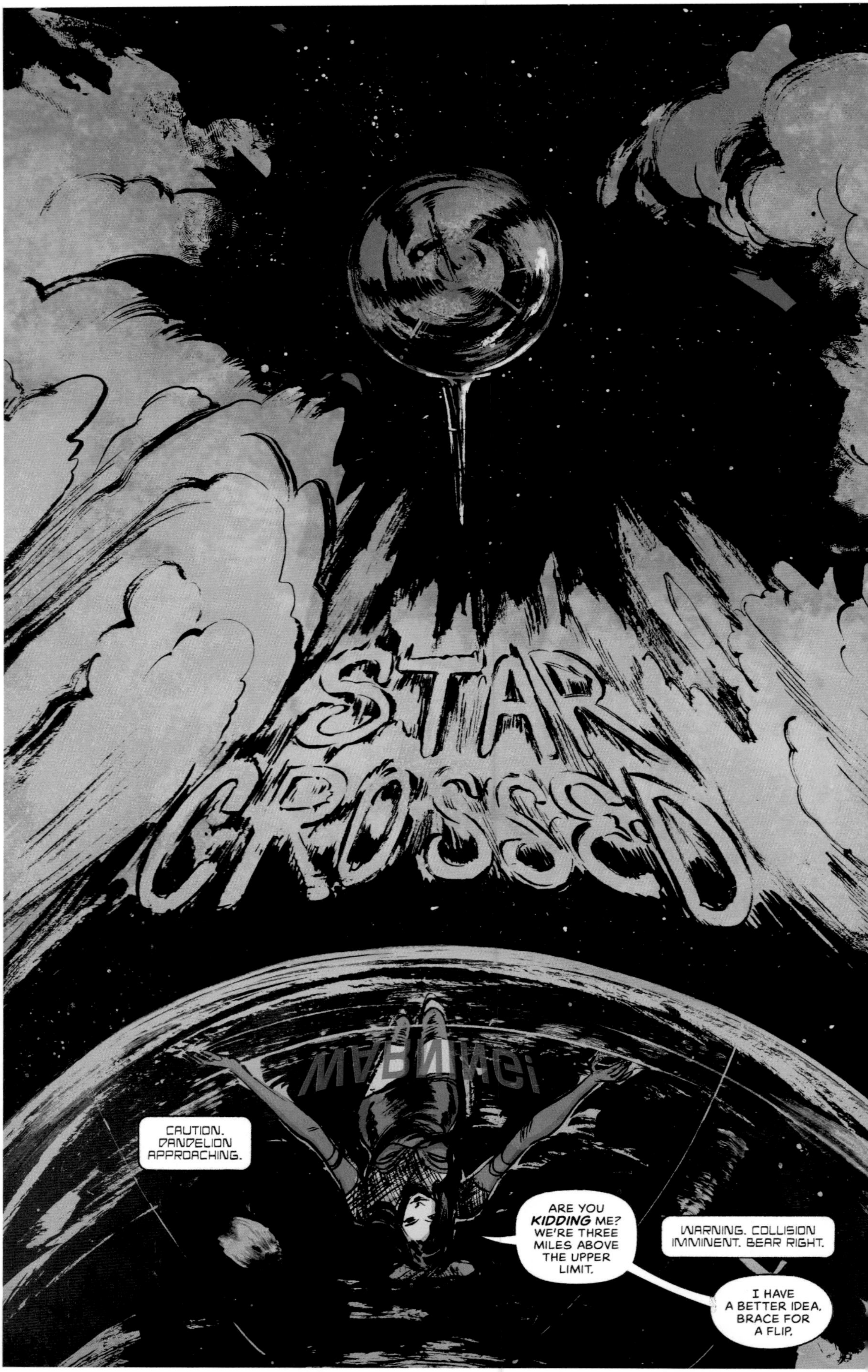
STAR CROSSED
CAUTION. DANDELION APPROACHING.
ARE YOU KIDDING ME? WE'RE THREE MILES ABOVE THE UPPER LIMIT.
WARNING. COLLISION IMMINENT. BEAR RIGHT.
I HAVE A BETTER IDEA. BRACE FOR A FLIP.

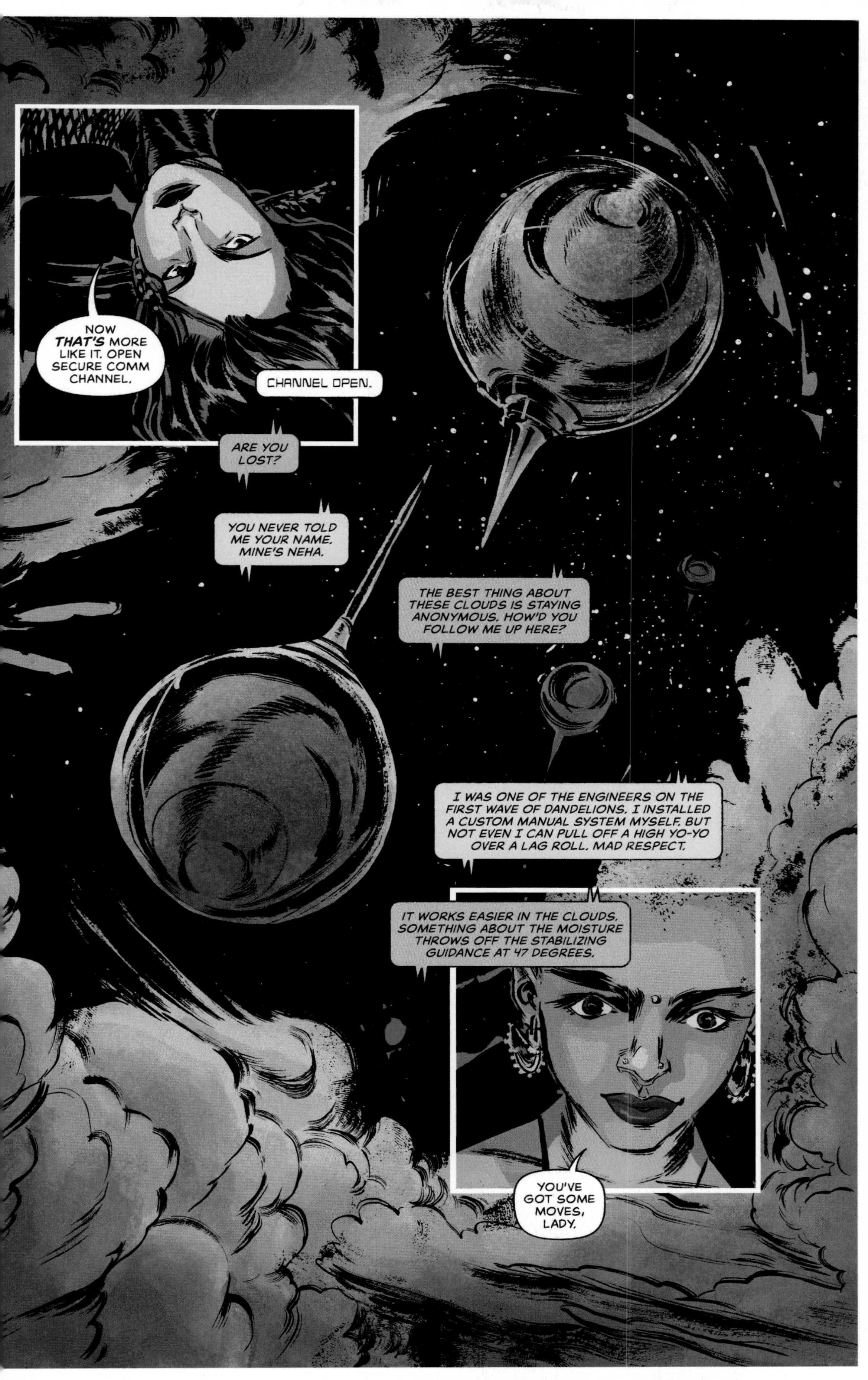
NOW THAT'S MORE LIKE IT. OPEN SECURE COMM CHANNEL.
CHANNEL OPEN.
ARE YOU LOST?
YOU NEVER TOLD ME YOUR NAME. MINE'S NEHA.
THE BEST THING ABOUT THESE CLOUDS IS STAYING ANONYMOUS. HOW'D YOU FOLLOW ME UP HERE?
I WAS ONE OF THE ENGINEERS ON THE FIRST WAVE OF DANDELIONS. I INSTALLED A CUSTOM MANUAL SYSTEM MYSELF. BUT NOT EVEN I CAN PULL OFF A HIGH YO-YO OVER A LAG ROLL. MAD RESPECT.
IT WORKS EASIER IN THE CLOUDS. SOMETHING ABOUT THE MOISTURE THROWS OFF THE STABILIZING GUIDANCE AT 47 DEGREES.
YOU'VE GOT SOME MOVES, LADY.

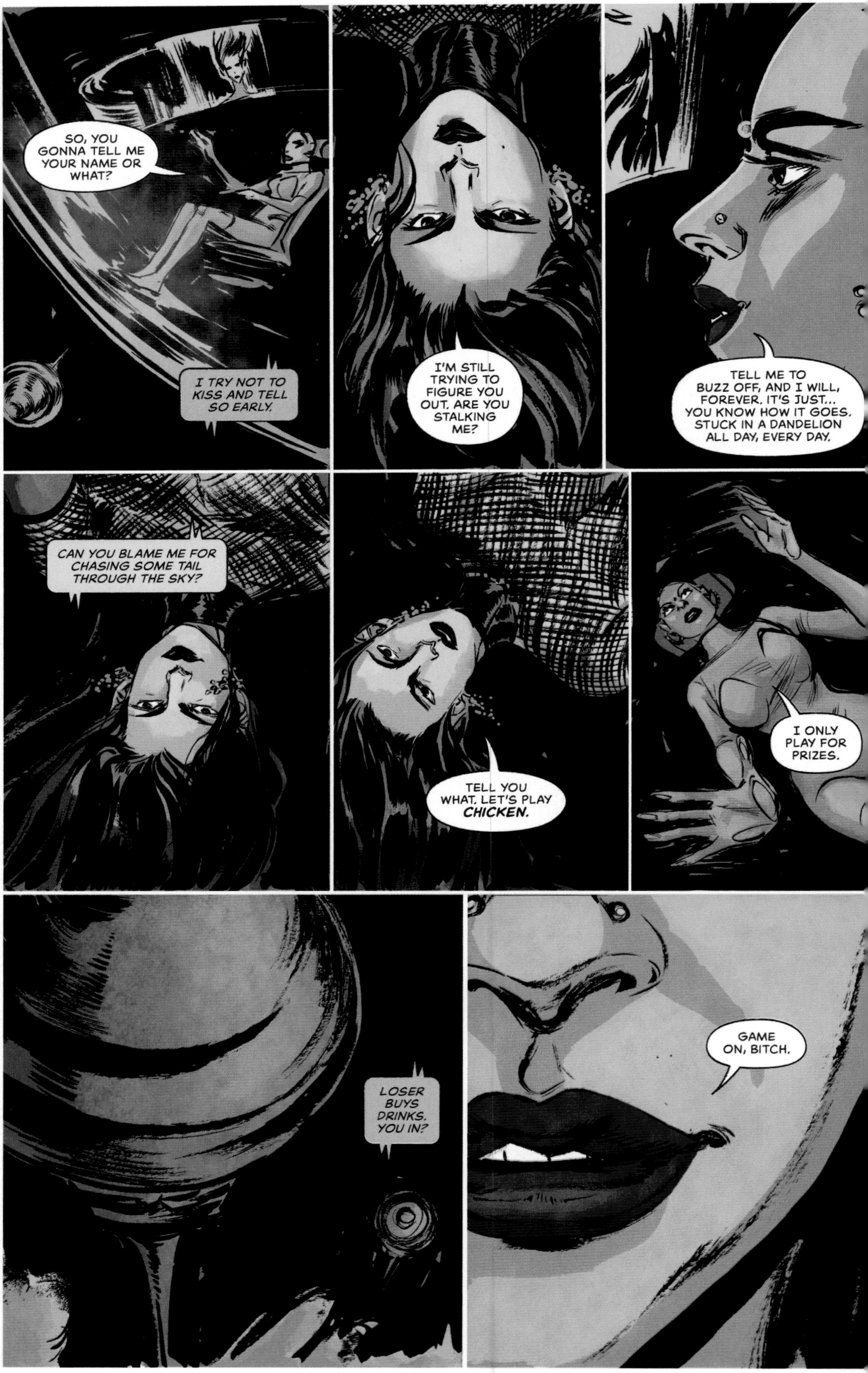
SO, YOU GONNA TELL ME YOUR NAME OR WHAT?
I TRY NOT TO KISS AND TELL SO EARLY.
I'M STILL TRYING TO FIGURE YOU OUT. ARE YOU STALKING ME?
TELL ME TO BUZZ OFF, AND I WILL, FOREVER. IT'S JUST... YOU KNOW HOW IT GOES. STUCK IN A DANDELION ALL DAY, EVERY DAY.
CAN YOU BLAME ME FOR CHASING SOME TAIL THROUGH THE SKY?
TELL YOU WHAT. LET'S PLAY CHICKEN.
I ONLY PLAY FOR PRIZES.
LOSER BUYS DRINKS. YOU IN?
GAME ON, BITCH.

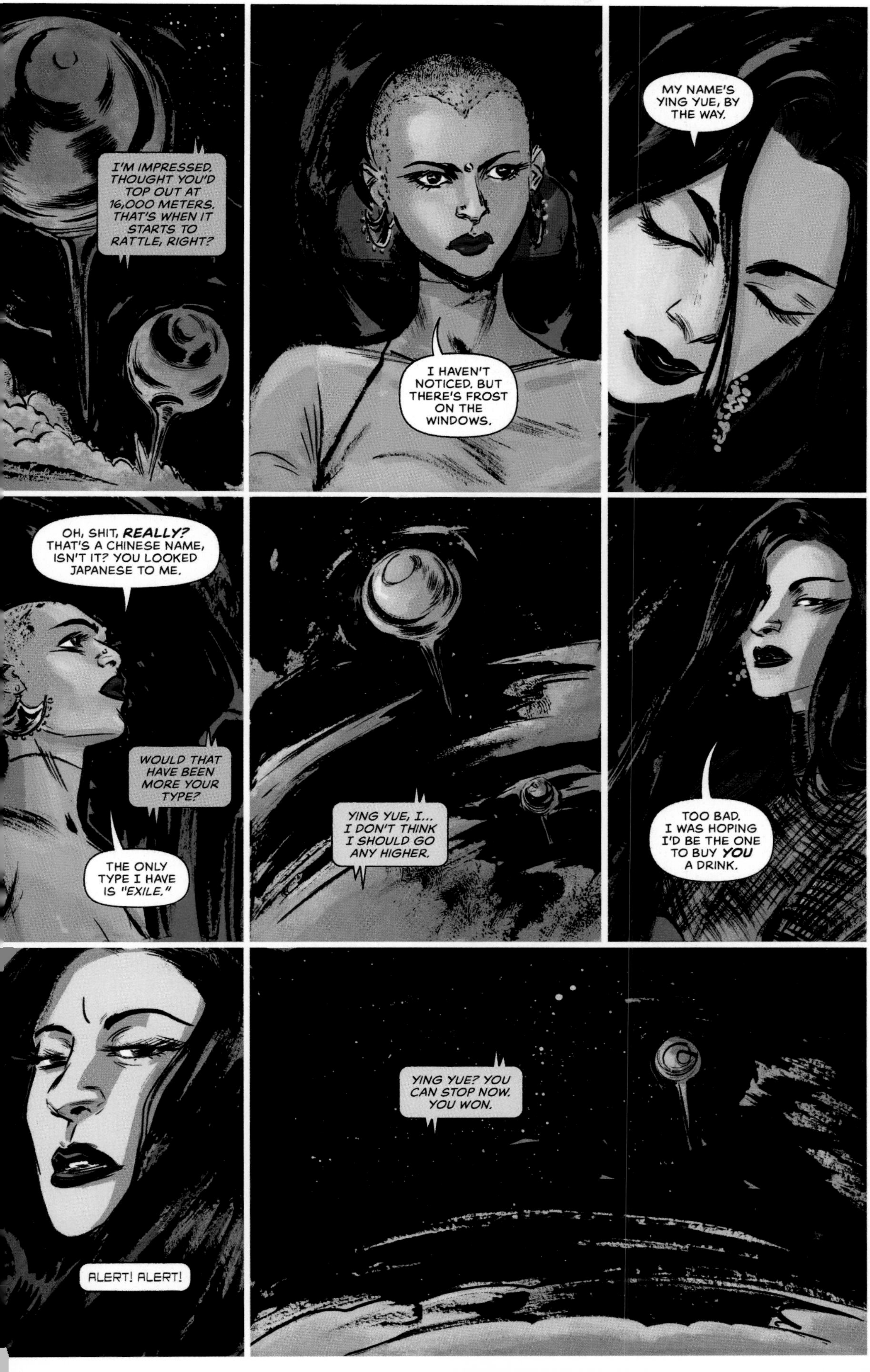
I'M IMPRESSED. THOUGHT YOU'D TOP OUT AT 16,000 METERS. THAT'S WHEN IT STARTS TO RATTLE, RIGHT?
I HAVEN'T NOTICED. BUT THERE'S FROST ON THE WINDOWS.
MY NAME'S YING YUE, BY THE WAY.
OH, SHIT, **REALLY?** THAT'S A CHINESE NAME, ISN'T IT? YOU LOOKED JAPANESE TO ME.
WOULD THAT HAVE BEEN MORE YOUR TYPE?
THE ONLY TYPE I HAVE IS "EXILE."
YING YUE, I... I DON'T THINK I SHOULD GO ANY HIGHER.
TOO BAD. I WAS HOPING I'D BE THE ONE TO BUY **YOU** A DRINK.
ALERT! ALERT!
YING YUE? YOU CAN STOP NOW. YOU WON.

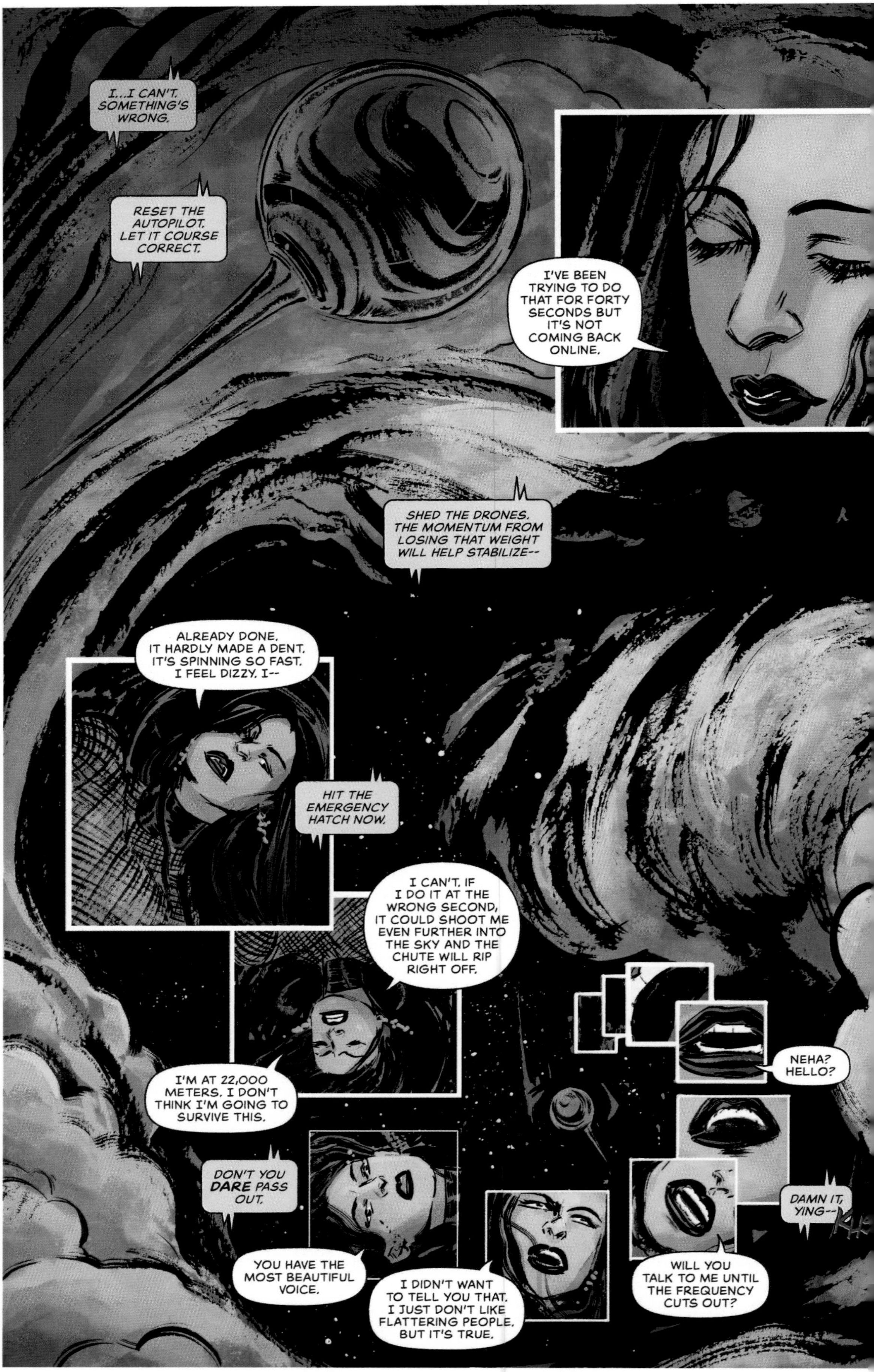

I...I CAN'T. SOMETHING'S WRONG.
RESET THE AUTOPILOT. LET IT COURSE CORRECT.
I'VE BEEN TRYING TO DO THAT FOR FORTY SECONDS BUT IT'S NOT COMING BACK ONLINE.
SHED THE DRONES. THE MOMENTUM FROM LOSING THAT WEIGHT WILL HELP STABILIZE--
ALREADY DONE. IT HARDLY MADE A DENT. IT'S SPINNING SO FAST. I FEEL DIZZY. I--
HIT THE EMERGENCY HATCH NOW.
I CAN'T. IF I DO IT AT THE WRONG SECOND, IT COULD SHOOT ME EVEN FURTHER INTO THE SKY AND THE CHUTE WILL RIP RIGHT OFF.
I'M AT 22,000 METERS. I DON'T THINK I'M GOING TO SURVIVE THIS.
DON'T YOU **DARE** PASS OUT.
YOU HAVE THE MOST BEAUTIFUL VOICE.
I DIDN'T WANT TO TELL YOU THAT. I JUST DON'T LIKE FLATTERING PEOPLE. BUT IT'S TRUE.
NEHA? HELLO?
DAMN IT, YING--
WILL YOU TALK TO ME UNTIL THE FREQUENCY CUTS OUT?

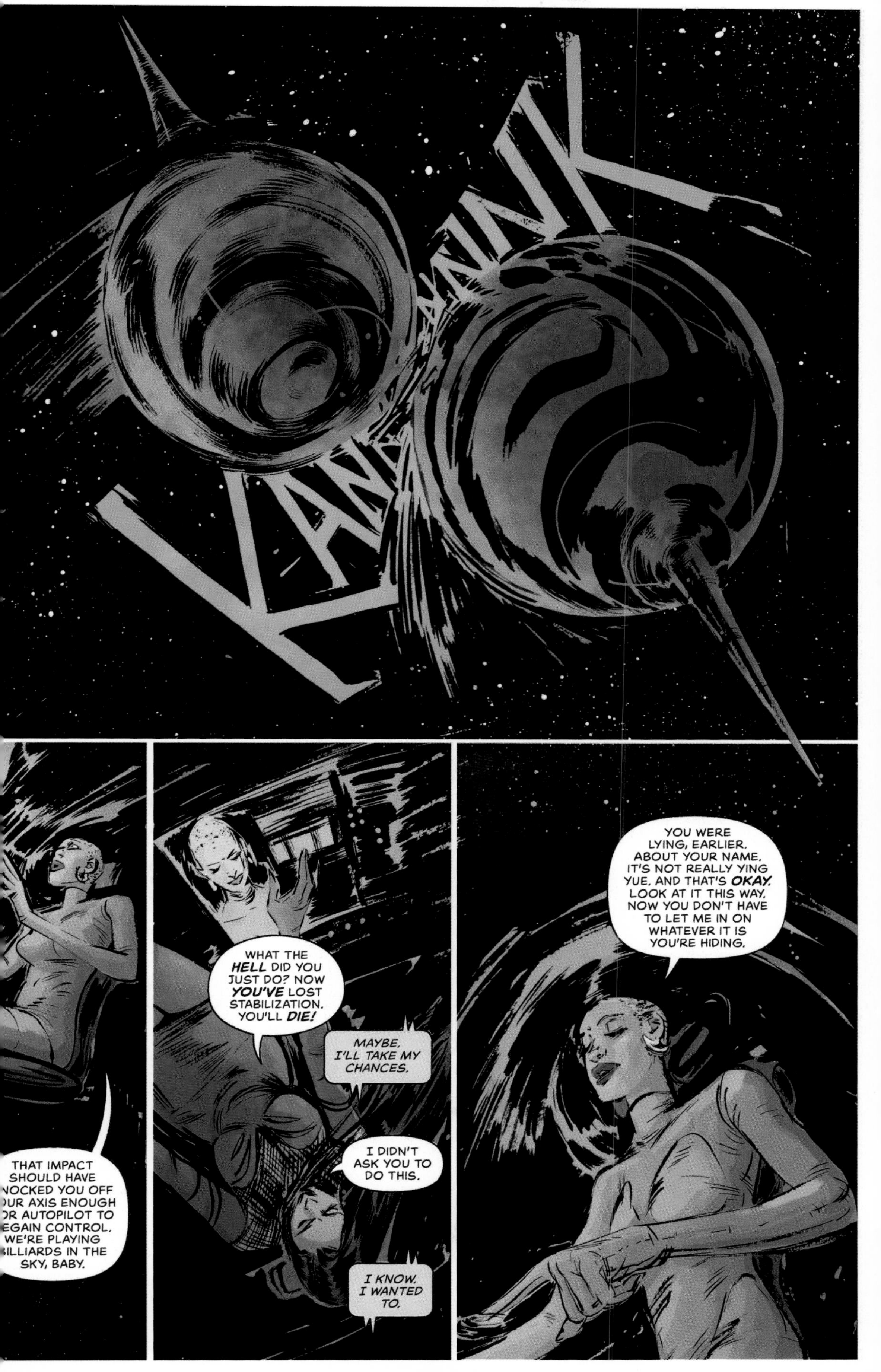
THAT IMPACT SHOULD HAVE NOCKED YOU OFF OUR AXIS ENOUGH OR AUTOPILOT TO EGAIN CONTROL. WE'RE PLAYING ILLIARDS IN THE SKY, BABY.
WHAT THE **HELL** DID YOU JUST DO? NOW **YOU'VE** LOST STABILIZATION. YOU'LL **DIE!**
MAYBE. I'LL TAKE MY CHANCES.
I DIDN'T ASK YOU TO DO THIS.
I KNOW. I WANTED TO.
YOU WERE LYING, EARLIER, ABOUT YOUR NAME. IT'S NOT REALLY YING YUE. AND THAT'S **OKAY.** LOOK AT IT THIS WAY. NOW YOU DON'T HAVE TO LET ME IN ON WHATEVER IT IS YOU'RE HIDING.

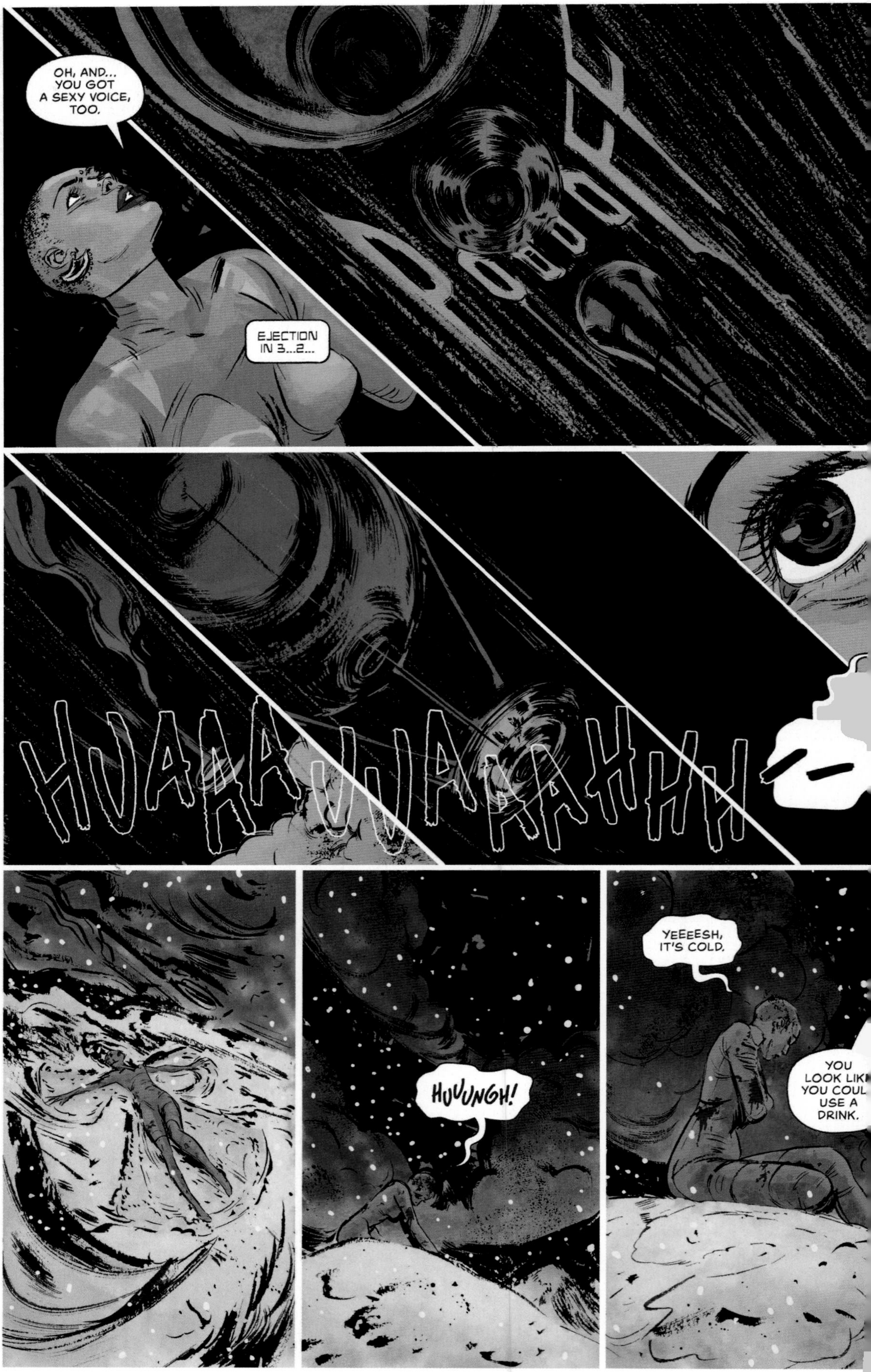

OH, AND... YOU GOT A SEXY VOICE, TOO.
EJECTION IN 3...2...
HUAAAUUAAAHHH—
HUUUNGH!
YEEEESH, IT'S COLD.
YOU LOOK LIK
YOU COUL
USE A DRINK.

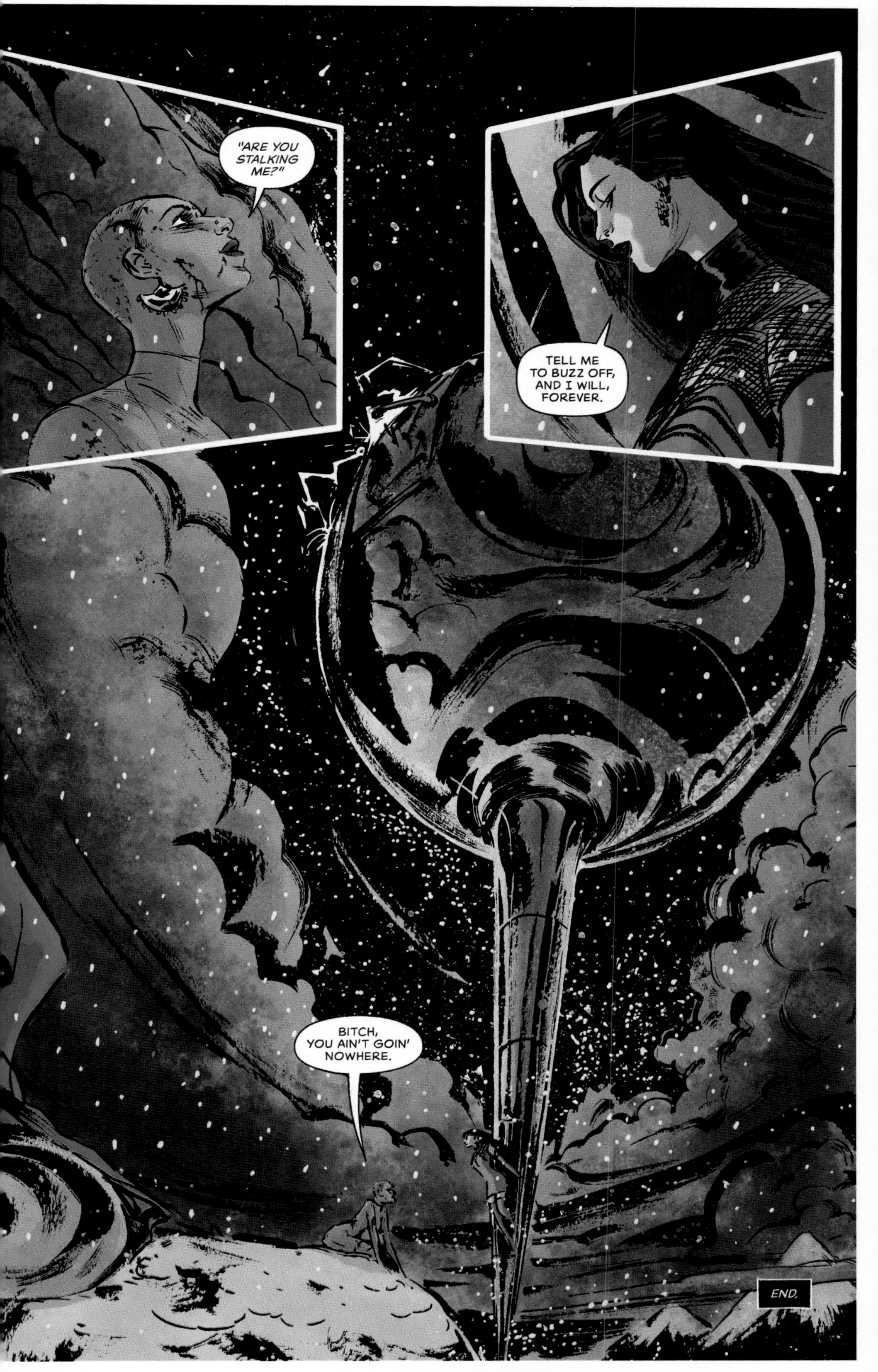
"ARE YOU STALKING ME?"
TELL ME TO BUZZ OFF, AND I WILL, FOREVER.
BITCH, YOU AIN'T GOIN' NOWHERE.
END.

"DANDELION" CONCEPT CONFERENCE TRANSCRIPT
21.11.2040 – 15:00 JST

ATTENDEES: Jen Nakamuto, Kanji Yamata

Translated from Japanese

KY: From one professional to another, maybe have someone with stronger English transliteration proof your work before you print. They spelled your name wrong. I've never seen a "u" in "Nakamoto" before.

JN: I guess that makes me special. If there's an error, it happened with my father's documents, but the "u" has stuck ever since. People sometimes correct it back to an "o" but I prefer it this way.

KY: Okay, anyway, I looked over your designs. It's really interesting. No one's taken a serious run at LTA travel in quite some time.

JN: They're all trying, trust me. Lighter-Than-Air vehicles get a bad rap because of the Hindenburg disaster, but as long as we avoid Hydrogen, we're good. The technology works, and soon enough there's going to be a race to dominate the market. But I'm going to get there first. As long as we've got the proper team in place to rebrand LTA travel –

KY: Let's not get ahead of ourselves. The scale seems a bit unwieldy to me. We're talking about the equivalent of a five-bedroom house. Even with lightweight materials and highly efficient solar conversion, I don't think you've factored in the weight accurately to get these things in the air.

JN: Nonsense. It'll work.

KY: I'm just trying to help you. They don't need to be so big, Jen. Just go a little smaller and the math makes more sense –

JN: We're not going smaller. This is the standard size. Anything smaller is a prison.

KY: But at least it'll work.

JN: Solar power's only part of it. The materials

harness the wind in between layers. Most of the time it's hardly using any energy at all.

KY: Sounds like a lot could go wrong.

JN: That's everything worthwhile ever invented, Kanji. We've checked every detail. The design is smart. The reason the sizing is looking odd to you is because the engineering is hidden so average consumers don't see it or think about it. They just board it and fly.

KY: [Inaudible]. And what's this antenna thing at the bottom?

JN: It's a lot of things. Mostly an atmospheric sensor and data receiver. But it folds in when the elevator descends.

KY: Right. Okay. An elevator to nowhere?

JN: To docking stations we're going to have. We've cracked it, Kanji. We're not wasting materials on a structure that's never meant to be on land. Eventually, we'll just launch them from the sky. That's how they make ships that float on water, don't they? They've got anchors to help them stop, but they simply don't work on land. This is no different.

KY: This thing here below the cabin?

JN: It's a cockpit but we're going to remove them in later models. We need to pass some inspections and get approvals first. Eventually we'll get more comfortable with autopilots and the cockpit won't be a measure for safety. It'll actually be a liability because human error is far worse than autopilot.

KY: You won't get that past regulation.

JN: Then you tell me. What will it take?

[RECORDING MISSING]

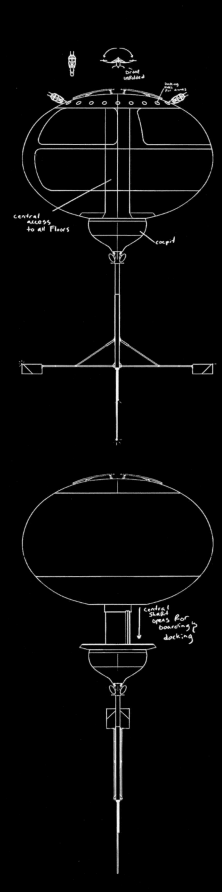

Drone unfolded
Docking holes for drones
central access to all floors
cocpit

central shaft opens for boarding & docking

KY: I can fund a prototype, sure, but to manufacture on this scale...

JN: I've got funds, too. The problem is the prototype of just the one Dandelion doesn't sell the concept. We need a fleet. A docking station.

KY: You're asking to build a city.

JN: We're this close, Kanji. The only thing that was holding this back were advancements in drone technology. Now that's taken care of –

KY: Slow down. Not all those patents are released yet.

JN: You can get them. I know you can. Just imagine it, Kanji. The drones go and retrieve the food supplies. They dispose of the waste. We can create a whole self-sustaining system in the skies.

KY: What's really going on here? The Jen that I know just wants to make soup and tend to her garden. Where is all this coming from?

JN: You've never woken up from a dream that was so real you had to chase it?

KY: The thing is, this doesn't sound like your dream.

JN: If you want in, you need to say so now. Because I already have seven backers. You'd be the eighth.

KY: What?

JN: Some of the normal players you'd expect. Some silent ones.

KY: Hold on a second. You said you'd come to me first.

JN: I knew you'd react like this. And that it would take convincing.

KY: I don't believe this. Who are the backers? Saito's under investigation, you know –

JN: His granddaughter isn't.

KY: Oh. Great. This is unbelievable.

JN: [Inaudible]. I'll tell you the others after we've gone through second round funding. But this is happening. Are you in or out?

KY: It's a lot of money, Jen.

JN: In or out, Kenji?

KY: Send me the papers. I'll sign them.

JN: That's my boy.

KY: Goodness. Woman, you are trouble.

TRUE NORTH

ART

ROY ALLAN **MARTINEZ**

COLORS

JACOB **PHILLIPS**

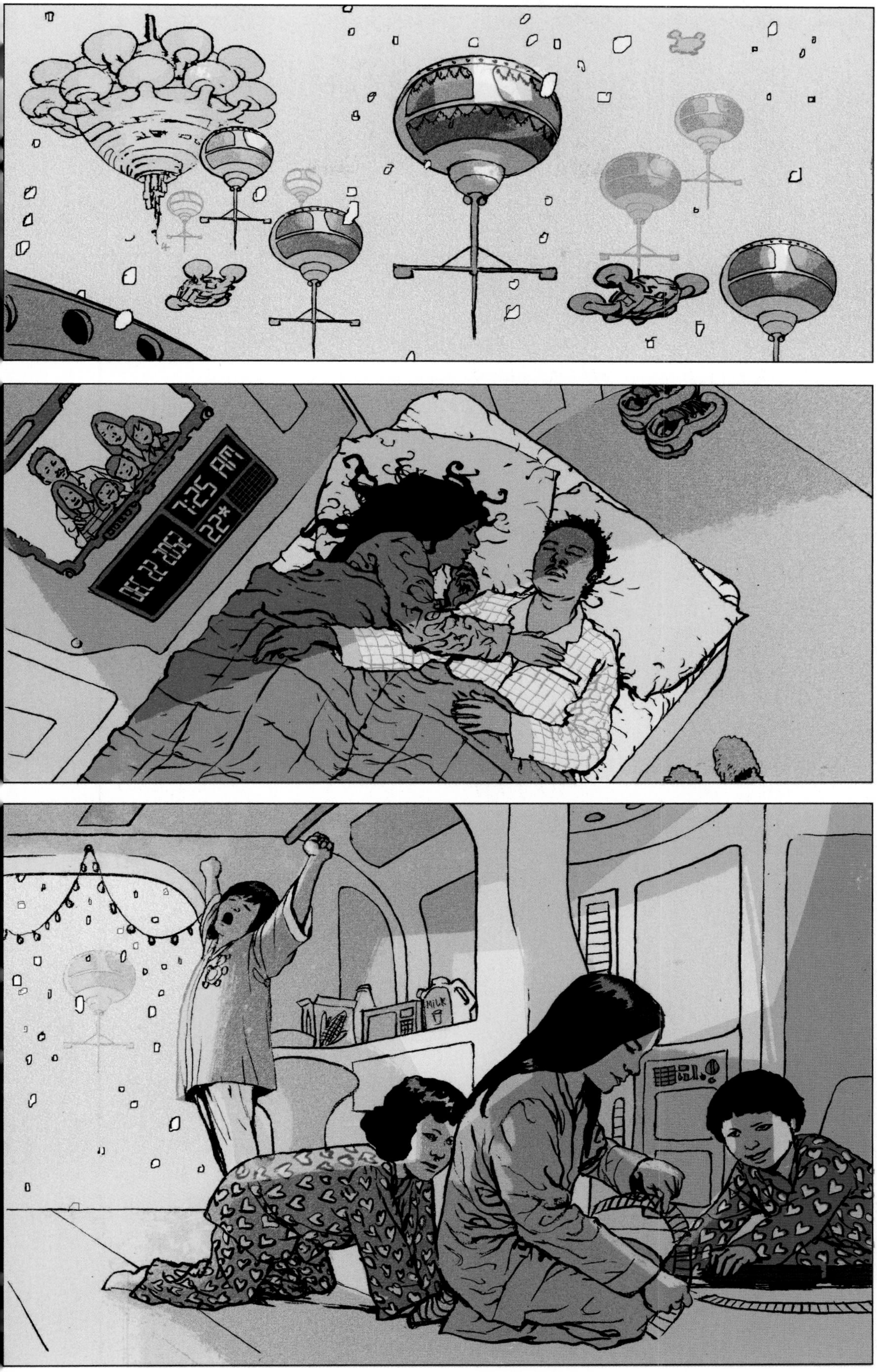

7:25 AM
22*
MILK

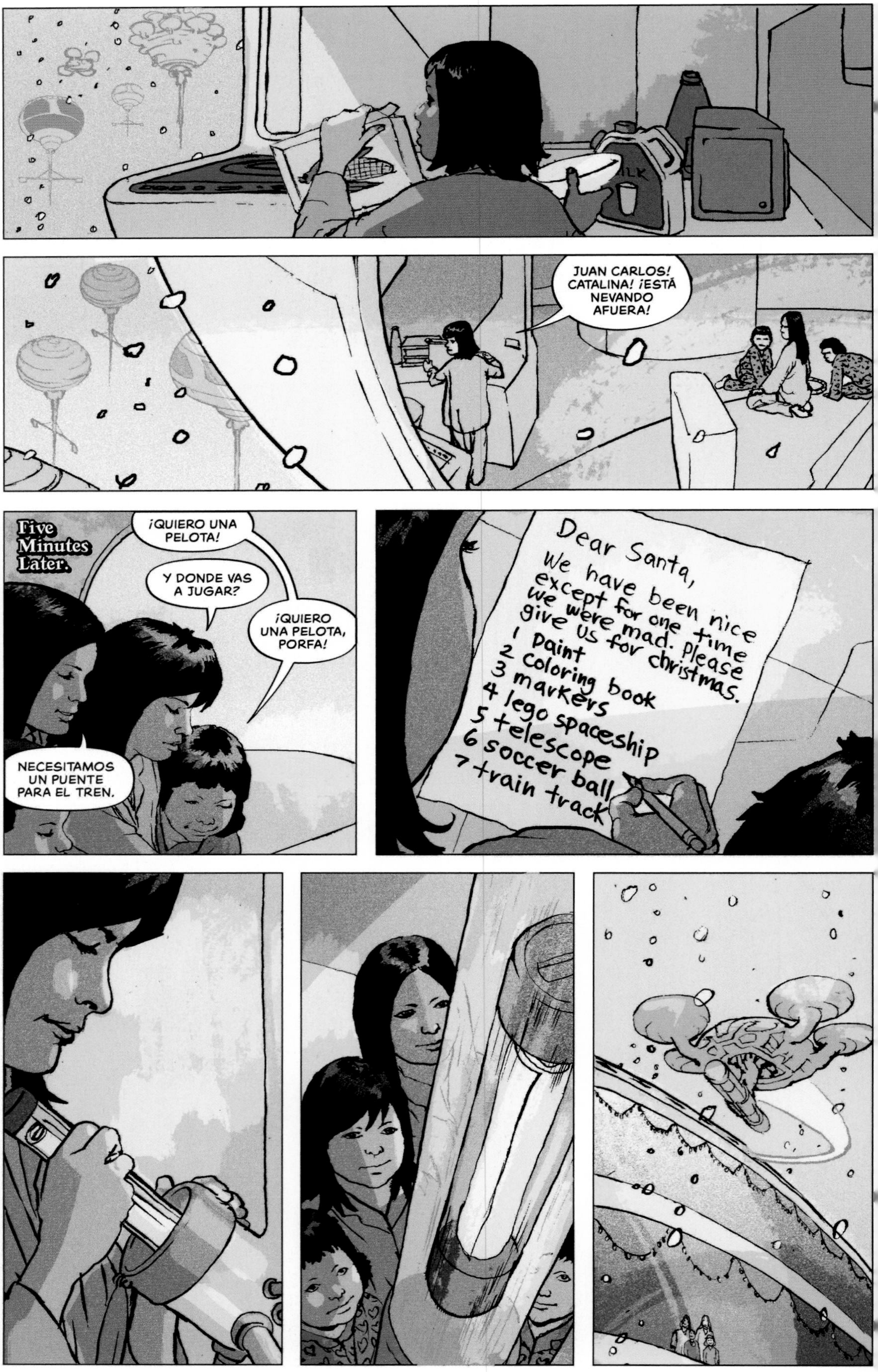
JUAN CARLOS! CATALINA! ¡ESTÁ NEVANDO AFUERA!
Five Minutes Later.
¡QUIERO UNA PELOTA!
Y DONDE VAS A JUGAR?
¡QUIERO UNA PELOTA, PORFA!
NECESITAMOS UN PUENTE PARA EL TREN.
Dear Santa,
We have been nice except for one time we were mad. please give us for christmas.
1 paint
2 coloring book
3 markers
4 lego spaceship
5 telescope
6 soccer ball
7 train track

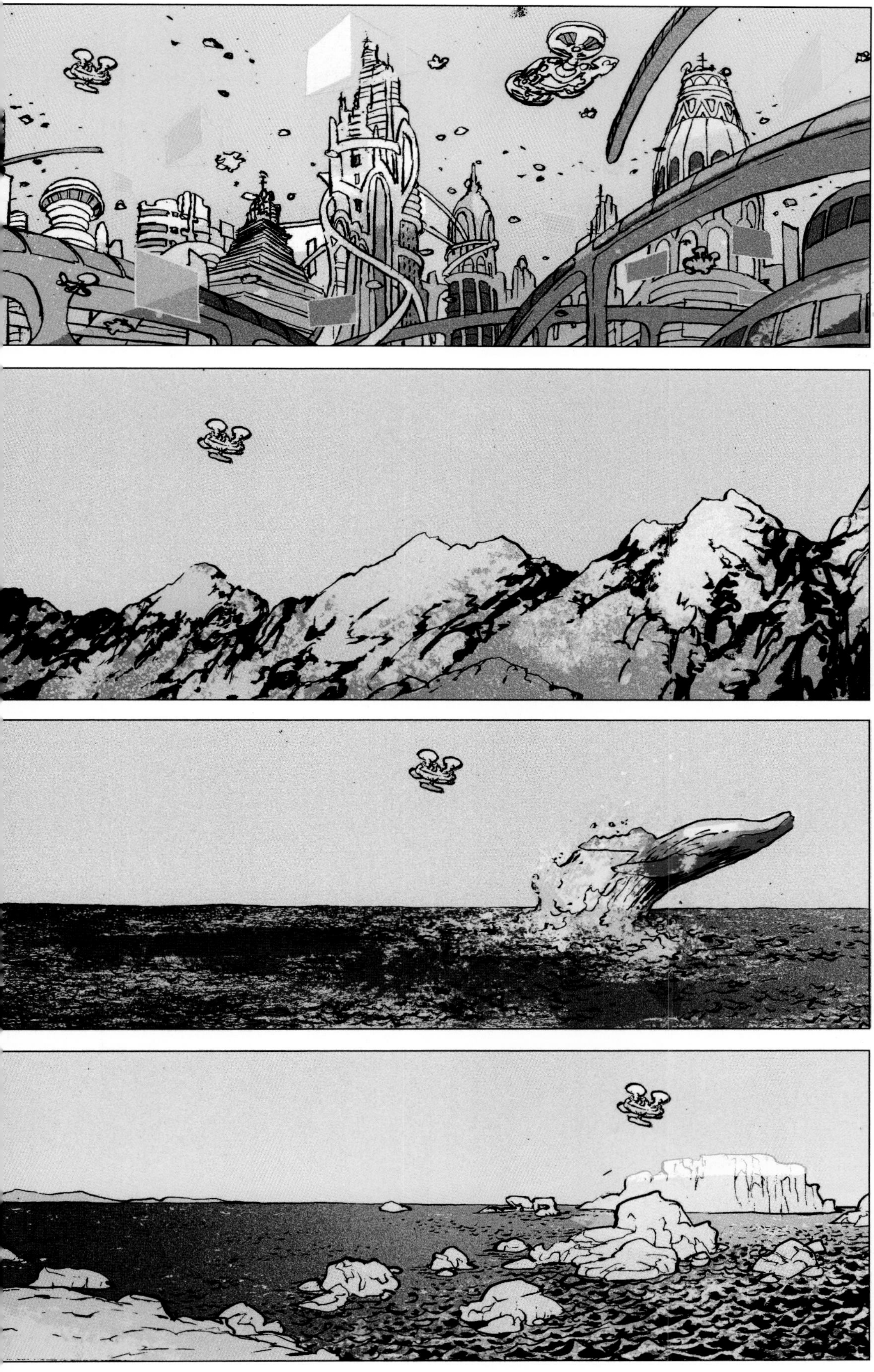

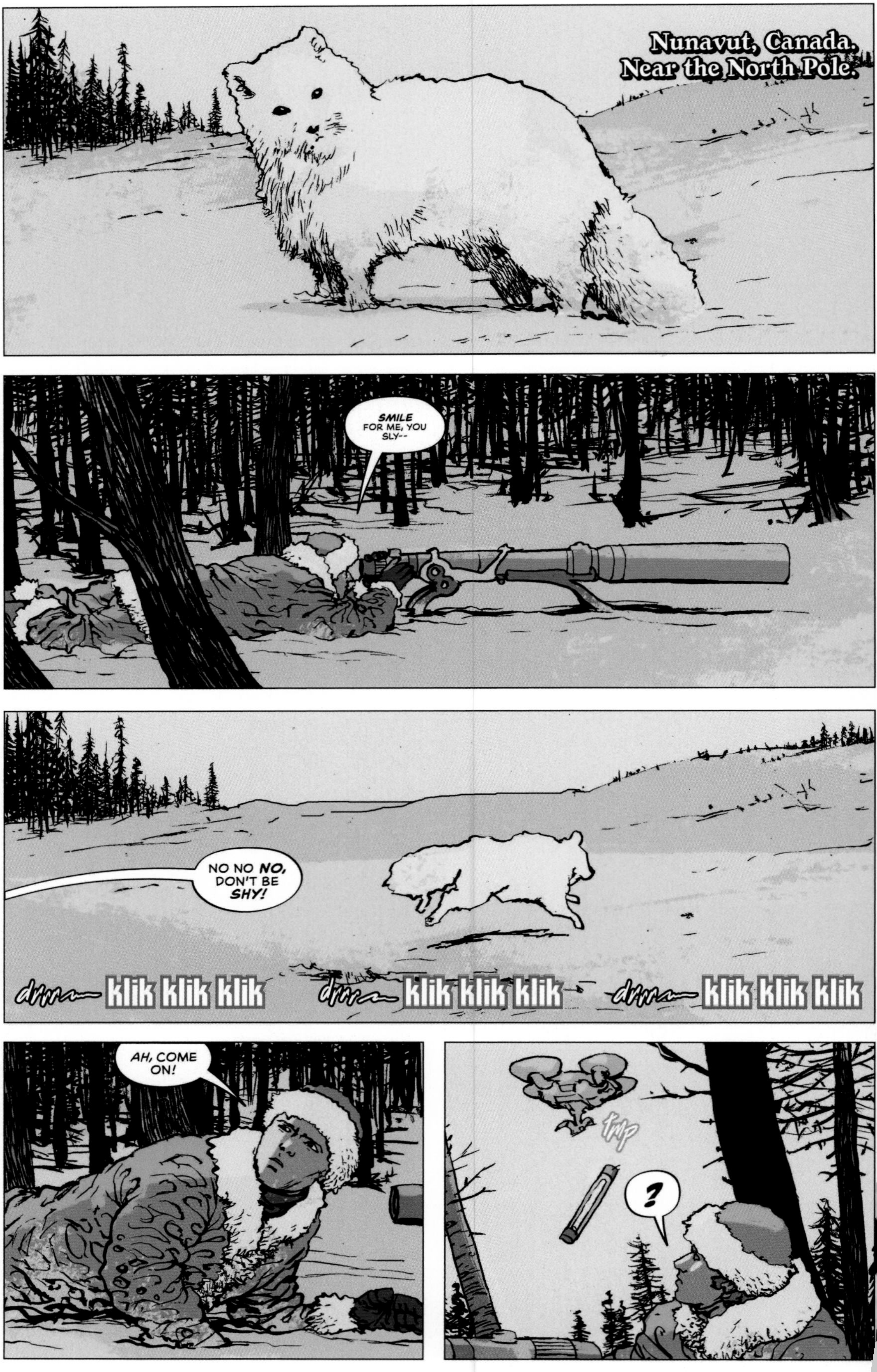

Nunavut, Canada. Near the North Pole.
SMILE FOR ME, YOU SLY--
NO NO NO, DON'T BE SHY!
klik klik klik
klik klik klik
klik klik klik
AH, COME ON!
?

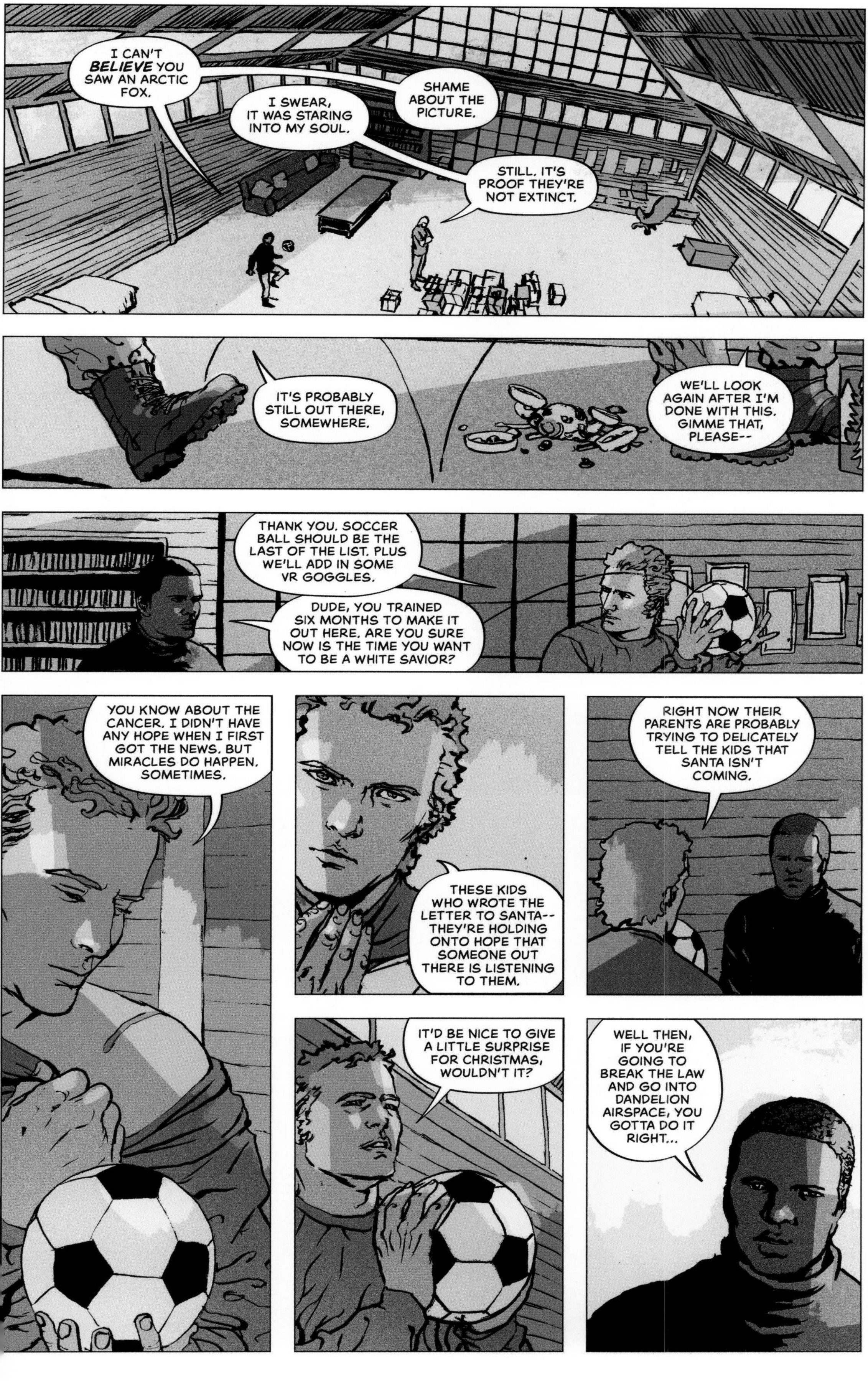
I CAN'T *BELIEVE* YOU SAW AN ARCTIC FOX.
I SWEAR, IT WAS STARING INTO MY SOUL.
SHAME ABOUT THE PICTURE.
STILL. IT'S PROOF THEY'RE NOT EXTINCT.
IT'S PROBABLY STILL OUT THERE, SOMEWHERE.
WE'LL LOOK AGAIN AFTER I'M DONE WITH THIS. GIMME THAT, PLEASE--
THANK YOU. SOCCER BALL SHOULD BE THE LAST OF THE LIST. PLUS WE'LL ADD IN SOME VR GOGGLES.
DUDE, YOU TRAINED SIX MONTHS TO MAKE IT OUT HERE. ARE YOU SURE NOW IS THE TIME YOU WANT TO BE A WHITE SAVIOR?
YOU KNOW ABOUT THE CANCER. I DIDN'T HAVE ANY HOPE WHEN I FIRST GOT THE NEWS. BUT MIRACLES DO HAPPEN, SOMETIMES.
THESE KIDS WHO WROTE THE LETTER TO SANTA-- THEY'RE HOLDING ONTO HOPE THAT SOMEONE OUT THERE IS LISTENING TO THEM.
RIGHT NOW THEIR PARENTS ARE PROBABLY TRYING TO DELICATELY TELL THE KIDS THAT SANTA ISN'T COMING.
IT'D BE NICE TO GIVE A LITTLE SURPRISE FOR CHRISTMAS, WOULDN'T IT?
WELL THEN, IF YOU'RE GOING TO BREAK THE LAW AND GO INTO DANDELION AIRSPACE, YOU GOTTA DO IT RIGHT...

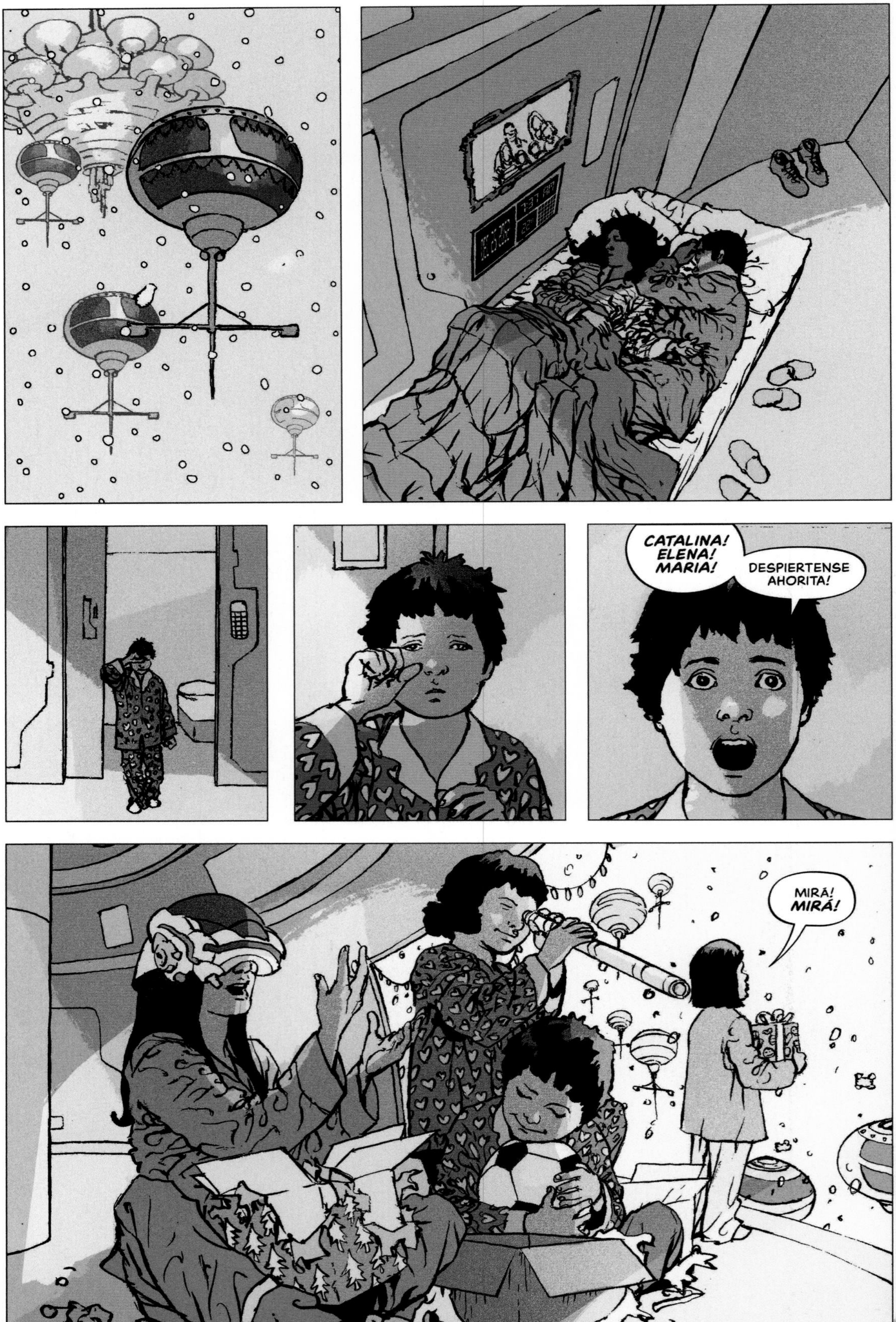
CATALINA! ELENA! MARIA!
DESPIERTENSE AHORITA!
MIRÁ! MIRÁ!

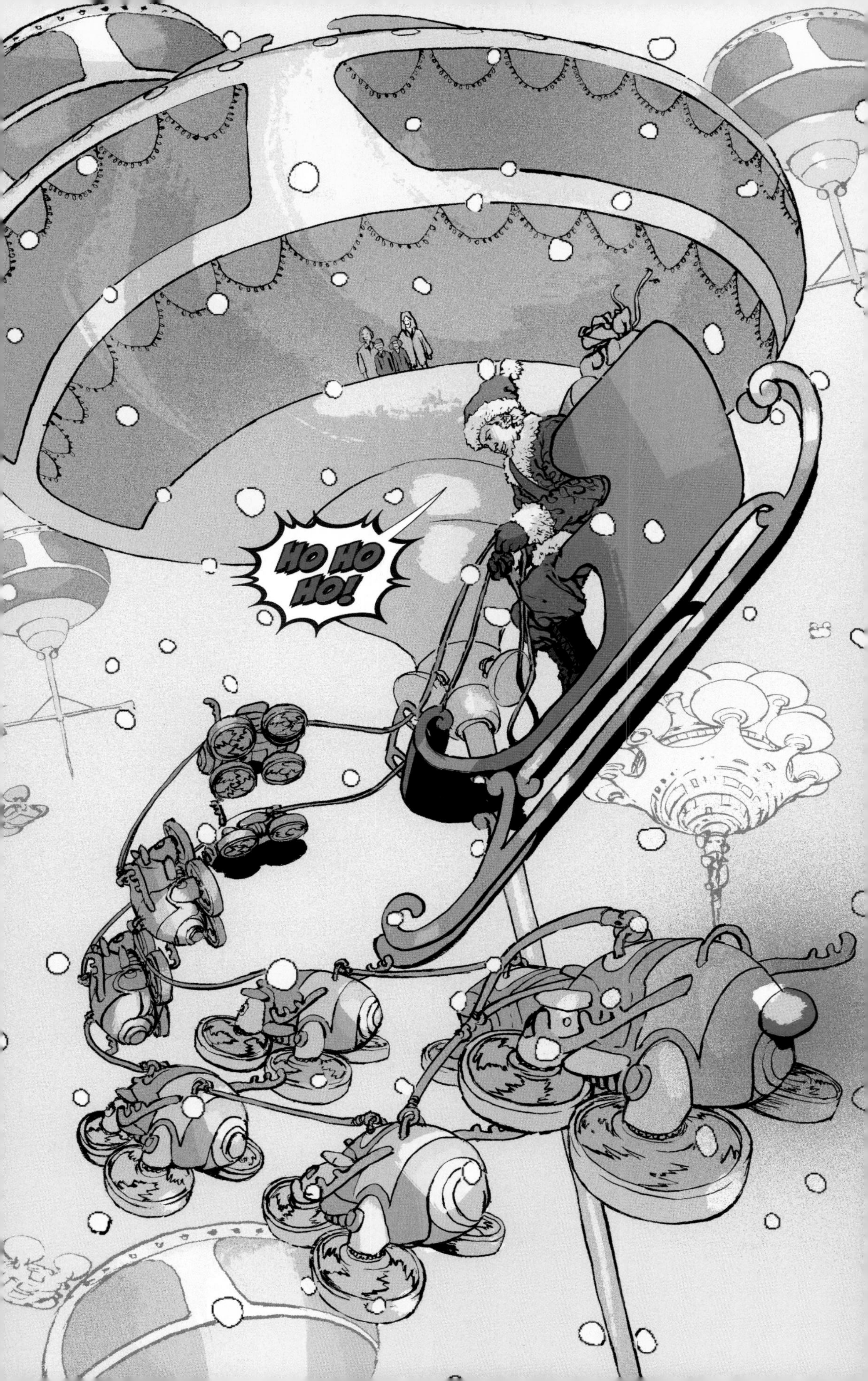
HO HO HO!

SECRET RECIPE

ART

GEGÊ **SCHALL**

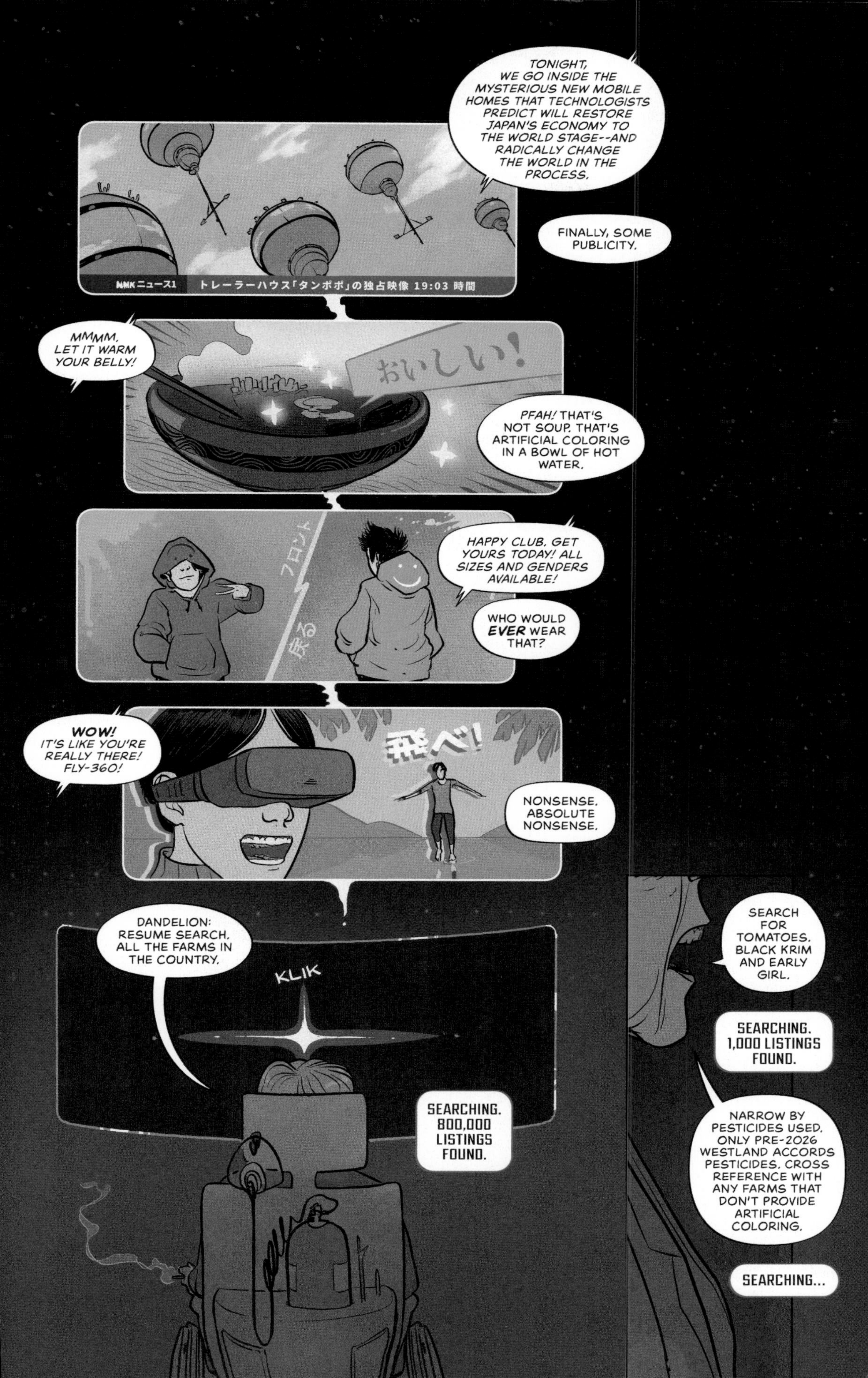
TONIGHT, WE GO INSIDE THE MYSTERIOUS NEW MOBILE HOMES THAT TECHNOLOGISTS PREDICT WILL RESTORE JAPAN'S ECONOMY TO THE WORLD STAGE--AND RADICALLY CHANGE THE WORLD IN THE PROCESS.
FINALLY, SOME PUBLICITY.
NMKニュース1
トレーラーハウス「タンポポ」の独占映像 19:03 時間
MMMM, LET IT WARM YOUR BELLY!
おいしい!
PFAH! THAT'S NOT SOUP. THAT'S ARTIFICIAL COLORING IN A BOWL OF HOT WATER.
フロント
戻る
HAPPY CLUB. GET YOURS TODAY! ALL SIZES AND GENDERS AVAILABLE!
WHO WOULD EVER WEAR THAT?
WOW! IT'S LIKE YOU'RE REALLY THERE! FLY-360!
飛べ!
NONSENSE. ABSOLUTE NONSENSE.
DANDELION: RESUME SEARCH. ALL THE FARMS IN THE COUNTRY.
KLIK
SEARCHING. 800,000 LISTINGS FOUND.
SEARCH FOR TOMATOES. BLACK KRIM AND EARLY GIRL.
SEARCHING. 1,000 LISTINGS FOUND.
NARROW BY PESTICIDES USED. ONLY PRE-2026 WESTLAND ACCORDS PESTICIDES. CROSS REFERENCE WITH ANY FARMS THAT DON'T PROVIDE ARTIFICIAL COLORING.
SEARCHING...

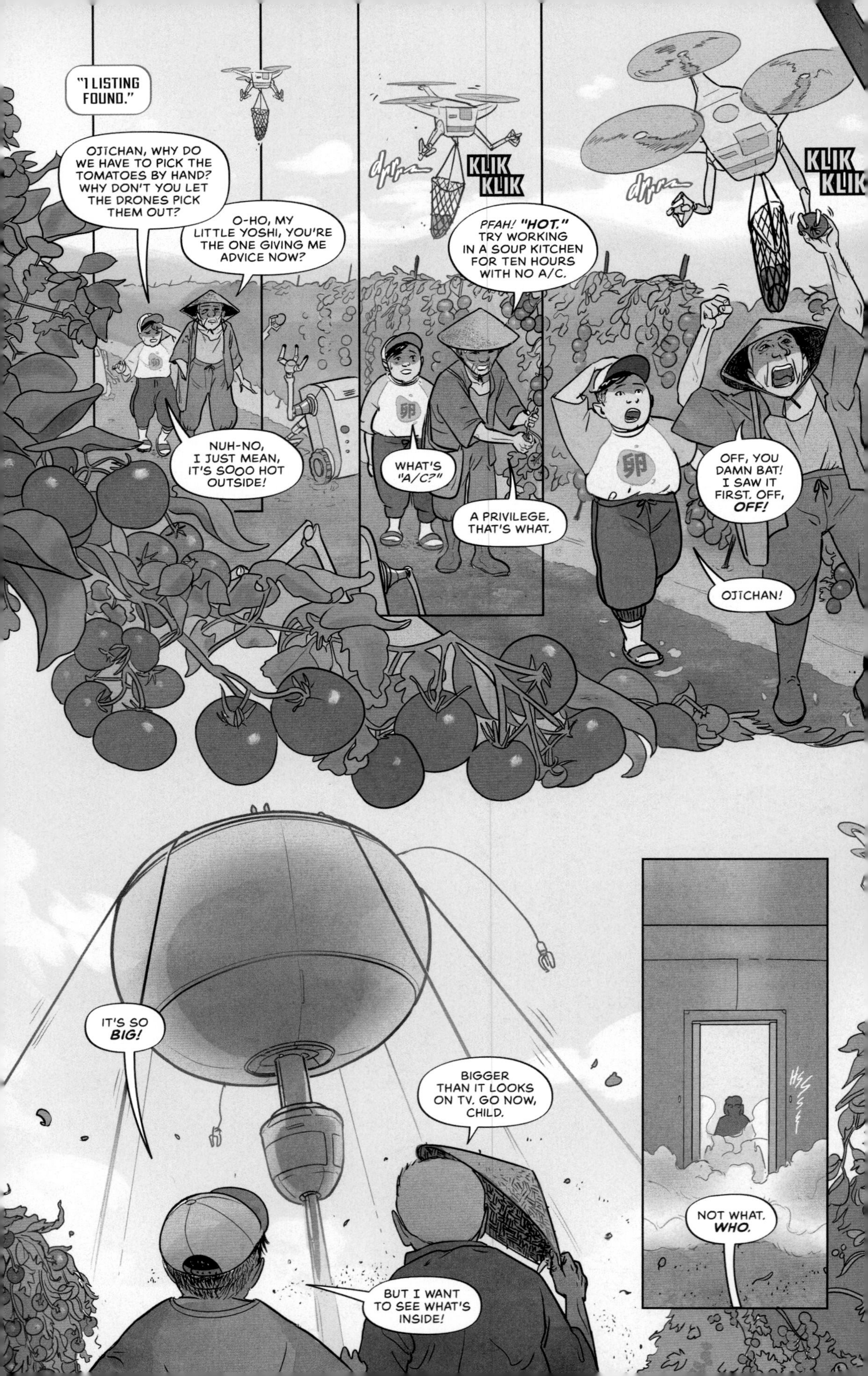
"1 LISTING FOUND."
OJĪCHAN, WHY DO WE HAVE TO PICK THE TOMATOES BY HAND? WHY DON'T YOU LET THE DRONES PICK THEM OUT?
O-HO, MY LITTLE YOSHI, YOU'RE THE ONE GIVING ME ADVICE NOW?
NUH-NO, I JUST MEAN, IT'S SOOO HOT OUTSIDE!
KLIK KLIK
PFAH! **"HOT."** TRY WORKING IN A SOUP KITCHEN FOR TEN HOURS WITH NO A/C.
WHAT'S "A/C?"
A PRIVILEGE. THAT'S WHAT.
KLIK KLIK
OFF, YOU DAMN BAT! I SAW IT FIRST. OFF, ***OFF!***
OJĪCHAN!
IT'S SO ***BIG!***
BIGGER THAN IT LOOKS ON TV. GO NOW, CHILD.
BUT I WANT TO SEE WHAT'S INSIDE!
NOT WHAT. ***WHO.***

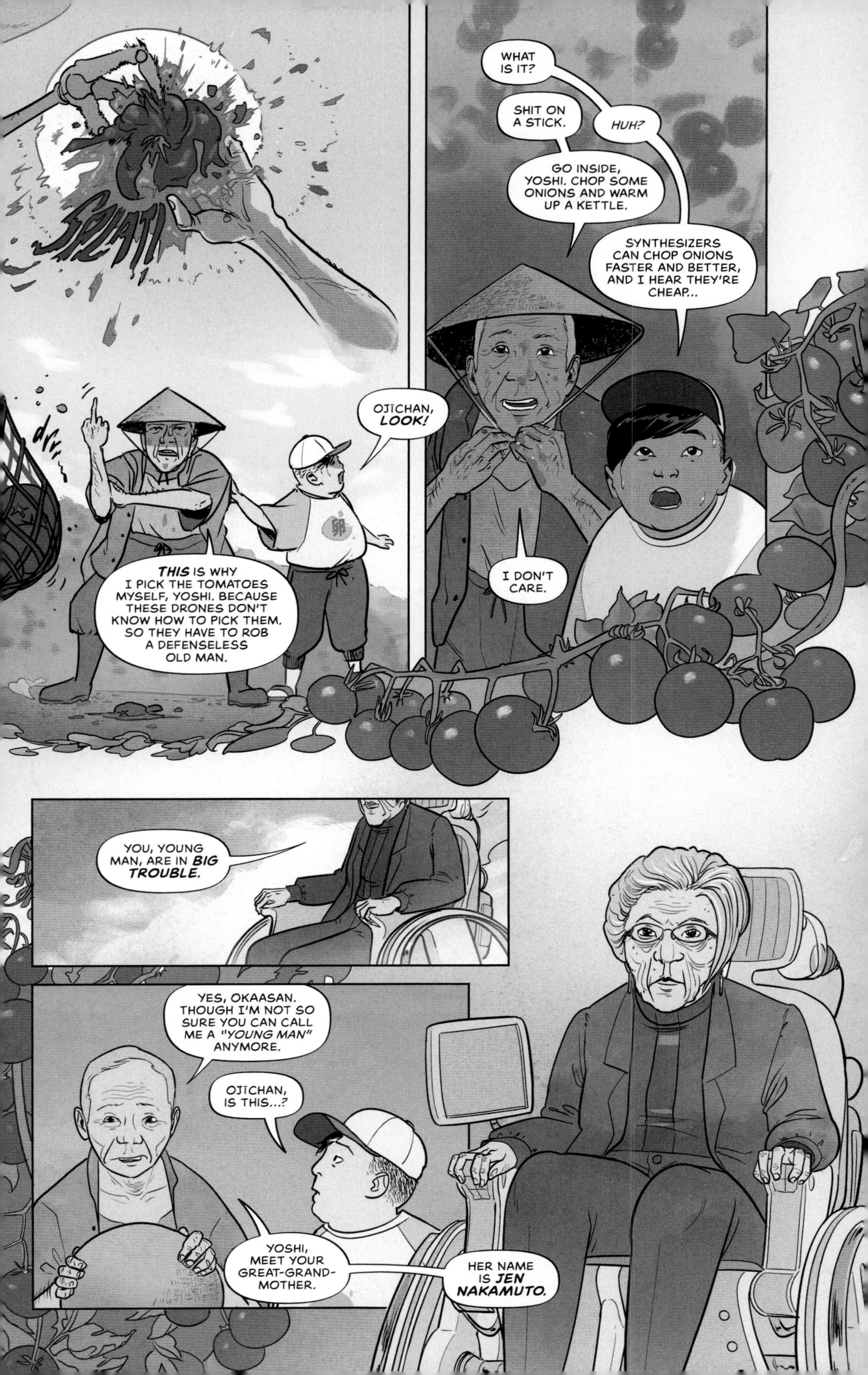
SPLAT!
THIS IS WHY I PICK THE TOMATOES MYSELF, YOSHI. BECAUSE THESE DRONES DON'T KNOW HOW TO PICK THEM. SO THEY HAVE TO ROB A DEFENSELESS OLD MAN.
OJĪCHAN, LOOK!
WHAT IS IT?
SHIT ON A STICK.
HUH?
GO INSIDE, YOSHI. CHOP SOME ONIONS AND WARM UP A KETTLE.
SYNTHESIZERS CAN CHOP ONIONS FASTER AND BETTER, AND I HEAR THEY'RE CHEAP...
I DON'T CARE.
YOU, YOUNG MAN, ARE IN BIG TROUBLE.
YES, OKAASAN. THOUGH I'M NOT SO SURE YOU CAN CALL ME A "YOUNG MAN" ANYMORE.
OJĪCHAN, IS THIS...?
YOSHI, MEET YOUR GREAT-GRAND-MOTHER.
HER NAME IS JEN NAKAMUTO.

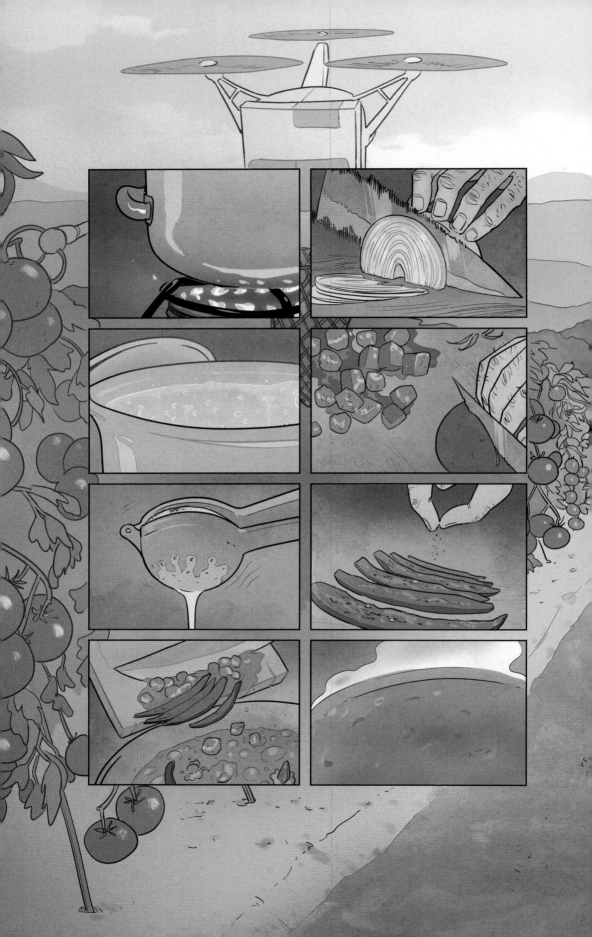

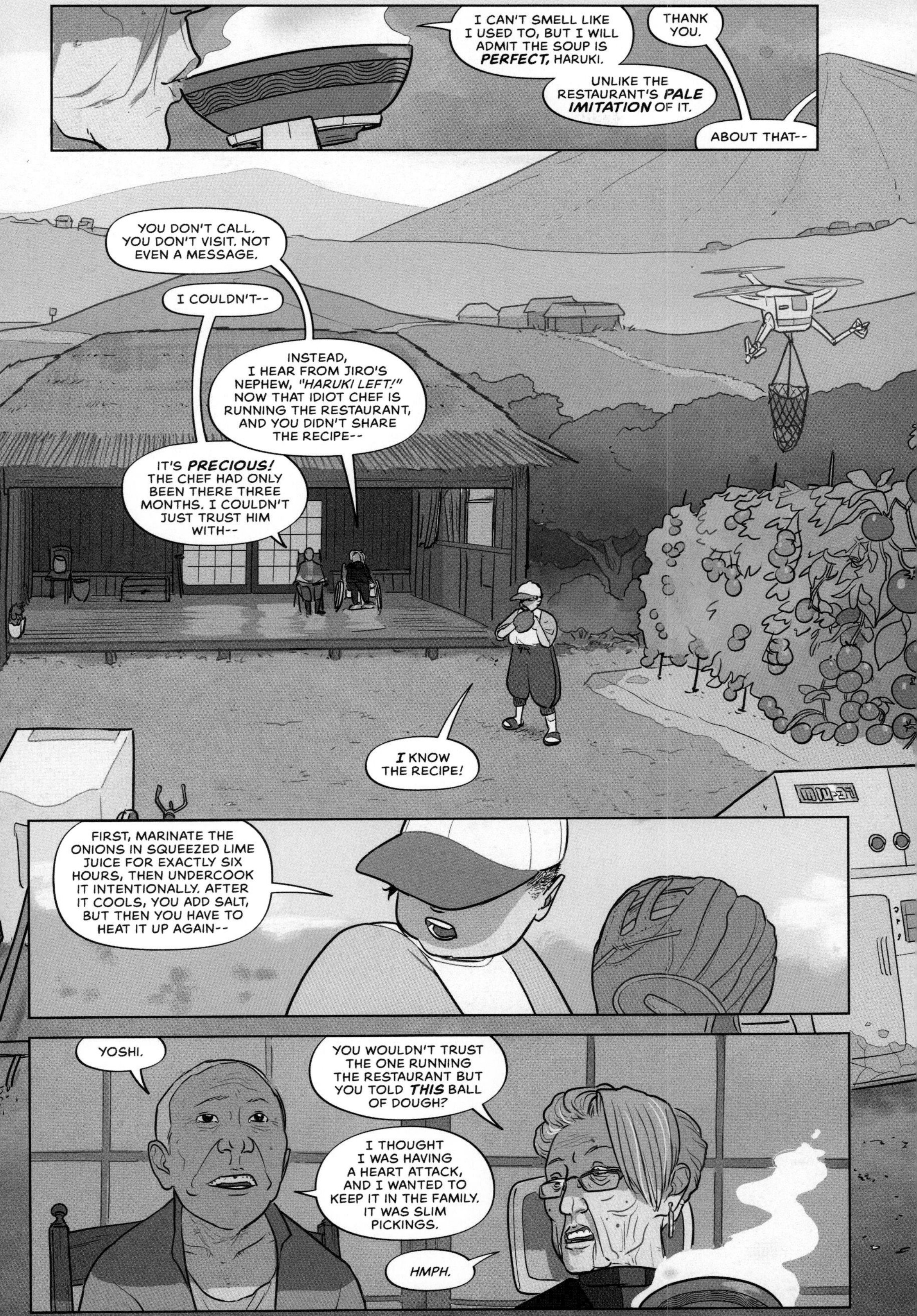
I CAN'T SMELL LIKE I USED TO, BUT I WILL ADMIT THE SOUP IS PERFECT, HARUKI.
UNLIKE THE RESTAURANT'S PALE IMITATION OF IT.
THANK YOU.
ABOUT THAT--
YOU DON'T CALL. YOU DON'T VISIT. NOT EVEN A MESSAGE.
I COULDN'T--
INSTEAD, I HEAR FROM JIRO'S NEPHEW, "HARUKI LEFT!" NOW THAT IDIOT CHEF IS RUNNING THE RESTAURANT, AND YOU DIDN'T SHARE THE RECIPE--
IT'S PRECIOUS! THE CHEF HAD ONLY BEEN THERE THREE MONTHS. I COULDN'T JUST TRUST HIM WITH--
I KNOW THE RECIPE!
FIRST, MARINATE THE ONIONS IN SQUEEZED LIME JUICE FOR EXACTLY SIX HOURS, THEN UNDERCOOK IT INTENTIONALLY. AFTER IT COOLS, YOU ADD SALT, BUT THEN YOU HAVE TO HEAT IT UP AGAIN--
YOSHI.
YOU WOULDN'T TRUST THE ONE RUNNING THE RESTAURANT BUT YOU TOLD THIS BALL OF DOUGH?
I THOUGHT I WAS HAVING A HEART ATTACK, AND I WANTED TO KEEP IT IN THE FAMILY. IT WAS SLIM PICKINGS.
HMPH.

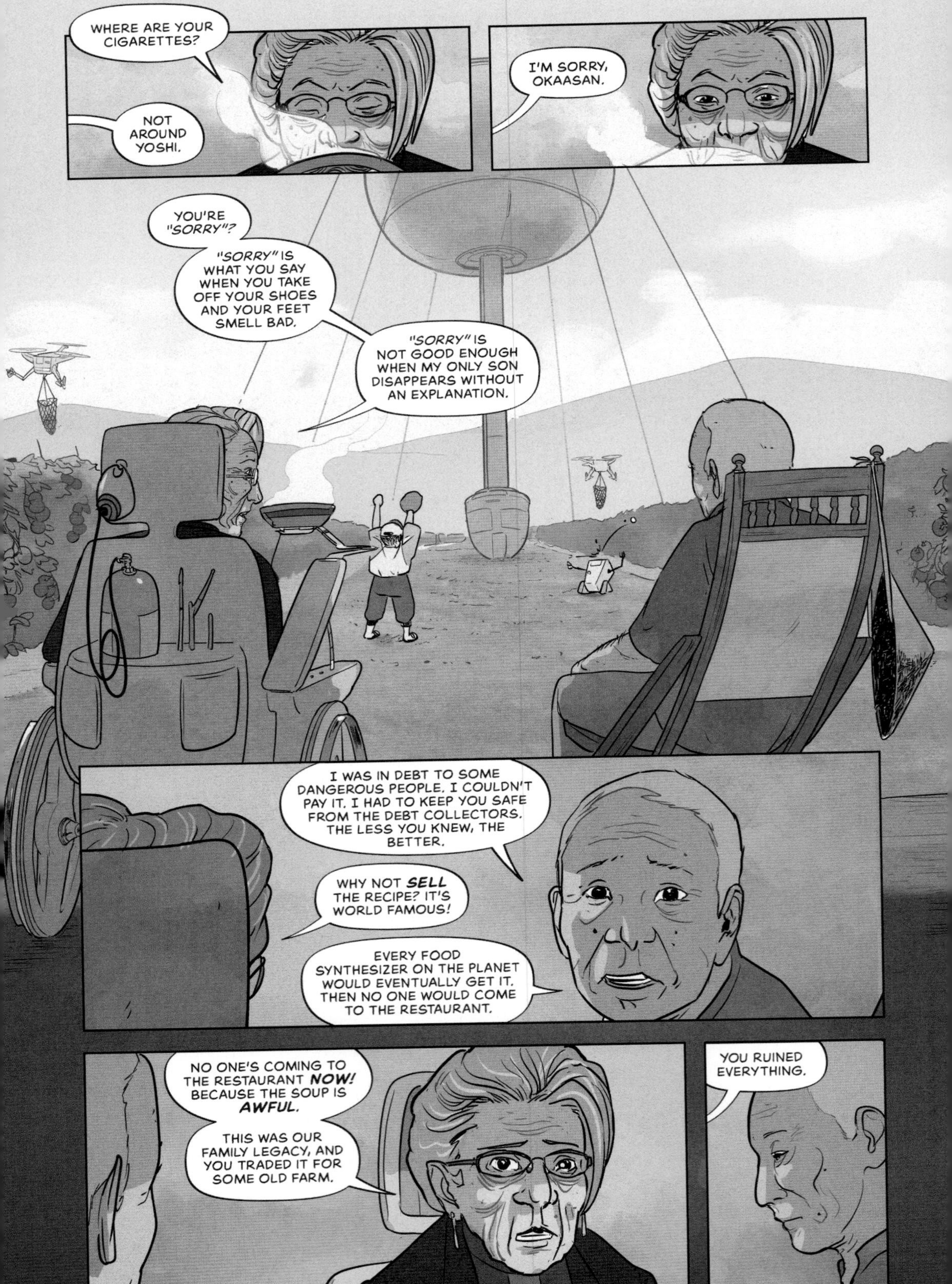
WHERE ARE YOUR CIGARETTES?
NOT AROUND YOSHI.
I'M SORRY, OKAASAN.
YOU'RE "SORRY"?
"SORRY" IS WHAT YOU SAY WHEN YOU TAKE OFF YOUR SHOES AND YOUR FEET SMELL BAD.
"SORRY" IS NOT GOOD ENOUGH WHEN MY ONLY SON DISAPPEARS WITHOUT AN EXPLANATION.
I WAS IN DEBT TO SOME DANGEROUS PEOPLE. I COULDN'T PAY IT. I HAD TO KEEP YOU SAFE FROM THE DEBT COLLECTORS. THE LESS YOU KNEW, THE BETTER.
WHY NOT SELL THE RECIPE? IT'S WORLD FAMOUS!
EVERY FOOD SYNTHESIZER ON THE PLANET WOULD EVENTUALLY GET IT. THEN NO ONE WOULD COME TO THE RESTAURANT.
NO ONE'S COMING TO THE RESTAURANT NOW! BECAUSE THE SOUP IS AWFUL.
THIS WAS OUR FAMILY LEGACY, AND YOU TRADED IT FOR SOME OLD FARM.
YOU RUINED EVERYTHING.

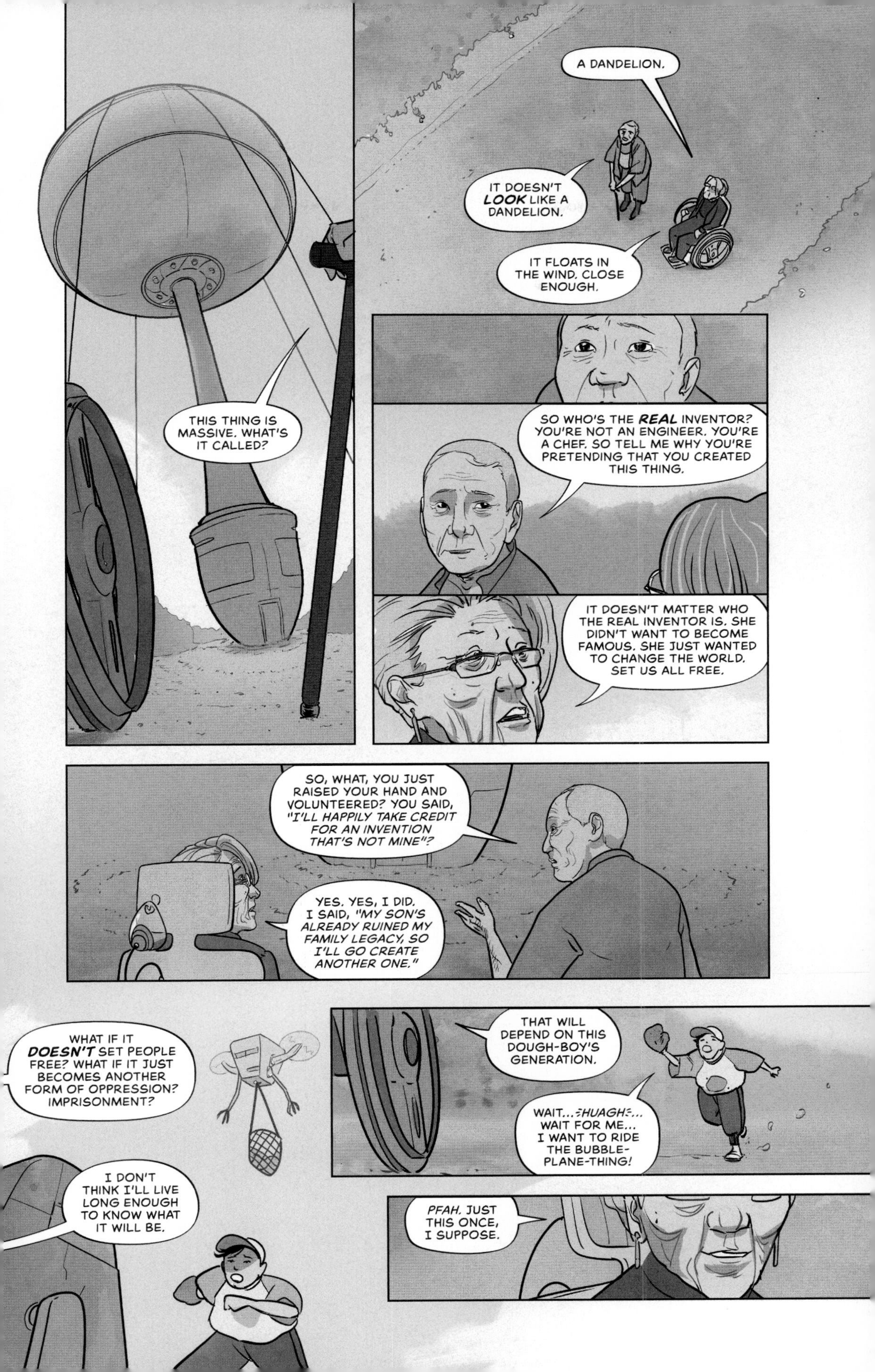
THIS THING IS MASSIVE. WHAT'S IT CALLED?
A DANDELION.
IT DOESN'T **LOOK** LIKE A DANDELION.
IT FLOATS IN THE WIND. CLOSE ENOUGH.
SO WHO'S THE ***REAL*** INVENTOR? YOU'RE NOT AN ENGINEER. YOU'RE A CHEF. SO TELL ME WHY YOU'RE PRETENDING THAT YOU CREATED THIS THING.
IT DOESN'T MATTER WHO THE REAL INVENTOR IS. SHE DIDN'T WANT TO BECOME FAMOUS. SHE JUST WANTED TO CHANGE THE WORLD. SET US ALL FREE.
SO, WHAT, YOU JUST RAISED YOUR HAND AND VOLUNTEERED? YOU SAID, *"I'LL HAPPILY TAKE CREDIT FOR AN INVENTION THAT'S NOT MINE"?*
YES. YES, I DID. I SAID, *"MY SON'S ALREADY RUINED MY FAMILY LEGACY, SO I'LL GO CREATE ANOTHER ONE."*
WHAT IF IT ***DOESN'T*** SET PEOPLE FREE? WHAT IF IT JUST BECOMES ANOTHER FORM OF OPPRESSION? IMPRISONMENT?
I DON'T THINK I'LL LIVE LONG ENOUGH TO KNOW WHAT IT WILL BE.
THAT WILL DEPEND ON THIS DOUGH-BOY'S GENERATION.
WAIT... HUAGH... WAIT FOR ME... I WANT TO RIDE THE BUBBLE-PLANE-THING!
PFAH. JUST THIS ONCE, I SUPPOSE.

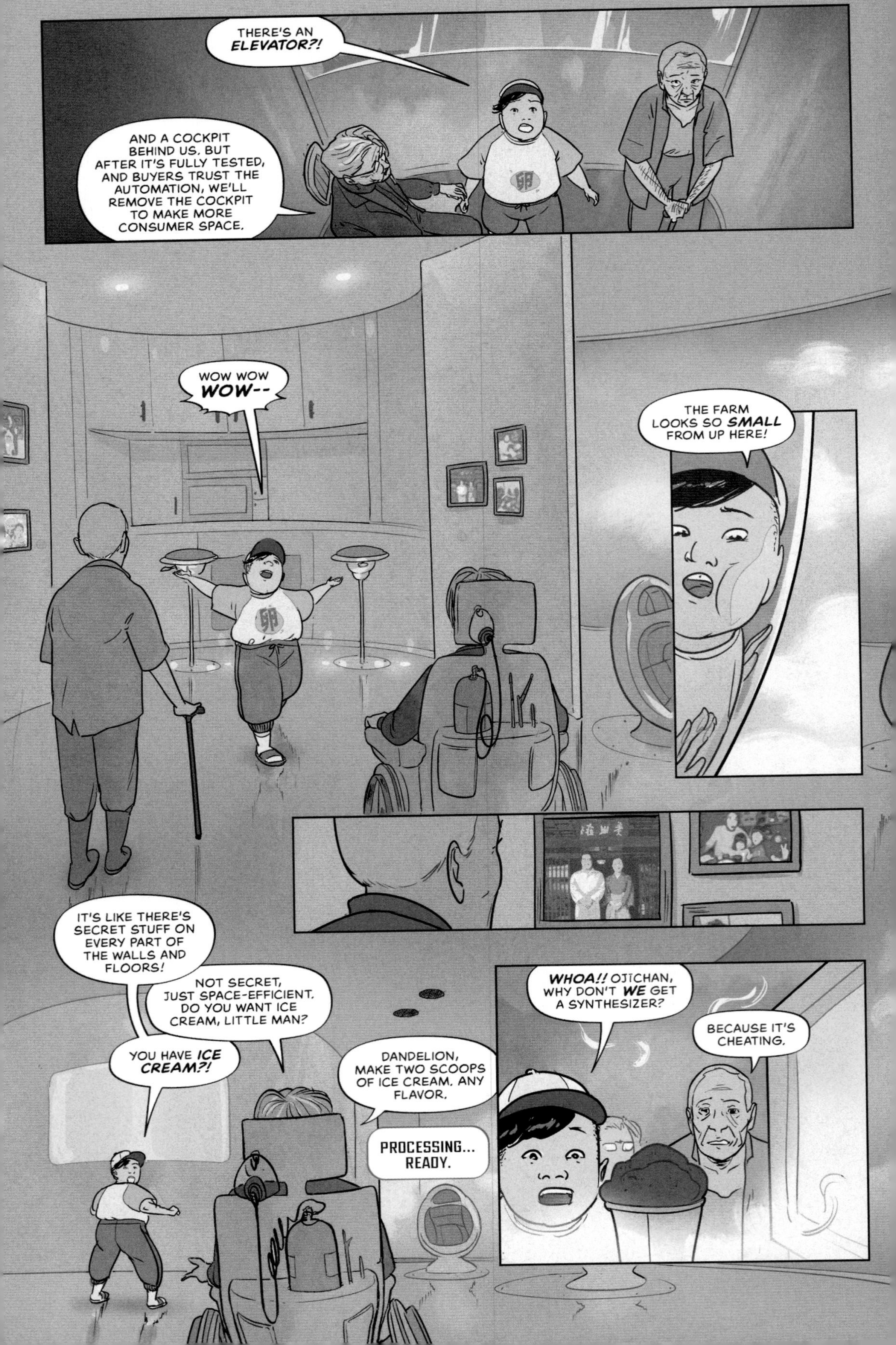
THERE'S AN *ELEVATOR?!*
AND A COCKPIT BEHIND US, BUT AFTER IT'S FULLY TESTED, AND BUYERS TRUST THE AUTOMATION, WE'LL REMOVE THE COCKPIT TO MAKE MORE CONSUMER SPACE.
WOW WOW *WOW--*
THE FARM LOOKS SO *SMALL* FROM UP HERE!
IT'S LIKE THERE'S SECRET STUFF ON EVERY PART OF THE WALLS AND FLOORS!
NOT SECRET, JUST SPACE-EFFICIENT. DO YOU WANT ICE CREAM, LITTLE MAN?
YOU HAVE *ICE CREAM?!*
DANDELION, MAKE TWO SCOOPS OF ICE CREAM, ANY FLAVOR.
PROCESSING... READY.
WHOA!! OJĪCHAN, WHY DON'T *WE* GET A SYNTHESIZER?
BECAUSE IT'S CHEATING.

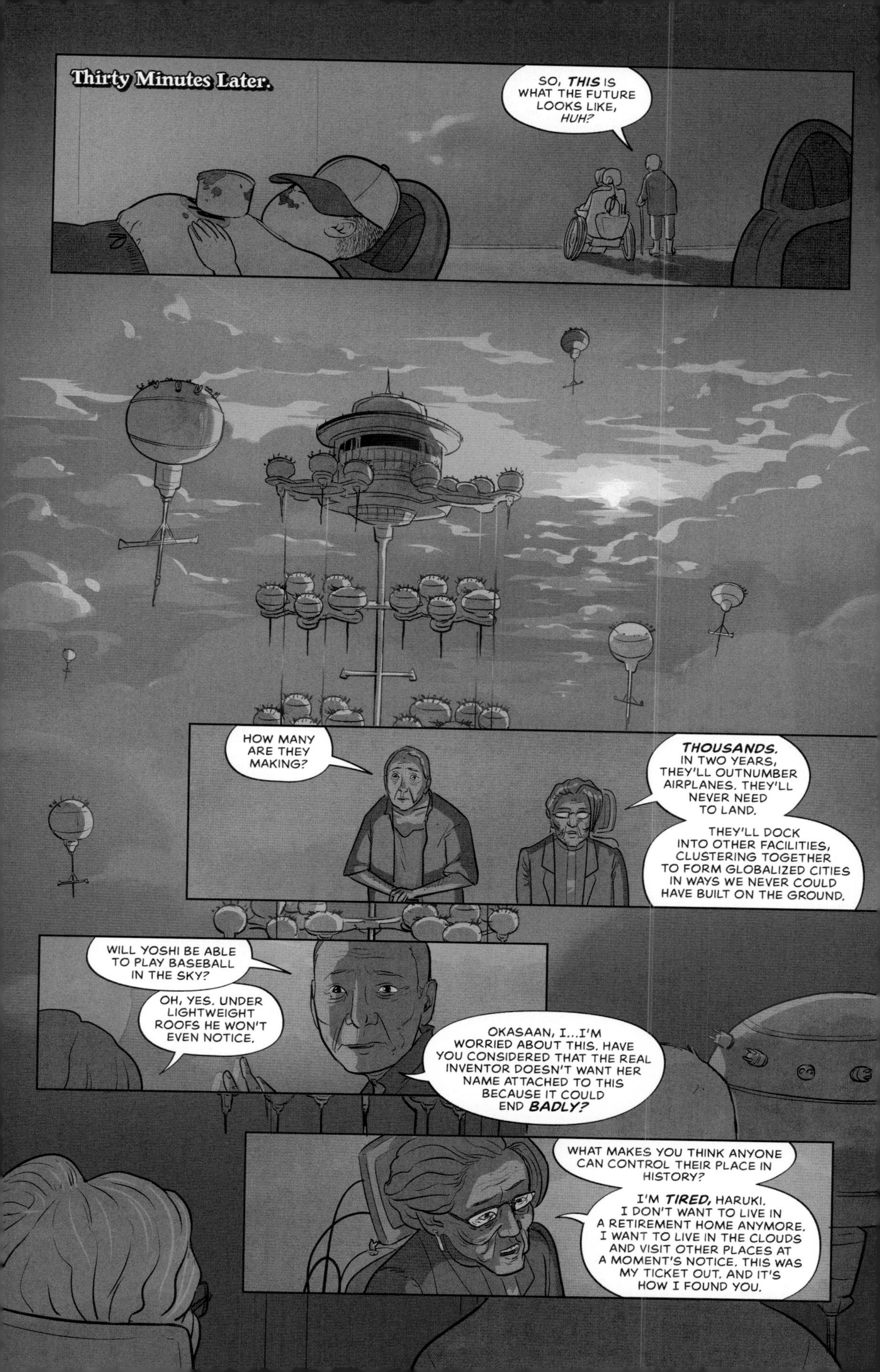
Thirty Minutes Later.
SO, THIS IS WHAT THE FUTURE LOOKS LIKE, HUH?
HOW MANY ARE THEY MAKING?
THOUSANDS. IN TWO YEARS, THEY'LL OUTNUMBER AIRPLANES. THEY'LL NEVER NEED TO LAND.
THEY'LL DOCK INTO OTHER FACILITIES, CLUSTERING TOGETHER TO FORM GLOBALIZED CITIES IN WAYS WE NEVER COULD HAVE BUILT ON THE GROUND.
WILL YOSHI BE ABLE TO PLAY BASEBALL IN THE SKY?
OH, YES. UNDER LIGHTWEIGHT ROOFS HE WON'T EVEN NOTICE.
OKASAAN, I...I'M WORRIED ABOUT THIS. HAVE YOU CONSIDERED THAT THE REAL INVENTOR DOESN'T WANT HER NAME ATTACHED TO THIS BECAUSE IT COULD END BADLY?
WHAT MAKES YOU THINK ANYONE CAN CONTROL THEIR PLACE IN HISTORY?
I'M TIRED, HARUKI. I DON'T WANT TO LIVE IN A RETIREMENT HOME ANYMORE. I WANT TO LIVE IN THE CLOUDS AND VISIT OTHER PLACES AT A MOMENT'S NOTICE. THIS WAS MY TICKET OUT. AND IT'S HOW I FOUND YOU.

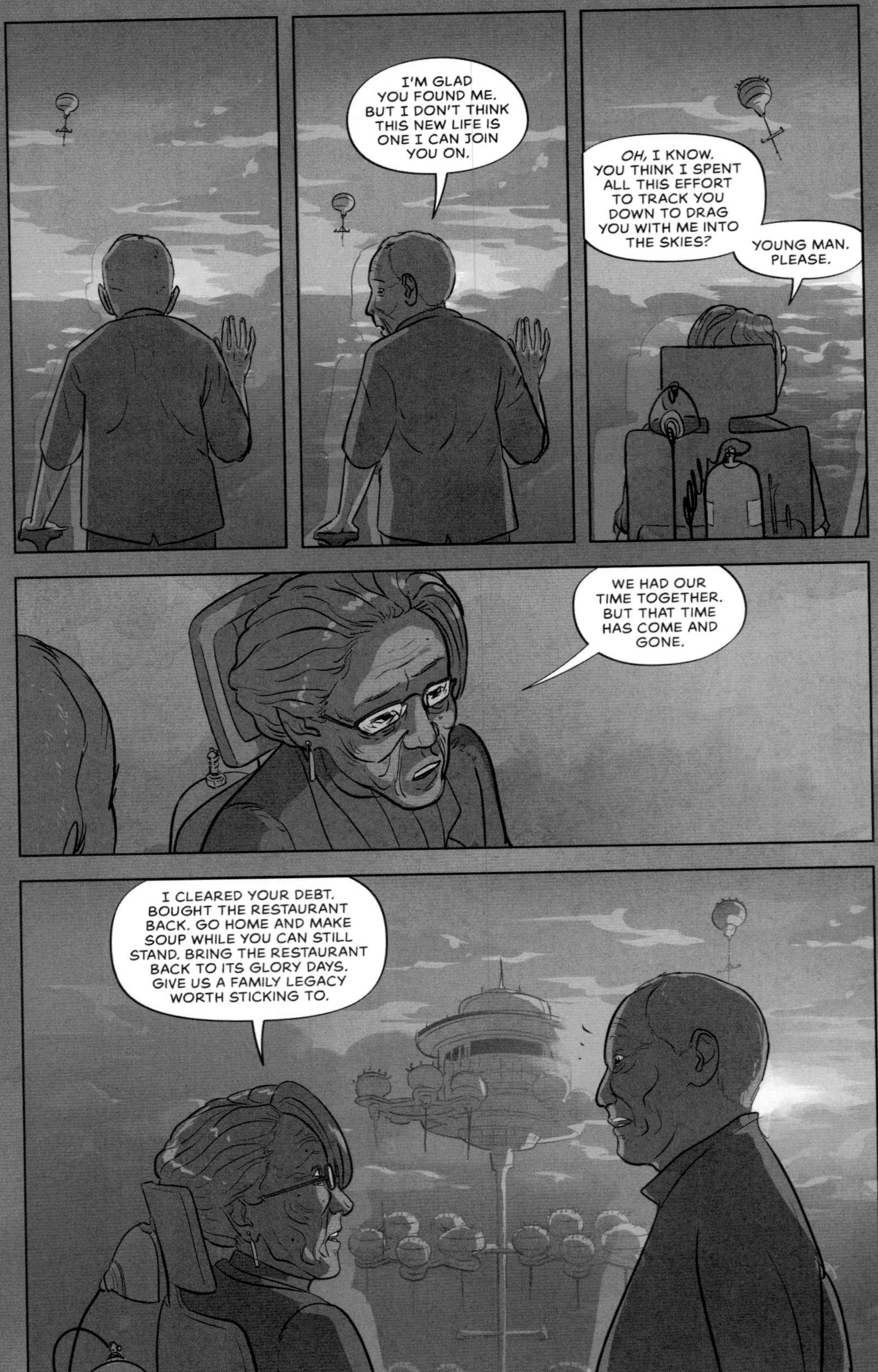
I'M GLAD YOU FOUND ME, BUT I DON'T THINK THIS NEW LIFE IS ONE I CAN JOIN YOU ON.
OH, I KNOW. YOU THINK I SPENT ALL THIS EFFORT TO TRACK YOU DOWN TO DRAG YOU WITH ME INTO THE SKIES?
YOUNG MAN. PLEASE.
WE HAD OUR TIME TOGETHER, BUT THAT TIME HAS COME AND GONE.
I CLEARED YOUR DEBT. BOUGHT THE RESTAURANT BACK. GO HOME AND MAKE SOUP WHILE YOU CAN STILL STAND. BRING THE RESTAURANT BACK TO ITS GLORY DAYS. GIVE US A FAMILY LEGACY WORTH STICKING TO.

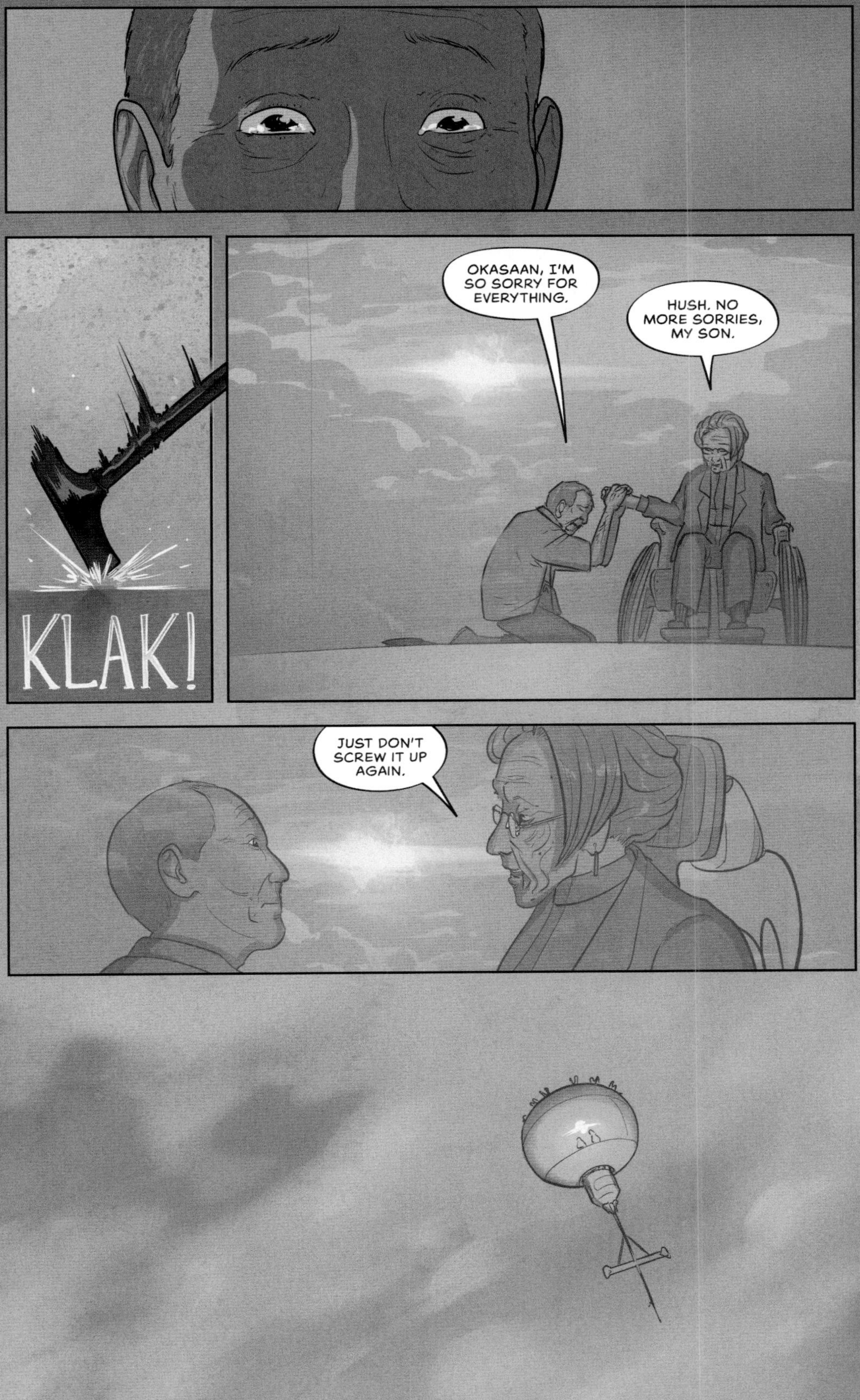
KLAK!
OKASAAN, I'M SO SORRY FOR EVERYTHING.
HUSH. NO MORE SORRIES, MY SON.
JUST DON'T SCREW IT UP AGAIN.

**Excerpt from the Stratosphere podcast:
Interview with Jen Nakamuto, inventor of the Dandelion.
Recorded on April 12th, 2047.**

I mean, it's a prison. Bigger than a solitary cell, mercifully. But there's no yard. That's what these people were forced to give up.

On the other hand, advances in virtual reality have helped considerably. So that's a silver lining. You might be stuck in a Dandelion, but just put on some goggles and all your senses are tricked into believing you're somewhere else.

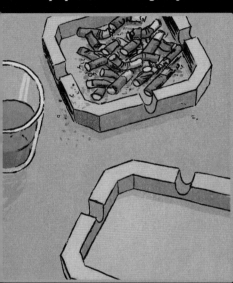

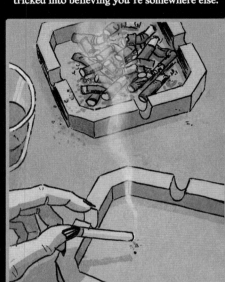

You won't **feel** like a prisoner. And there are all these programs that have more than passed the turing test to keep people company for those who live in solitude. So the issues of captivity and solitude have been somewhat solved.

But a prison is still a prison.

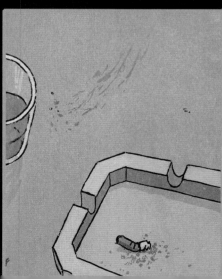

THE BIRD

ART

MARTÍN **MORAZZO**

COLORS

JUHA **VELTTI**

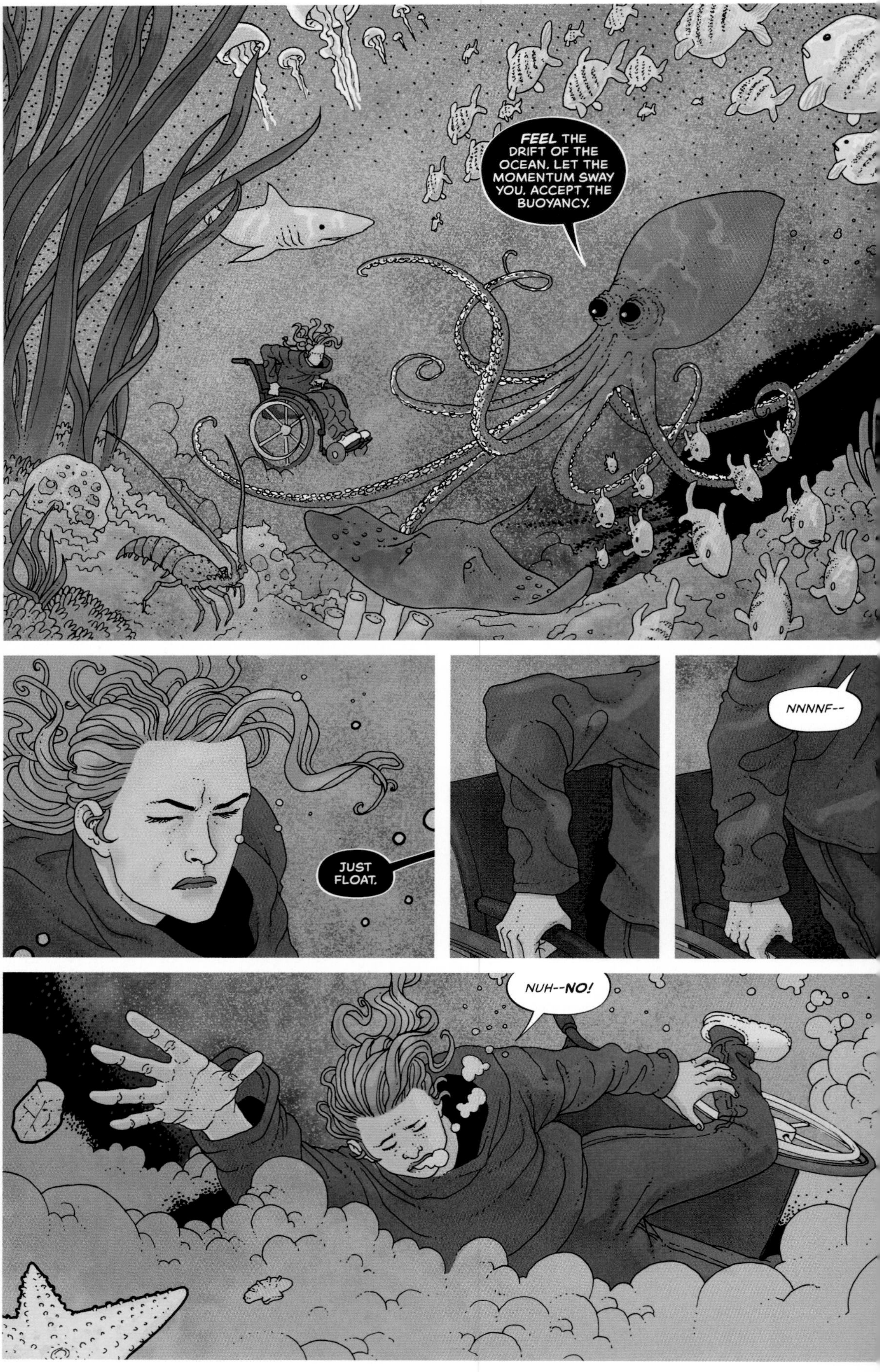
FEEL THE DRIFT OF THE OCEAN. LET THE MOMENTUM SWAY YOU. ACCEPT THE BUOYANCY.
JUST FLOAT.
NNNNF--
NUH--NO!

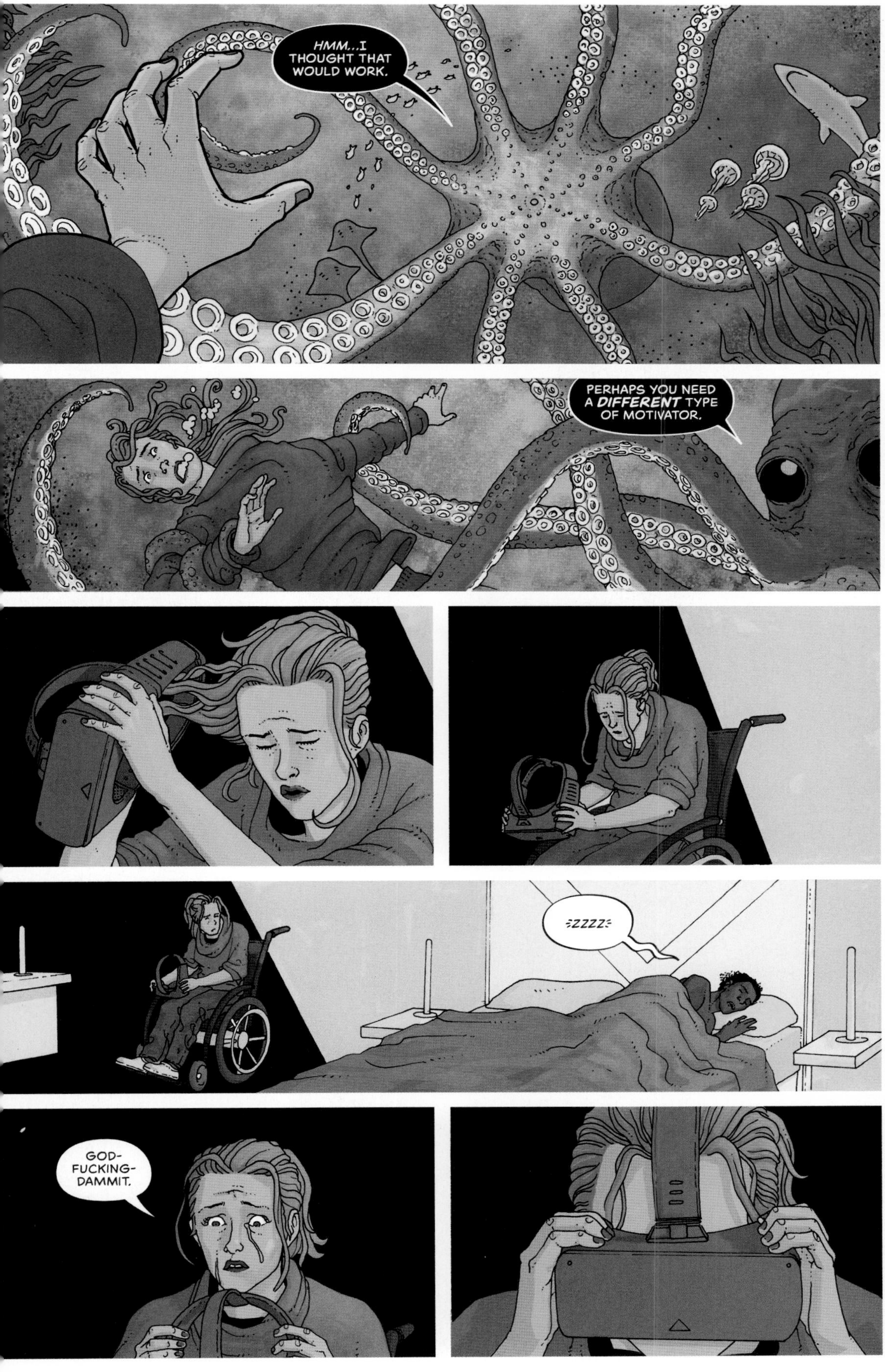
HMM...I THOUGHT THAT WOULD WORK.
PERHAPS YOU NEED A DIFFERENT TYPE OF MOTIVATOR.
ZZZZ
GOD-FUCKING-DAMMIT.

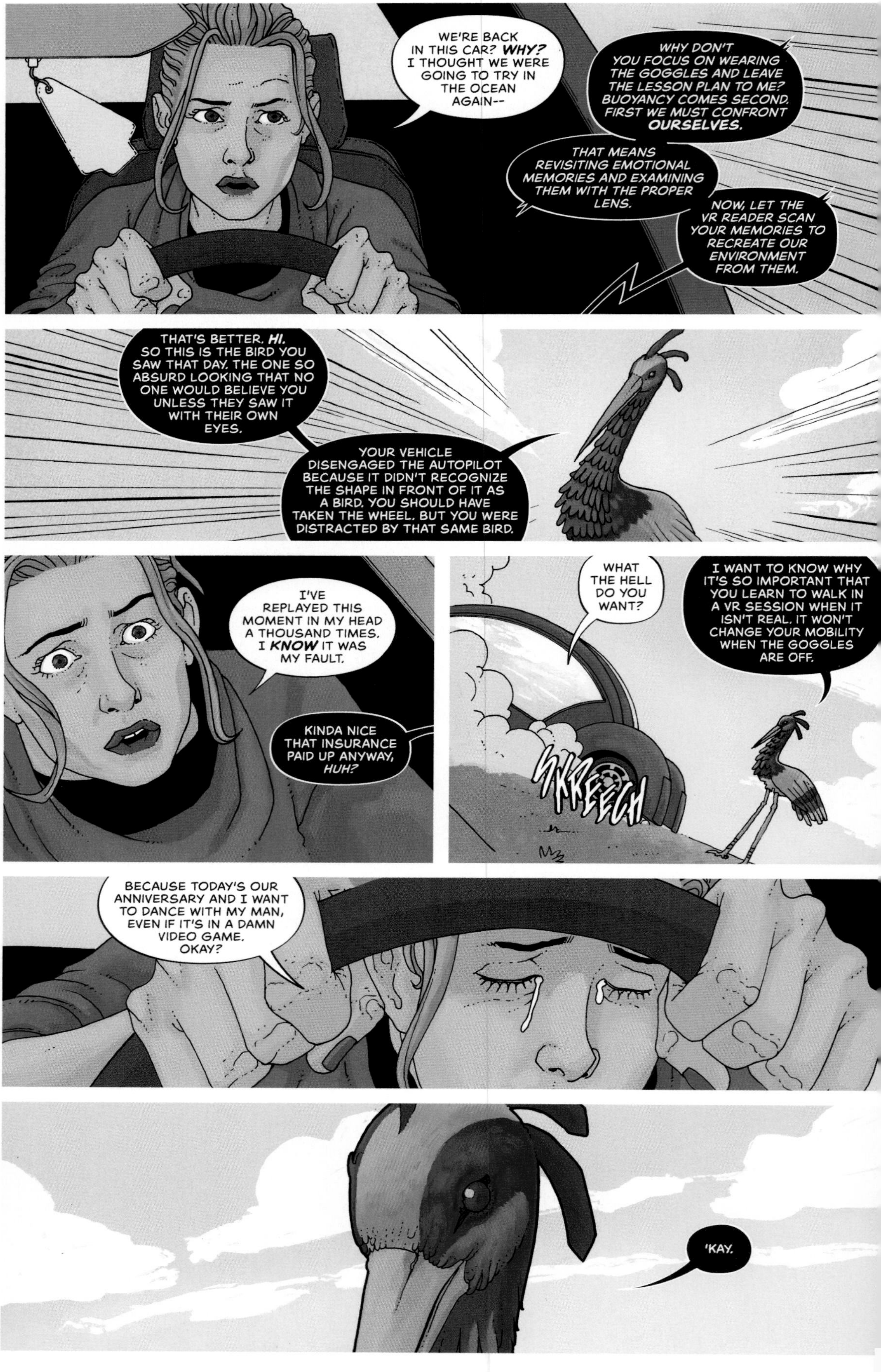

WE'RE BACK IN THIS CAR? WHY? I THOUGHT WE WERE GOING TO TRY IN THE OCEAN AGAIN--
WHY DON'T YOU FOCUS ON WEARING THE GOGGLES AND LEAVE THE LESSON PLAN TO ME? BUOYANCY COMES SECOND. FIRST WE MUST CONFRONT OURSELVES.
THAT MEANS REVISITING EMOTIONAL MEMORIES AND EXAMINING THEM WITH THE PROPER LENS.
NOW, LET THE VR READER SCAN YOUR MEMORIES TO RECREATE OUR ENVIRONMENT FROM THEM.
THAT'S BETTER. HI. SO THIS IS THE BIRD YOU SAW THAT DAY. THE ONE SO ABSURD LOOKING THAT NO ONE WOULD BELIEVE YOU UNLESS THEY SAW IT WITH THEIR OWN EYES.
YOUR VEHICLE DISENGAGED THE AUTOPILOT BECAUSE IT DIDN'T RECOGNIZE THE SHAPE IN FRONT OF IT AS A BIRD. YOU SHOULD HAVE TAKEN THE WHEEL. BUT YOU WERE DISTRACTED BY THAT SAME BIRD.
I'VE REPLAYED THIS MOMENT IN MY HEAD A THOUSAND TIMES. I KNOW IT WAS MY FAULT.
KINDA NICE THAT INSURANCE PAID UP ANYWAY, HUH?
WHAT THE HELL DO YOU WANT?
I WANT TO KNOW WHY IT'S SO IMPORTANT THAT YOU LEARN TO WALK IN A VR SESSION WHEN IT ISN'T REAL. IT WON'T CHANGE YOUR MOBILITY WHEN THE GOGGLES ARE OFF.
SKREECH
BECAUSE TODAY'S OUR ANNIVERSARY AND I WANT TO DANCE WITH MY MAN, EVEN IF IT'S IN A DAMN VIDEO GAME. OKAY?
'KAY.

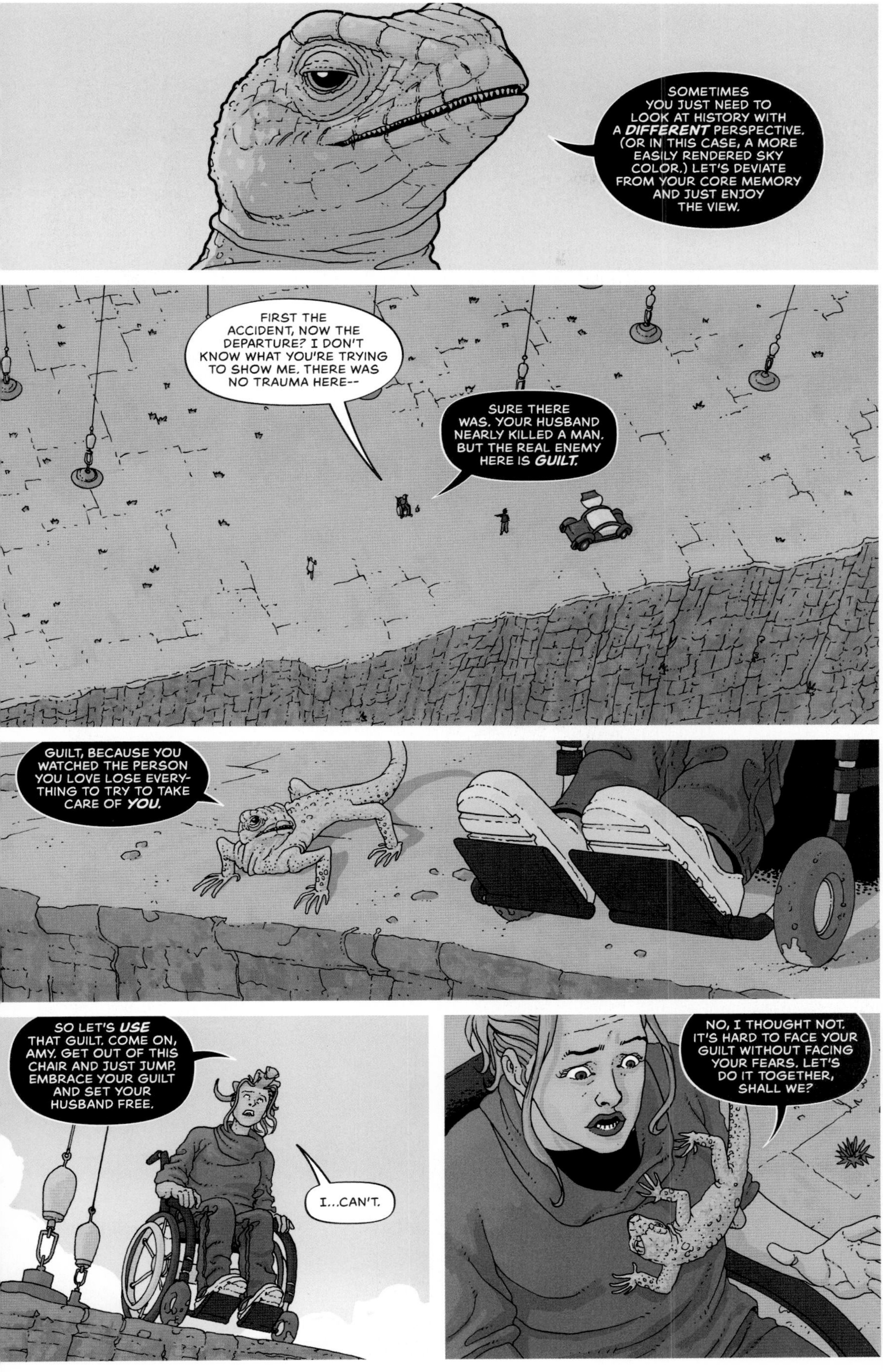
SOMETIMES YOU JUST NEED TO LOOK AT HISTORY WITH A *DIFFERENT* PERSPECTIVE. (OR IN THIS CASE, A MORE EASILY RENDERED SKY COLOR.) LET'S DEVIATE FROM YOUR CORE MEMORY AND JUST ENJOY THE VIEW.
FIRST THE ACCIDENT, NOW THE DEPARTURE? I DON'T KNOW WHAT YOU'RE TRYING TO SHOW ME. THERE WAS NO TRAUMA HERE--
SURE THERE WAS. YOUR HUSBAND NEARLY KILLED A MAN. BUT THE REAL ENEMY HERE IS *GUILT.*
GUILT, BECAUSE YOU WATCHED THE PERSON YOU LOVE LOSE EVERY-THING TO TRY TO TAKE CARE OF *YOU.*
SO LET'S *USE* THAT GUILT. COME ON, AMY. GET OUT OF THIS CHAIR AND JUST JUMP. EMBRACE YOUR GUILT AND SET YOUR HUSBAND FREE.
I...CAN'T.
NO, I THOUGHT NOT. IT'S HARD TO FACE YOUR GUILT WITHOUT FACING YOUR FEARS. LET'S DO IT TOGETHER, SHALL WE?

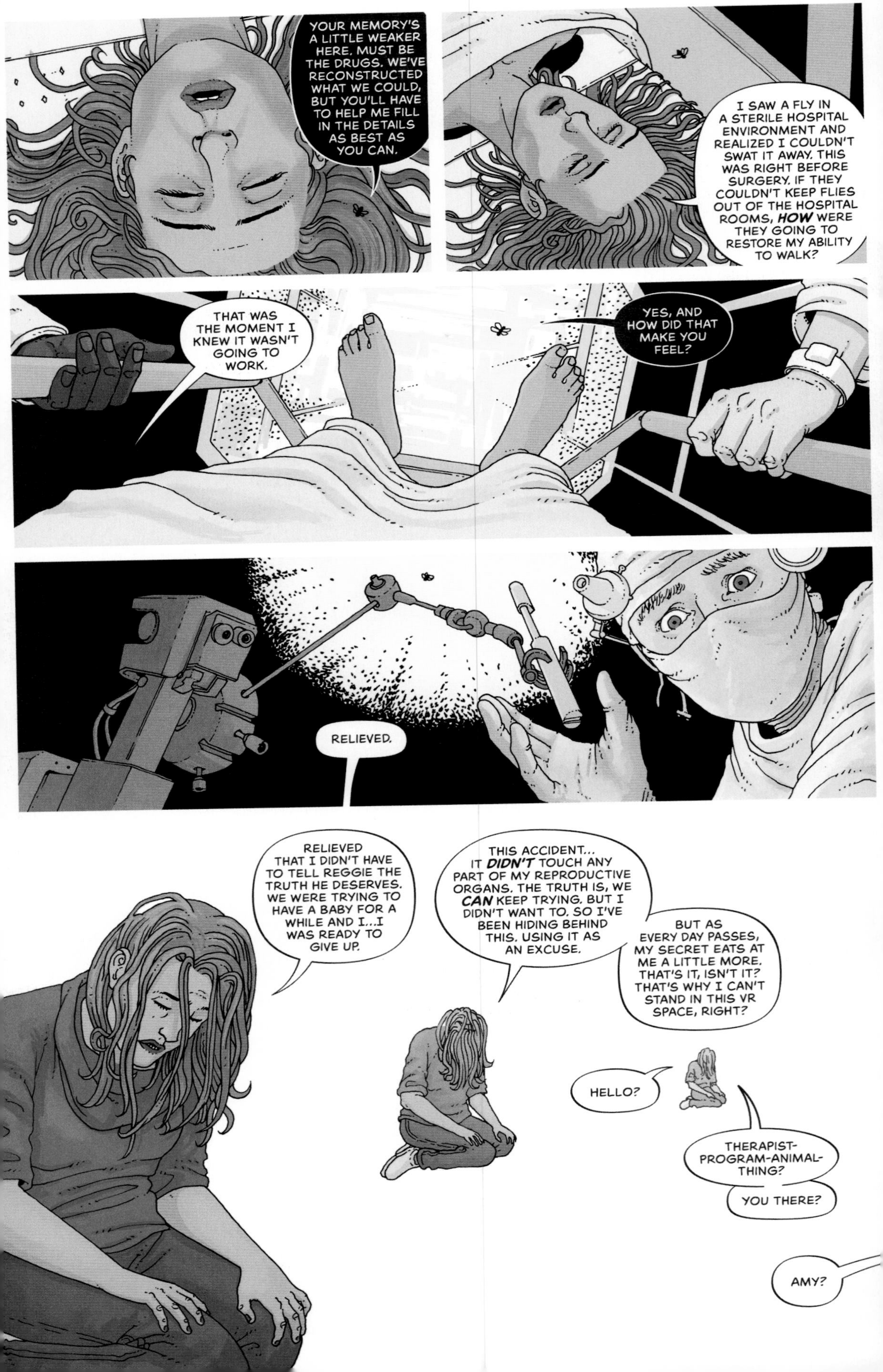

YOUR MEMORY'S A LITTLE WEAKER HERE. MUST BE THE DRUGS. WE'VE RECONSTRUCTED WHAT WE COULD, BUT YOU'LL HAVE TO HELP ME FILL IN THE DETAILS AS BEST AS YOU CAN.
I SAW A FLY IN A STERILE HOSPITAL ENVIRONMENT AND REALIZED I COULDN'T SWAT IT AWAY. THIS WAS RIGHT BEFORE SURGERY. IF THEY COULDN'T KEEP FLIES OUT OF THE HOSPITAL ROOMS, **HOW** WERE THEY GOING TO RESTORE MY ABILITY TO WALK?
THAT WAS THE MOMENT I KNEW IT WASN'T GOING TO WORK.
YES, AND HOW DID THAT MAKE YOU FEEL?
RELIEVED.
RELIEVED THAT I DIDN'T HAVE TO TELL REGGIE THE TRUTH HE DESERVES. WE WERE TRYING TO HAVE A BABY FOR A WHILE AND I... I WAS READY TO GIVE UP.
THIS ACCIDENT... IT ***DIDN'T*** TOUCH ANY PART OF MY REPRODUCTIVE ORGANS. THE TRUTH IS, WE ***CAN*** KEEP TRYING. BUT I DIDN'T WANT TO. SO I'VE BEEN HIDING BEHIND THIS. USING IT AS AN EXCUSE.
BUT AS EVERY DAY PASSES, MY SECRET EATS AT ME A LITTLE MORE. THAT'S IT, ISN'T IT? THAT'S WHY I CAN'T STAND IN THIS VR SPACE, RIGHT?
HELLO?
THERAPIST-PROGRAM-ANIMAL-THING?
YOU THERE?
AMY?

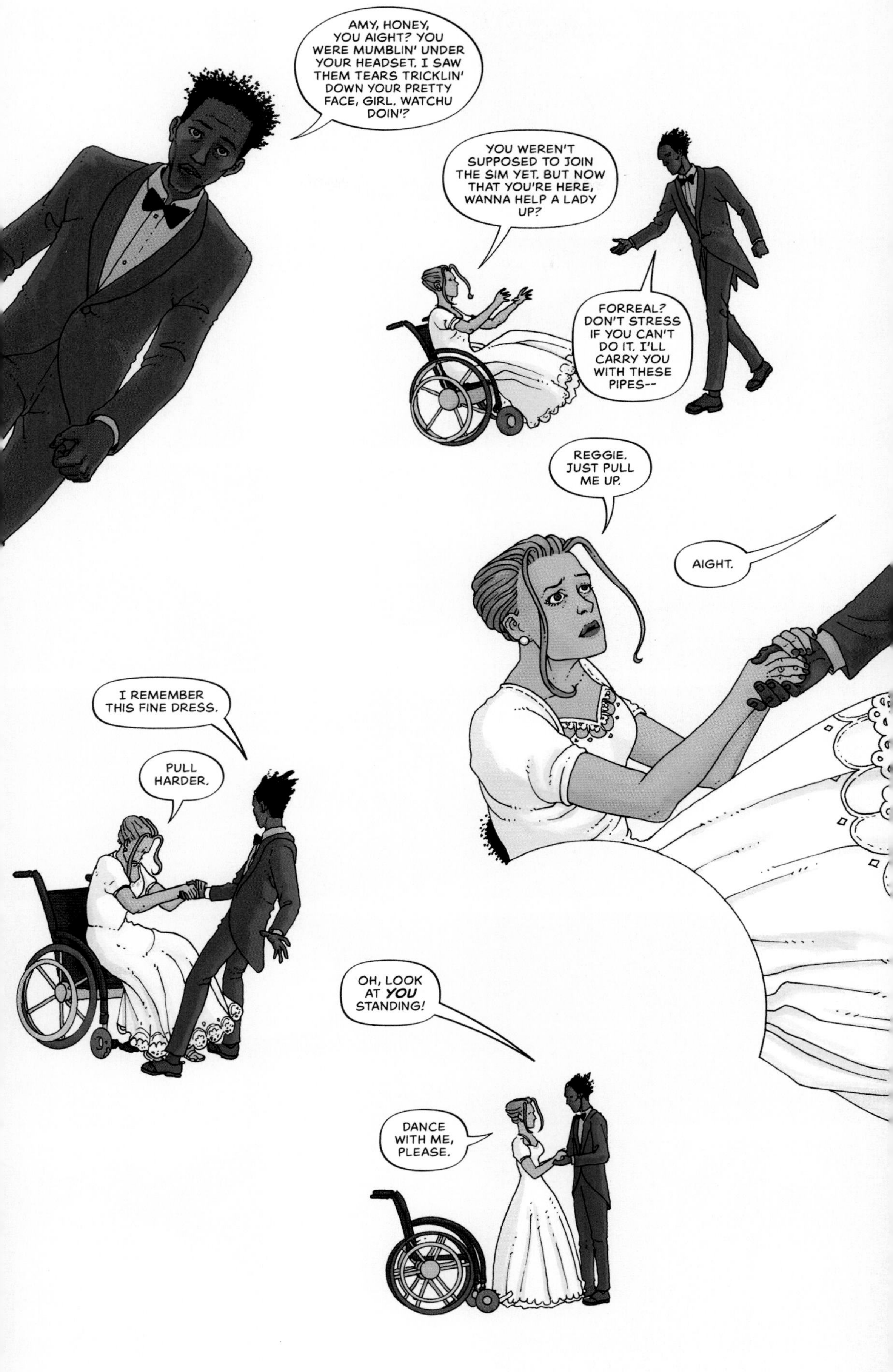
AMY, HONEY, YOU AIGHT? YOU WERE MUMBLIN' UNDER YOUR HEADSET. I SAW THEM TEARS TRICKLIN' DOWN YOUR PRETTY FACE, GIRL. WATCHU DOIN'?
YOU WEREN'T SUPPOSED TO JOIN THE SIM YET. BUT NOW THAT YOU'RE HERE, WANNA HELP A LADY UP?
FORREAL? DON'T STRESS IF YOU CAN'T DO IT. I'LL CARRY YOU WITH THESE PIPES--
REGGIE. JUST PULL ME UP.
AIGHT.
I REMEMBER THIS FINE DRESS.
PULL HARDER.
OH, LOOK AT ***YOU*** STANDING!
DANCE WITH ME, PLEASE.

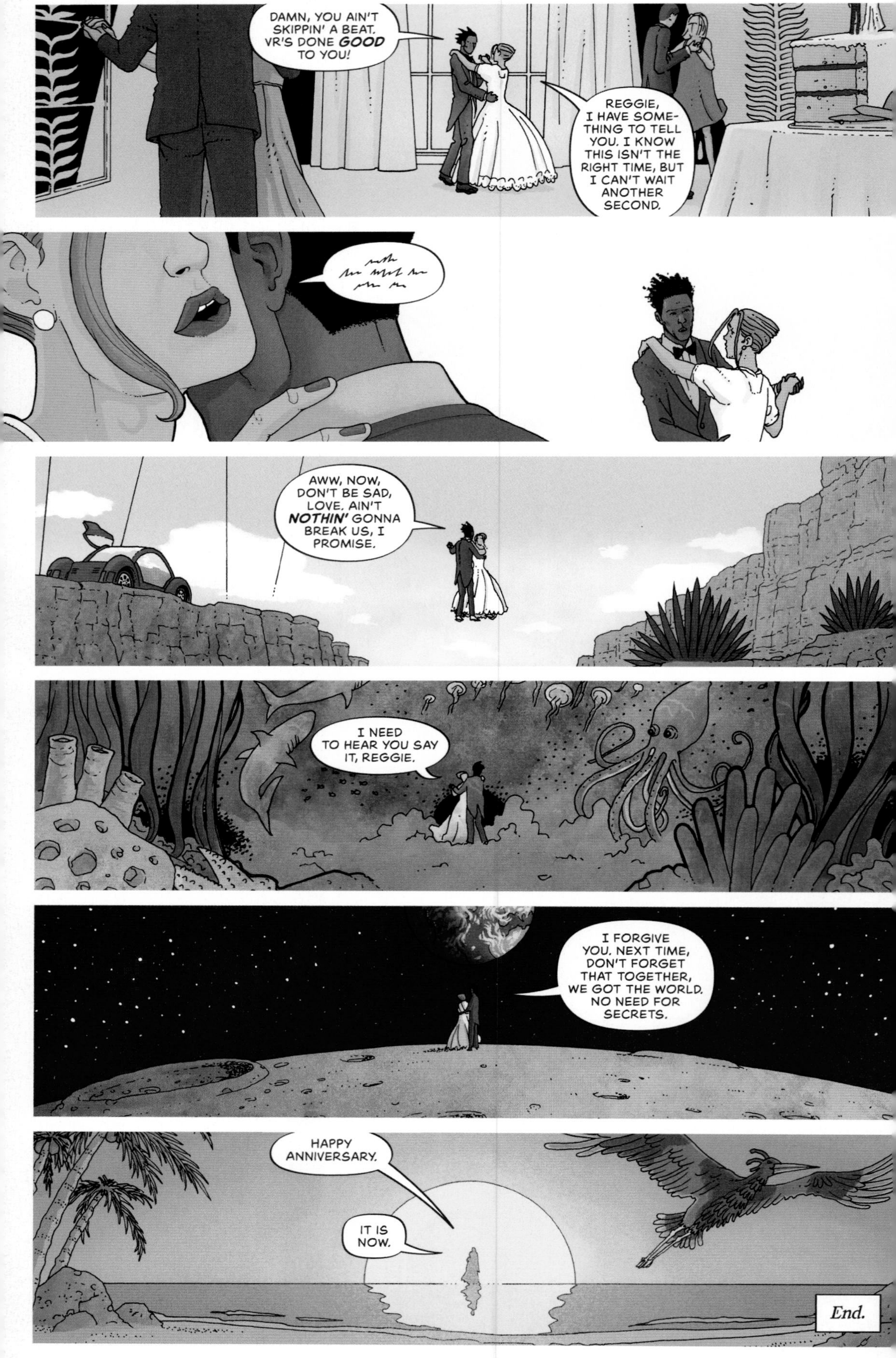
DAMN, YOU AIN'T SKIPPIN' A BEAT. VR'S DONE **GOOD** TO YOU!
REGGIE, I HAVE SOME-THING TO TELL YOU. I KNOW THIS ISN'T THE RIGHT TIME, BUT I CAN'T WAIT ANOTHER SECOND.
AWW, NOW, DON'T BE SAD, LOVE. AIN'T ***NOTHIN'*** GONNA BREAK US, I PROMISE.
I NEED TO HEAR YOU SAY IT, REGGIE.
I FORGIVE YOU. NEXT TIME, DON'T FORGET THAT TOGETHER, WE GOT THE WORLD. NO NEED FOR SECRETS.
HAPPY ANNIVERSARY.
IT IS NOW.
End.

Excerpt from the Stratosphere podcast:
Interview with Jen Nakamuto, inventor of the Dandelion.
Recorded on April 12th, 2047.

Dandelions were designed to float in the skies endlessly. **People** were not. The idea was, you'd visit the skies and then return to land. You'd vacation in the clouds. Take the scenic route through the mountains back. Not this permanent exile.

There should have been studies conducted. Years of research on the long-term effects of life in the skies. But, no. We saw an opportunity and we rushed it into law. I see now that I was too eager.

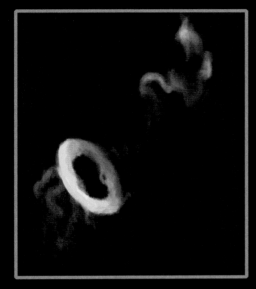

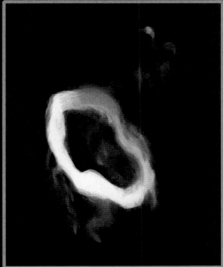

The Dandelions are networked and automated. They don't have a choice — they **have** to keep on floating forever.

But people? I don't know. I just don't know.

OIL AND WATER

ART

THOMAS CAMPI

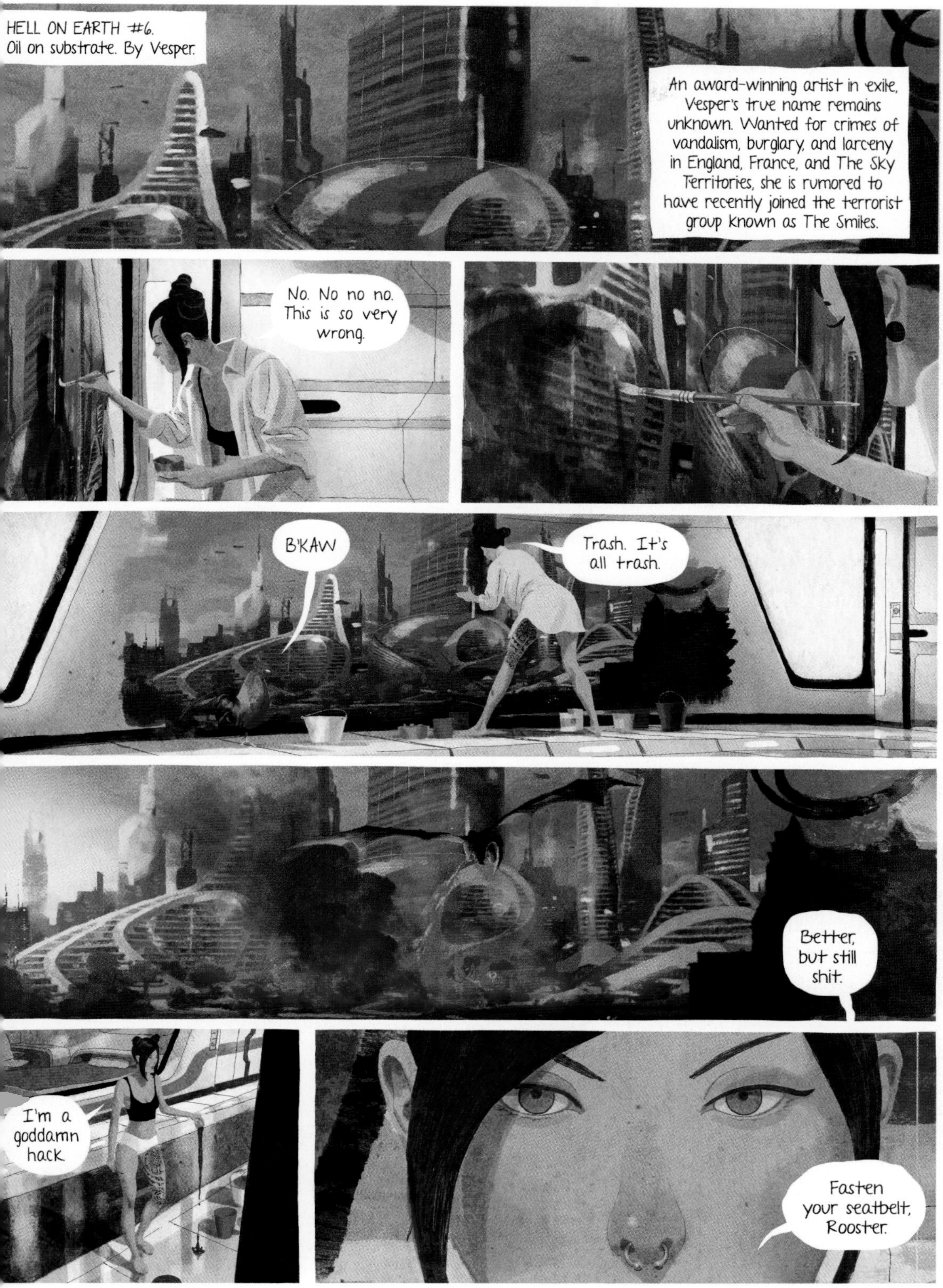
HELL ON EARTH #6.
Oil on substrate. By Vesper.
An award-winning artist in exile, Vesper's true name remains unknown. Wanted for crimes of vandalism, burglary, and larceny in England, France, and The Sky Territories, she is rumored to have recently joined the terrorist group known as The Smiles.
No. No no no. This is so very wrong.
B'KAW
Trash. It's all trash.
Better, but still shit.
I'm a goddamn hack.
Fasten your seatbelt, Rooster.

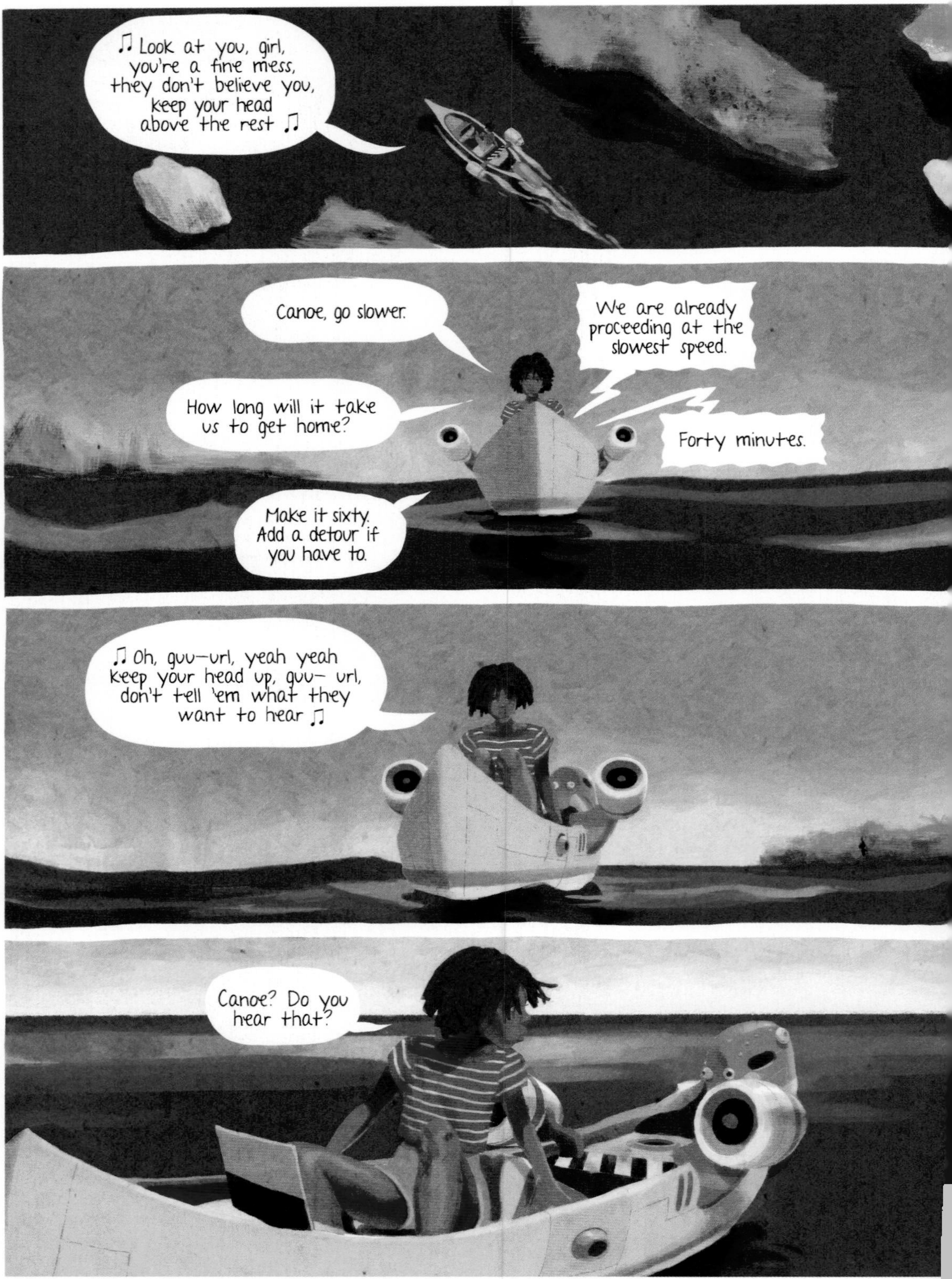
♫ Look at you, girl, you're a fine mess, they don't believe you, keep your head above the rest ♫
Canoe, go slower.
We are already proceeding at the slowest speed.
How long will it take us to get home?
Forty minutes.
Make it sixty. Add a detour if you have to.
♫ Oh, guu—url, yeah yeah keep your head up, guu— url, don't tell 'em what they want to hear ♫
Canoe? Do you hear that?

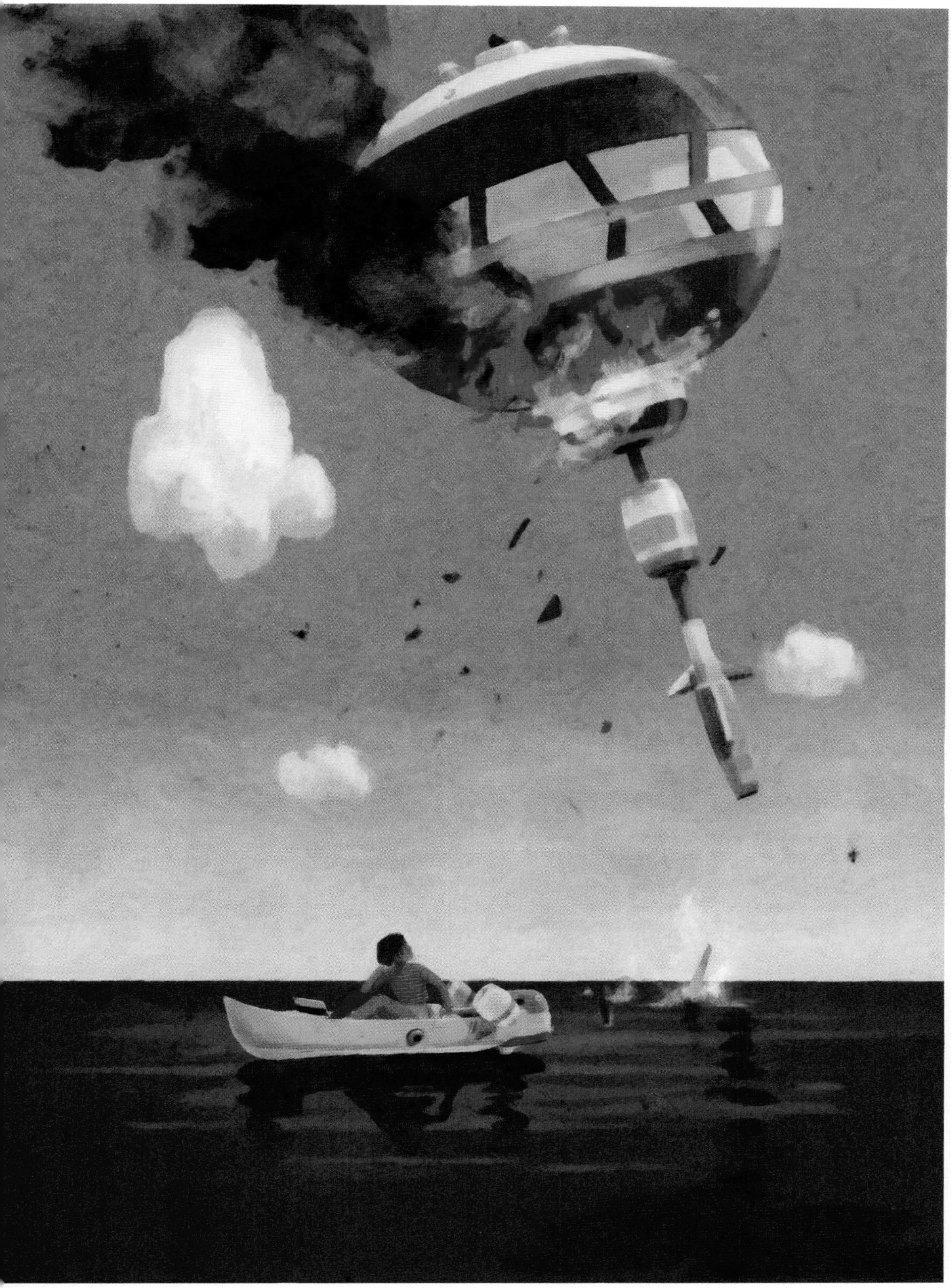

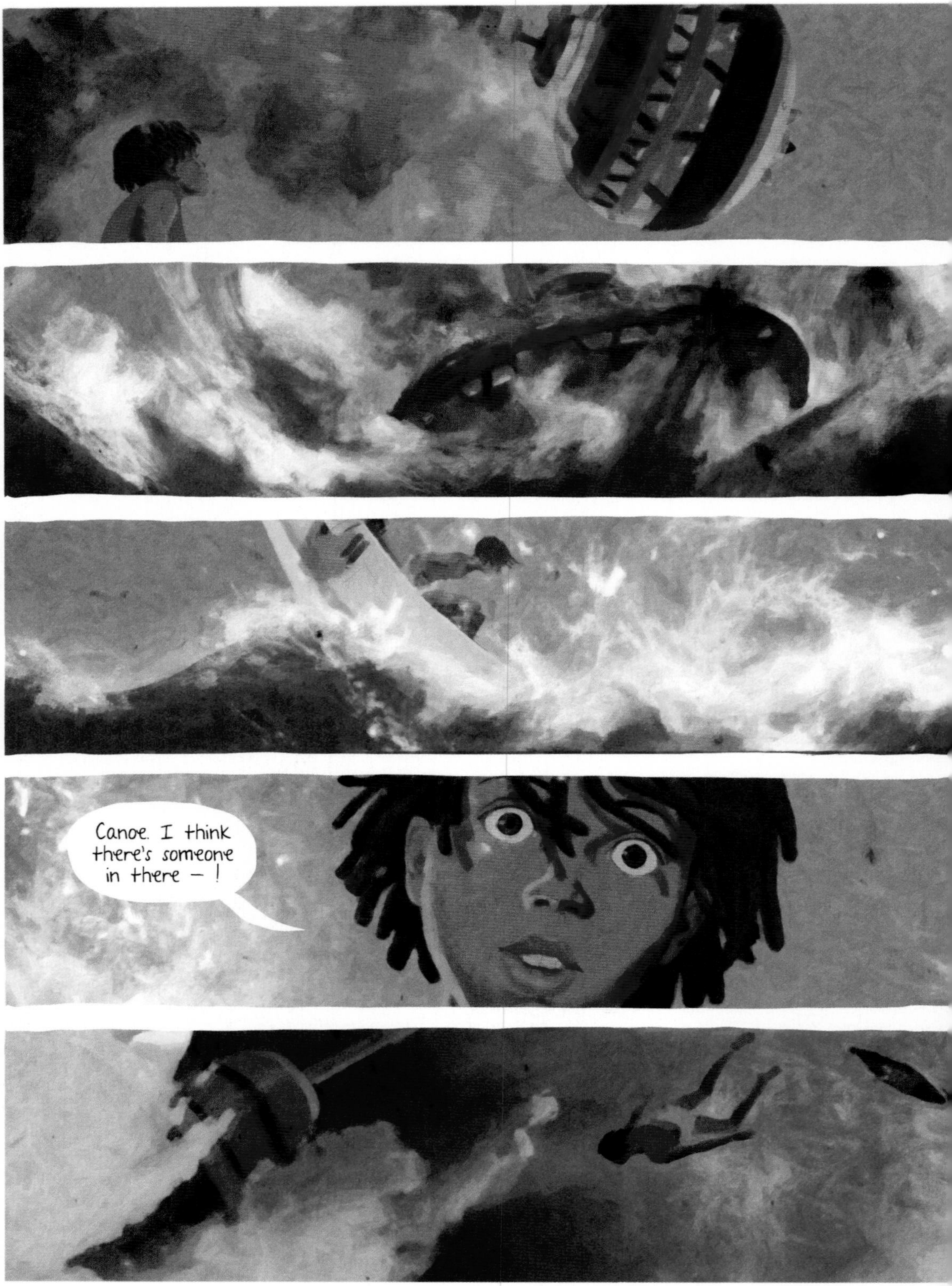
Canoe. I think there's someone in there — !

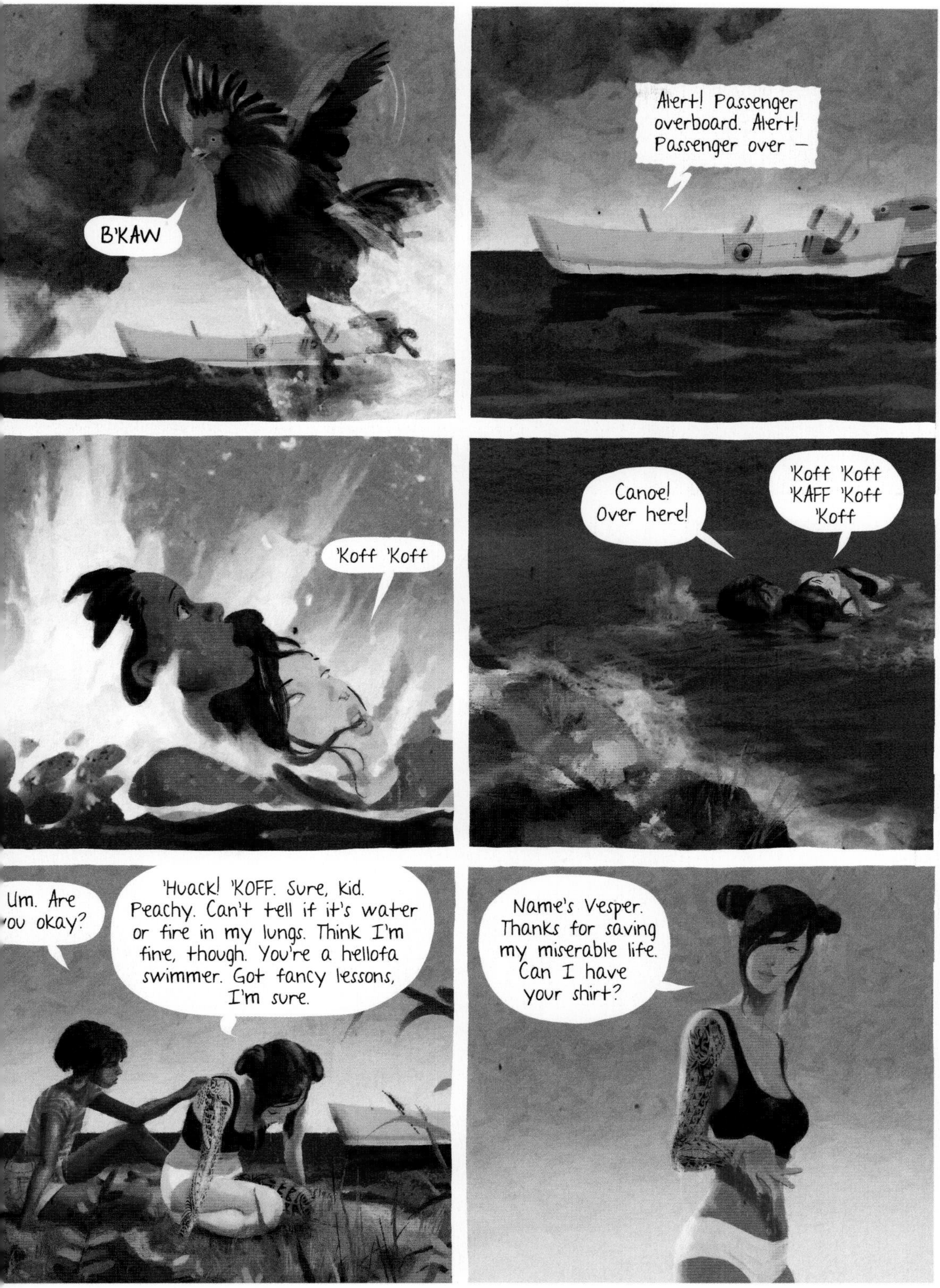
B'KAW
Alert! Passenger overboard. Alert! Passenger over —
'Koff 'Koff
Canoe! Over here!
'Koff 'Koff 'KAFF 'Koff 'Koff
Um. Are ou okay?
'Huack! 'KOFF. Sure, kid. Peachy. Can't tell if it's water or fire in my lungs. Think I'm fine, though. You're a hellofa swimmer. Got fancy lessons, I'm sure.
Name's Vesper. Thanks for saving my miserable life. Can I have your shirt?

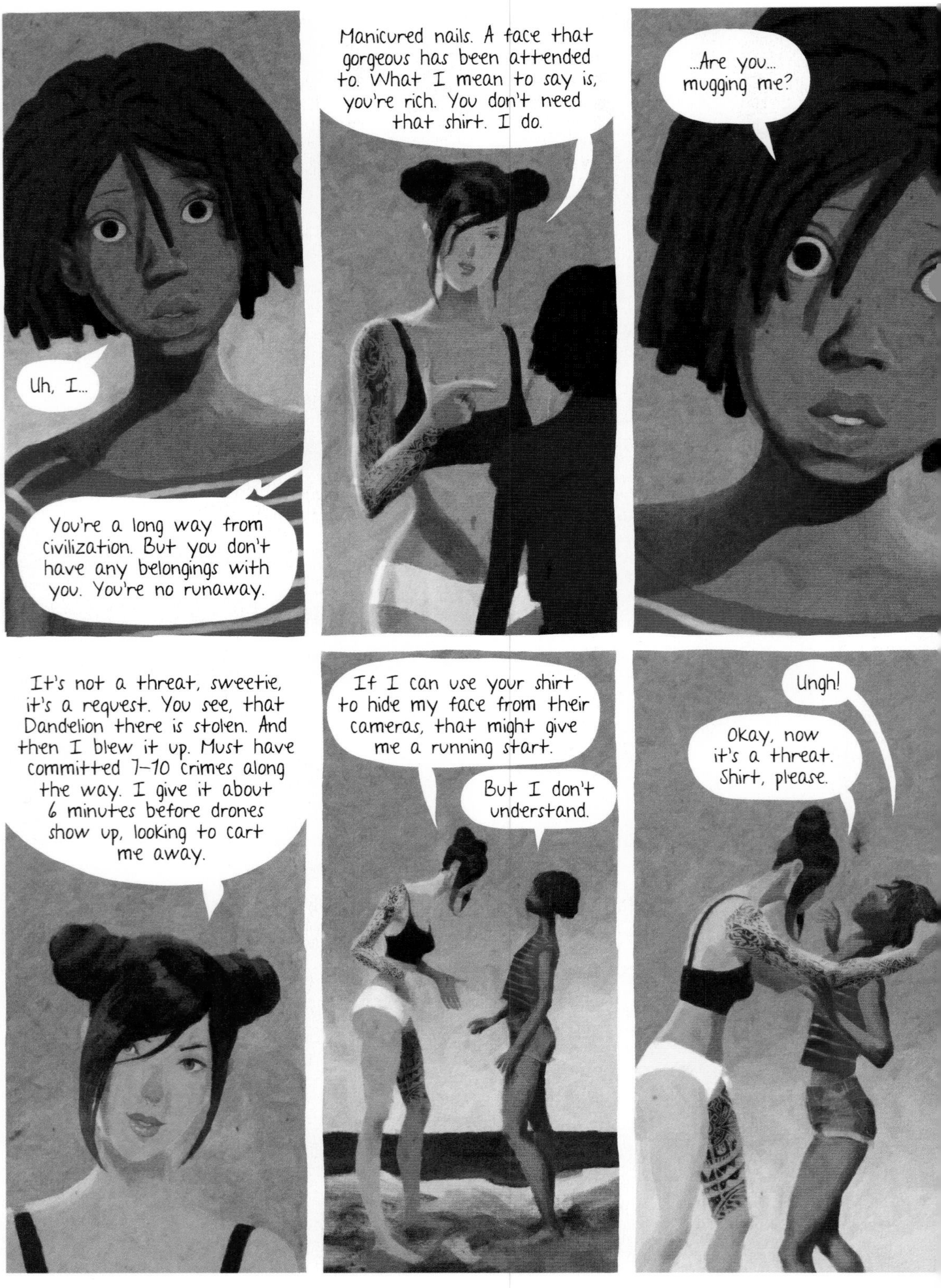
Uh, I...
You're a long way from civilization. But you don't have any belongings with you. You're no runaway.
Manicured nails. A face that gorgeous has been attended to. What I mean to say is, you're rich. You don't need that shirt. I do.
...Are you... mugging me?
It's not a threat, sweetie, it's a request. You see, that Dandelion there is stolen. And then I blew it up. Must have committed 7–10 crimes along the way. I give it about 6 minutes before drones show up, looking to cart me away.
If I can use your shirt to hide my face from their cameras, that might give me a running start.
But I don't understand.
Ungh!
Okay, now it's a threat. Shirt, please.

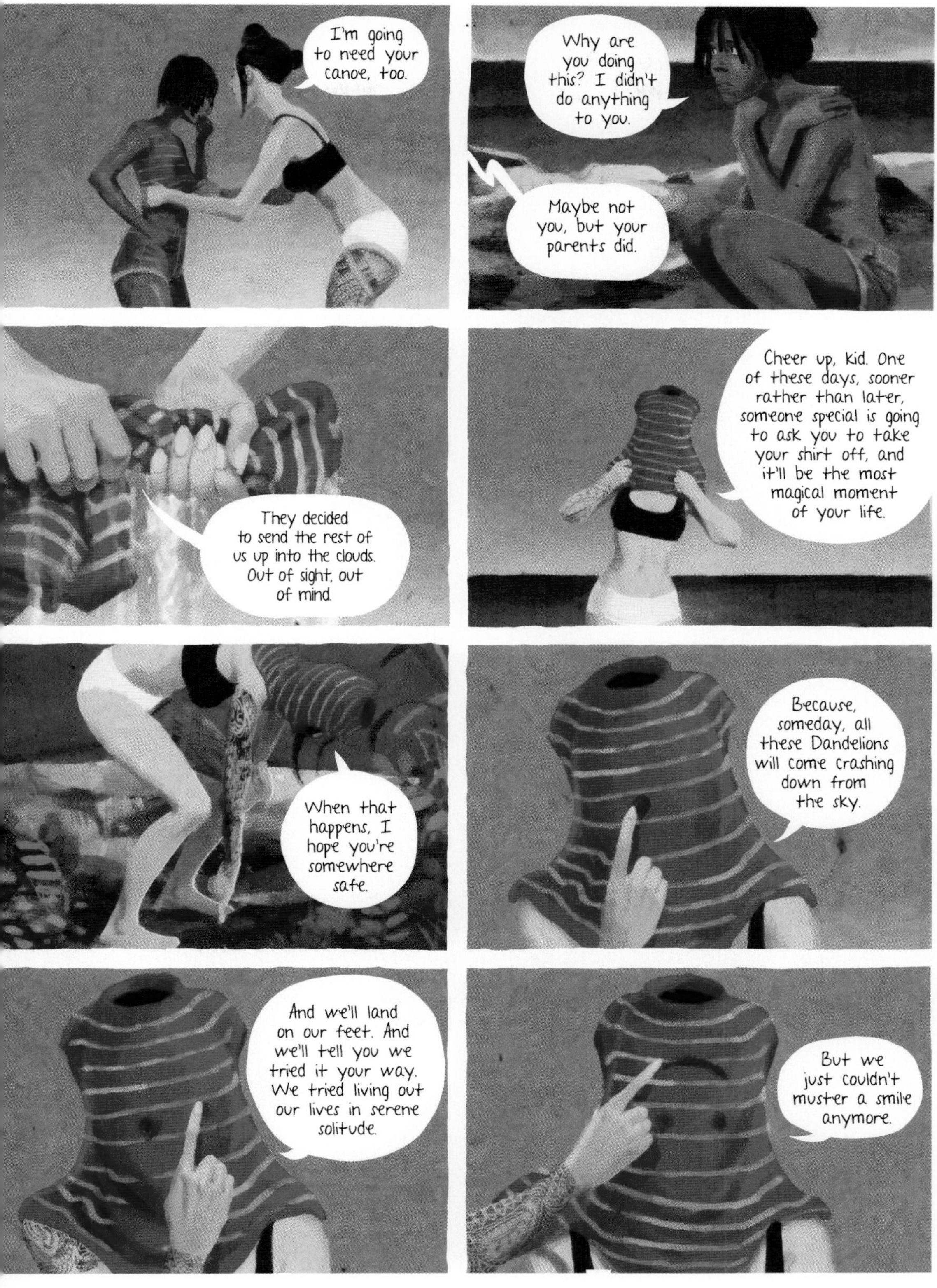
I'm going to need your canoe, too.
Why are you doing this? I didn't do anything to you.
Maybe not you, but your parents did.
They decided to send the rest of us up into the clouds. Out of sight, out of mind.
Cheer up, kid. One of these days, sooner rather than later, someone special is going to ask you to take your shirt off, and it'll be the most magical moment of your life.
When that happens, I hope you're somewhere safe.
Because, someday, all these Dandelions will come crashing down from the sky.
And we'll land on our feet. And we'll tell you we tried it your way. We tried living out our lives in serene solitude.
But we just couldn't muster a smile anymore.

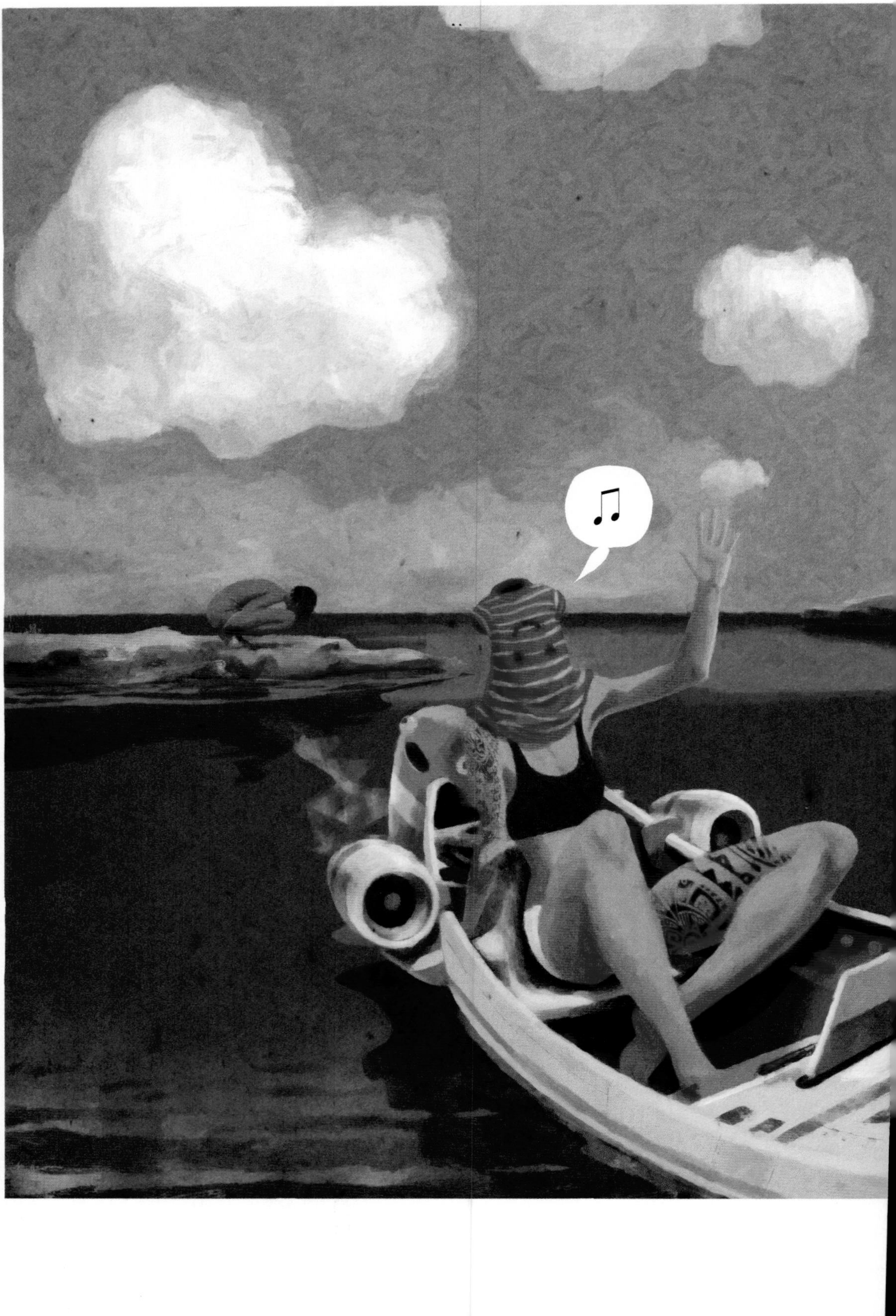

Excerpt from the Stratosphere podcast:
Interview with Jen Nakamuto, inventor of the Dandelion.
Recorded on April 12th, 2047.

It's a tragedy, is what it is. And we all saw it coming. The reports kept warning us, again and again. The ice caps are melting. Cities will be underwater. The AI and the robots are coming for our jobs. The proposed solution was always the same: government regulation.

The problem was, the only people in a position to do anything about it were the rich people, who only cared about getting richer. I'll be honest with you, I was one of them. Sort of. I paid my share of charity, but I could have done more.

I guess, in a way, the Dandelion was meant to atone for my mistakes. I think it's horrible how it came at the cost of citizenship. That wasn't the intention. I just wanted people to have a roof over their heads and the freedom to go wherever the wind blows.

But the bureaucratic bastards out-smarted me. They found a way to work the Dandelion into giving them every-thing they ever wanted. So, I guess, I have even more to atone for.

THE PIRATE AND THE FISHERMAN

ART

ERIC KODA

COLORS

JUHA VELTTI

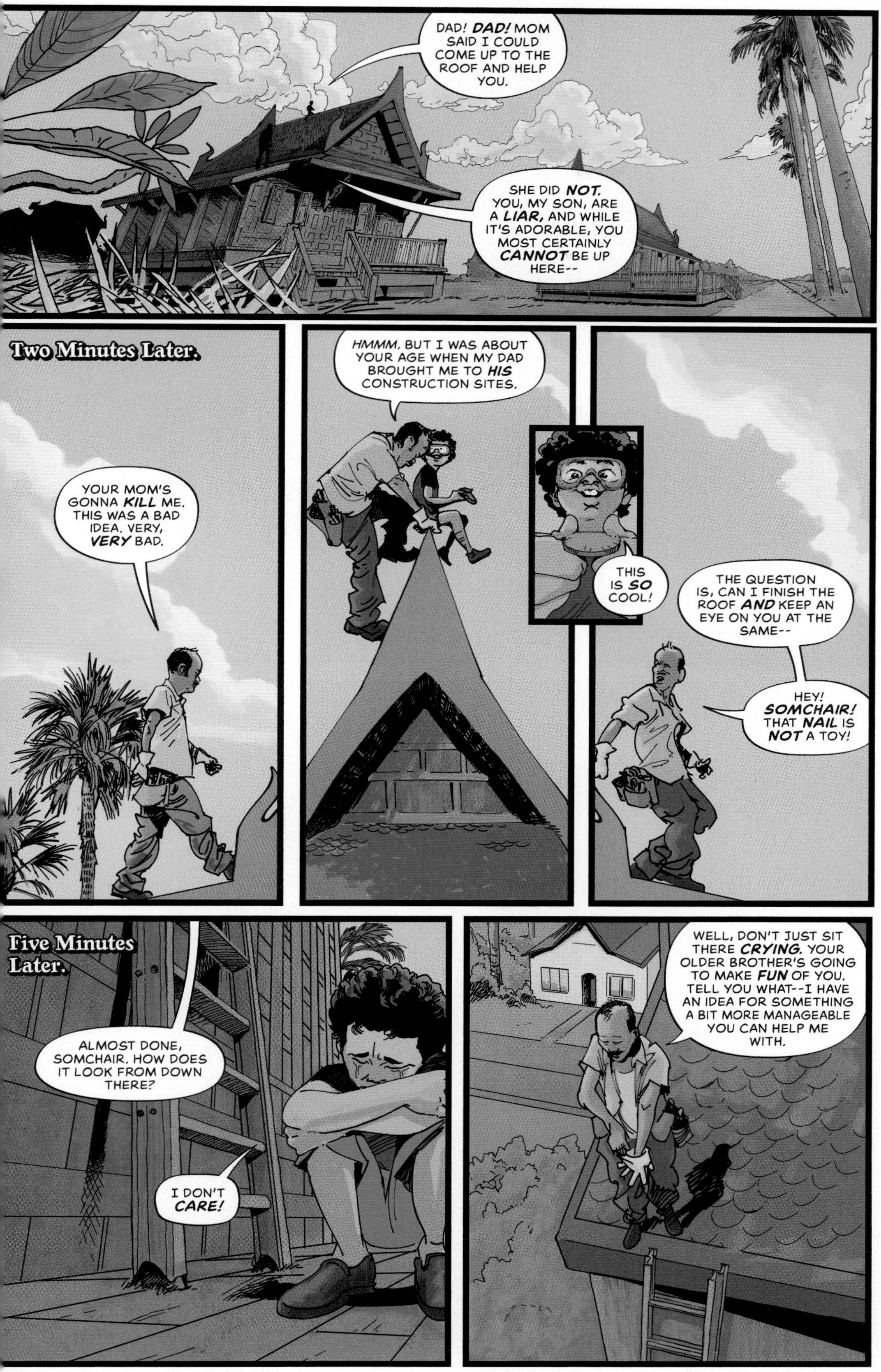
DAD! DAD! MOM SAID I COULD COME UP TO THE ROOF AND HELP YOU.
SHE DID NOT. YOU, MY SON, ARE A LIAR, AND WHILE IT'S ADORABLE, YOU MOST CERTAINLY CANNOT BE UP HERE--
Two Minutes Later.
YOUR MOM'S GONNA KILL ME. THIS WAS A BAD IDEA. VERY, VERY BAD.
HMMM. BUT I WAS ABOUT YOUR AGE WHEN MY DAD BROUGHT ME TO HIS CONSTRUCTION SITES.
THIS IS SO COOL!
THE QUESTION IS, CAN I FINISH THE ROOF AND KEEP AN EYE ON YOU AT THE SAME--
HEY! SOMCHAIR! THAT NAIL IS NOT A TOY!
Five Minutes Later.
ALMOST DONE, SOMCHAIR. HOW DOES IT LOOK FROM DOWN THERE?
I DON'T CARE!
WELL, DON'T JUST SIT THERE CRYING. YOUR OLDER BROTHER'S GOING TO MAKE FUN OF YOU. TELL YOU WHAT--I HAVE AN IDEA FOR SOMETHING A BIT MORE MANAGEABLE YOU CAN HELP ME WITH.

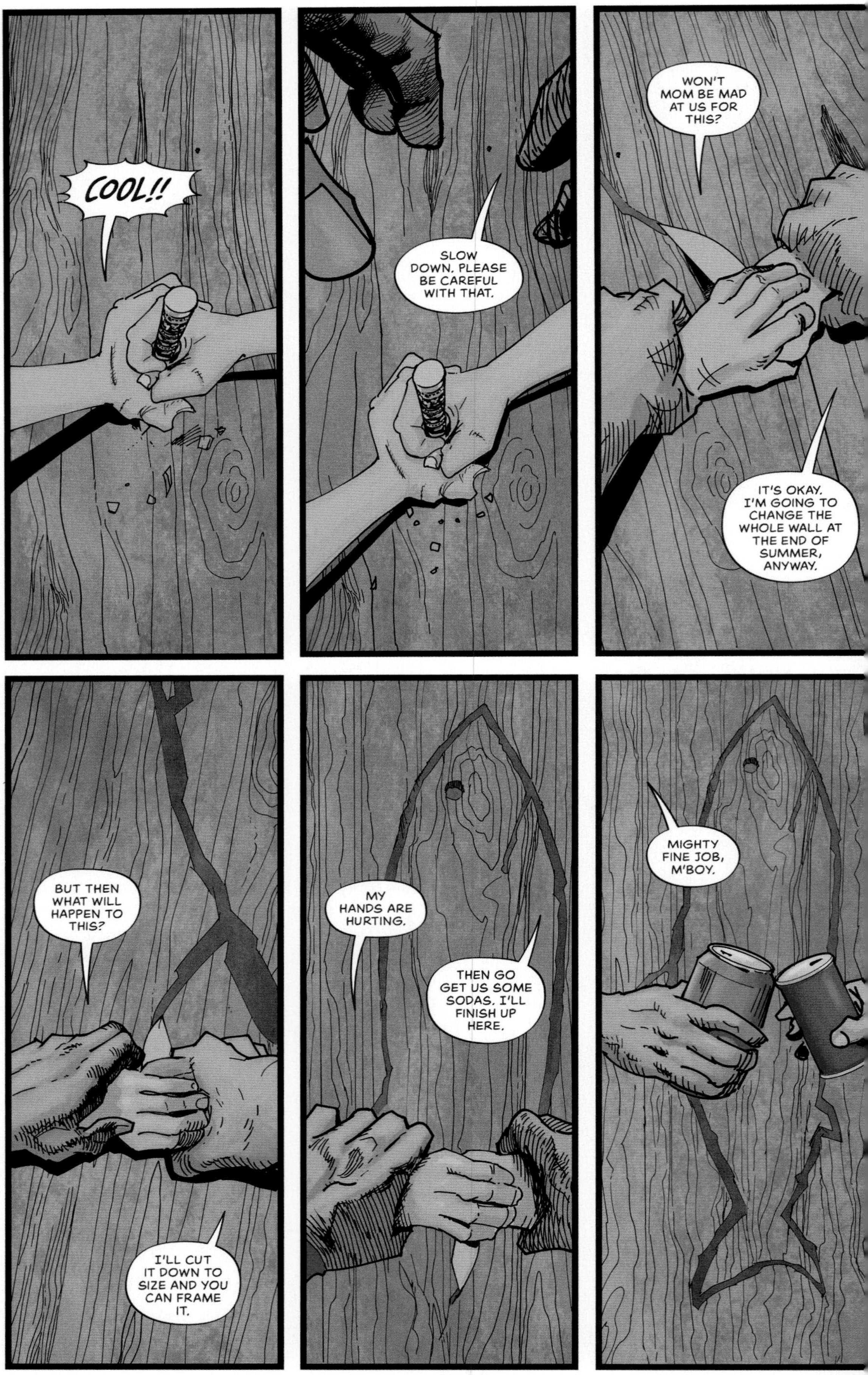
COOL!!
SLOW DOWN. PLEASE BE CAREFUL WITH THAT.
WON'T MOM BE MAD AT US FOR THIS?
IT'S OKAY. I'M GOING TO CHANGE THE WHOLE WALL AT THE END OF SUMMER, ANYWAY.
BUT THEN WHAT WILL HAPPEN TO THIS?
I'LL CUT IT DOWN TO SIZE AND YOU CAN FRAME IT.
MY HANDS ARE HURTING.
THEN GO GET US SOME SODAS. I'LL FINISH UP HERE.
MIGHTY FINE JOB, M'BOY.

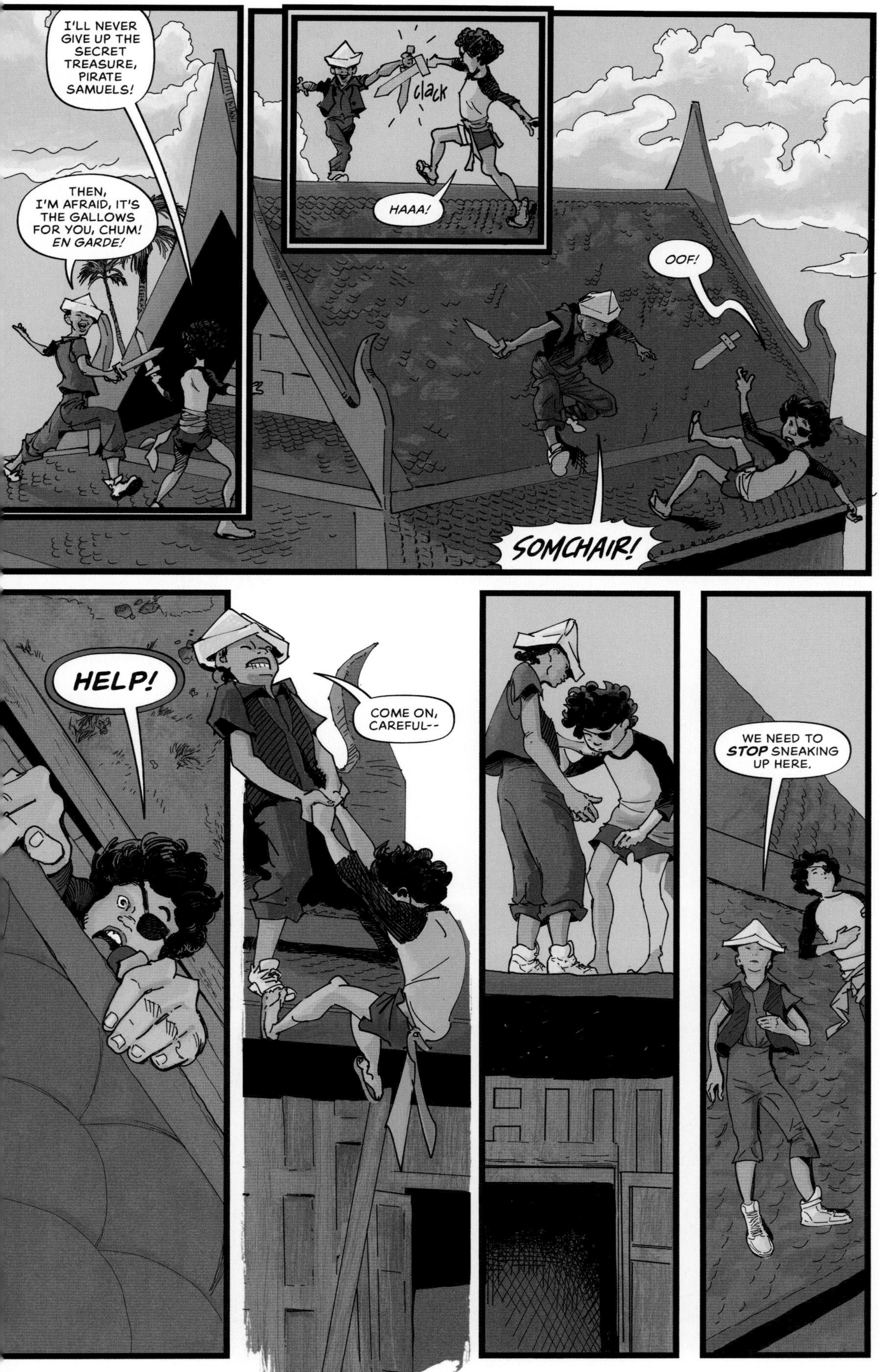
I'LL NEVER GIVE UP THE SECRET TREASURE, PIRATE SAMUELS!
THEN, I'M AFRAID, IT'S THE GALLOWS FOR YOU, CHUM! *EN GARDE!*
CLACK
HAAA!
OOF!
SOMCHAIR!
HELP!
COME ON, CAREFUL--
WE NEED TO **STOP** SNEAKING UP HERE.

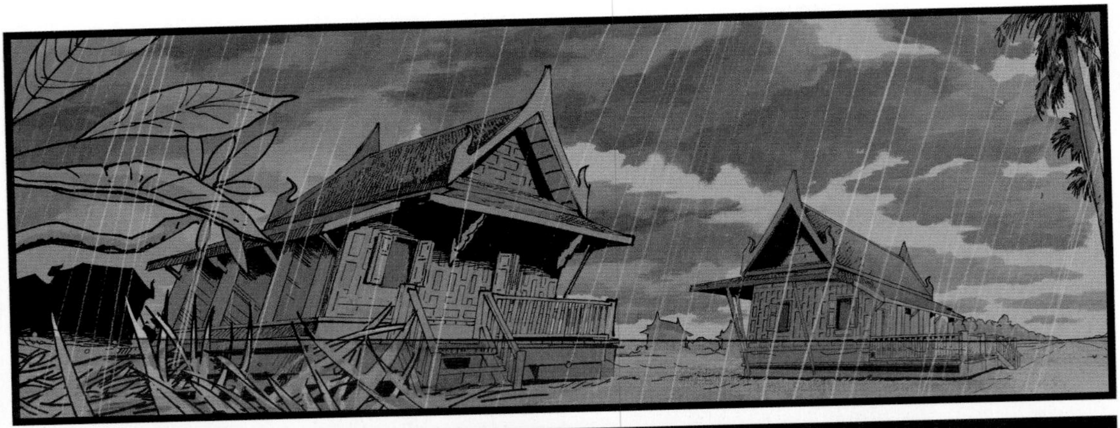

Bangkok was among the first cities
to flood from rising sea levels.

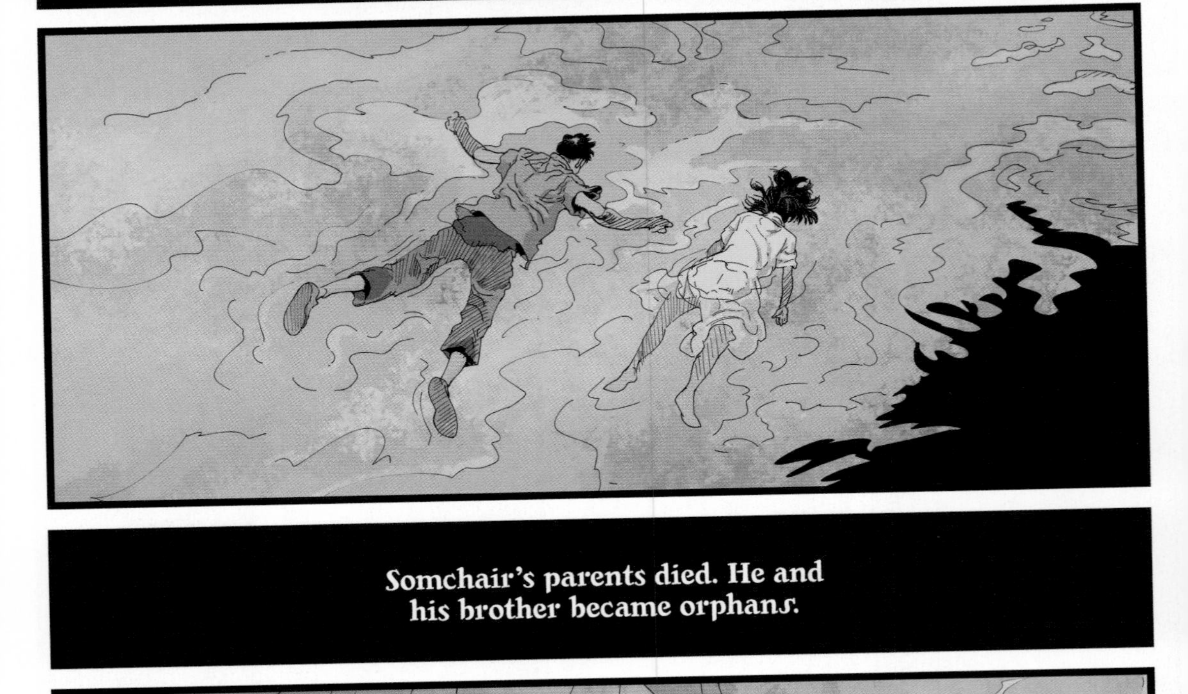

Somchair's parents died. He and
his brother became orphans.

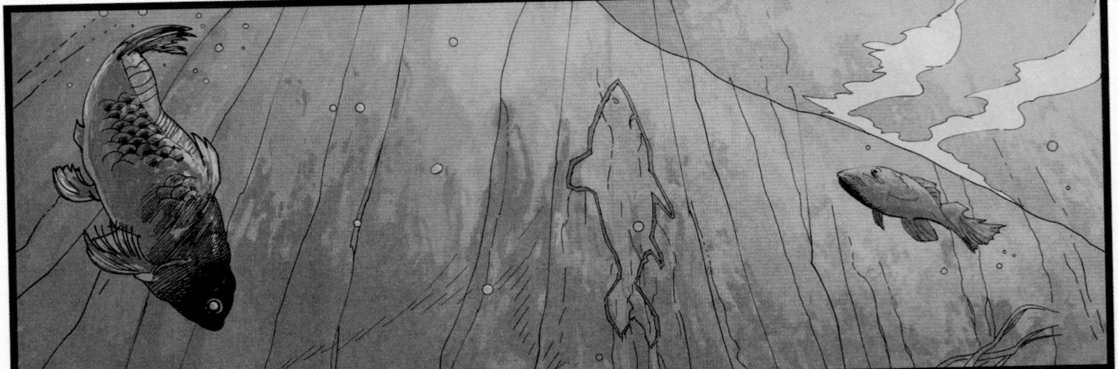

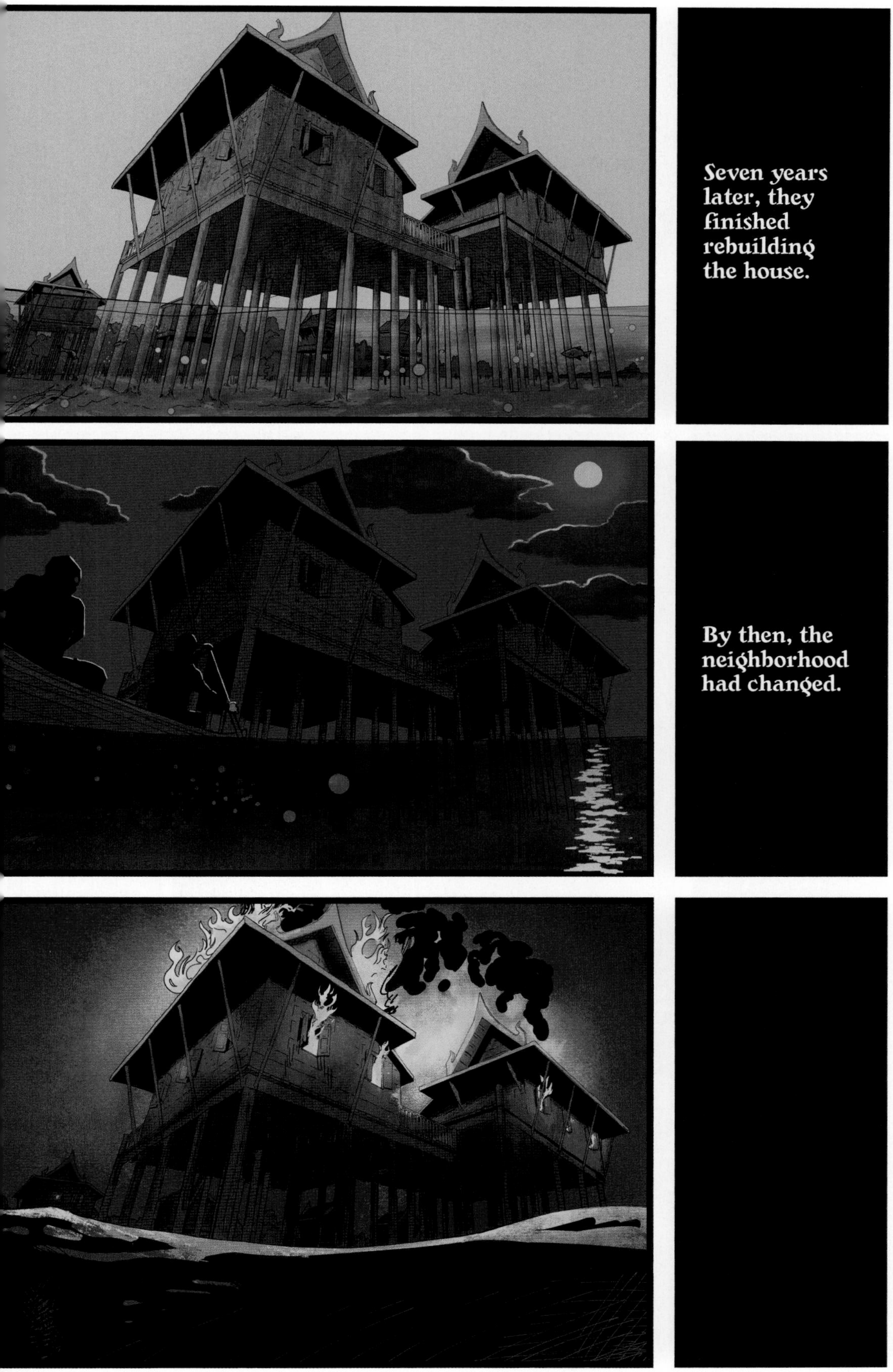
Seven years later, they finished rebuilding the house.
By then, the neighborhood had changed.

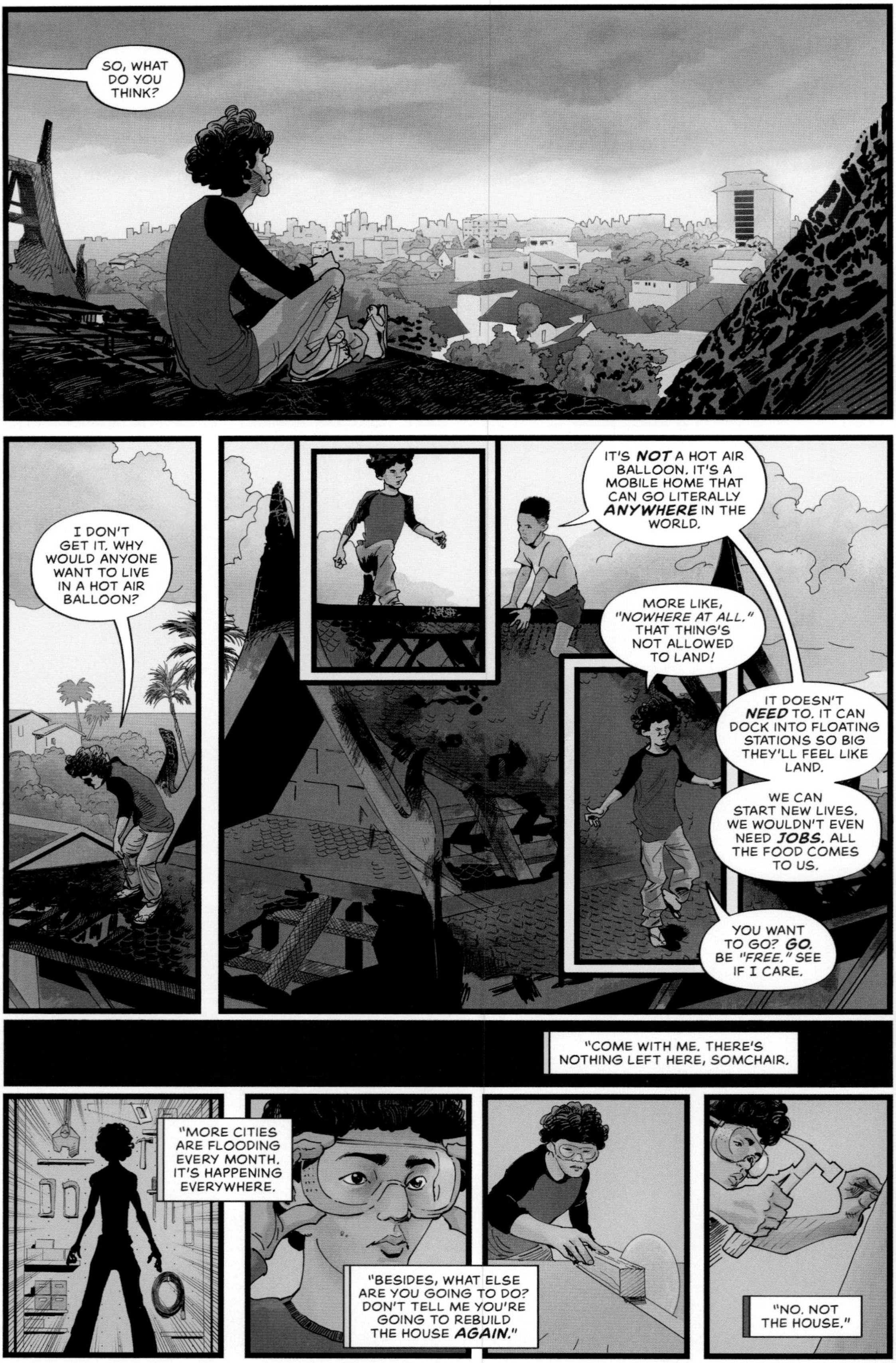
SO, WHAT DO YOU THINK?
I DON'T GET IT. WHY WOULD ANYONE WANT TO LIVE IN A HOT AIR BALLOON?
IT'S NOT A HOT AIR BALLOON. IT'S A MOBILE HOME THAT CAN GO LITERALLY ANYWHERE IN THE WORLD.
MORE LIKE, "NOWHERE AT ALL." THAT THING'S NOT ALLOWED TO LAND!
IT DOESN'T NEED TO. IT CAN DOCK INTO FLOATING STATIONS SO BIG THEY'LL FEEL LIKE LAND.
WE CAN START NEW LIVES. WE WOULDN'T EVEN NEED JOBS. ALL THE FOOD COMES TO US.
YOU WANT TO GO? GO. BE "FREE." SEE IF I CARE.
"COME WITH ME. THERE'S NOTHING LEFT HERE, SOMCHAIR.
"MORE CITIES ARE FLOODING EVERY MONTH. IT'S HAPPENING EVERYWHERE.
"BESIDES, WHAT ELSE ARE YOU GOING TO DO? DON'T TELL ME YOU'RE GOING TO REBUILD THE HOUSE AGAIN."
"NO. NOT THE HOUSE."

The Pirate

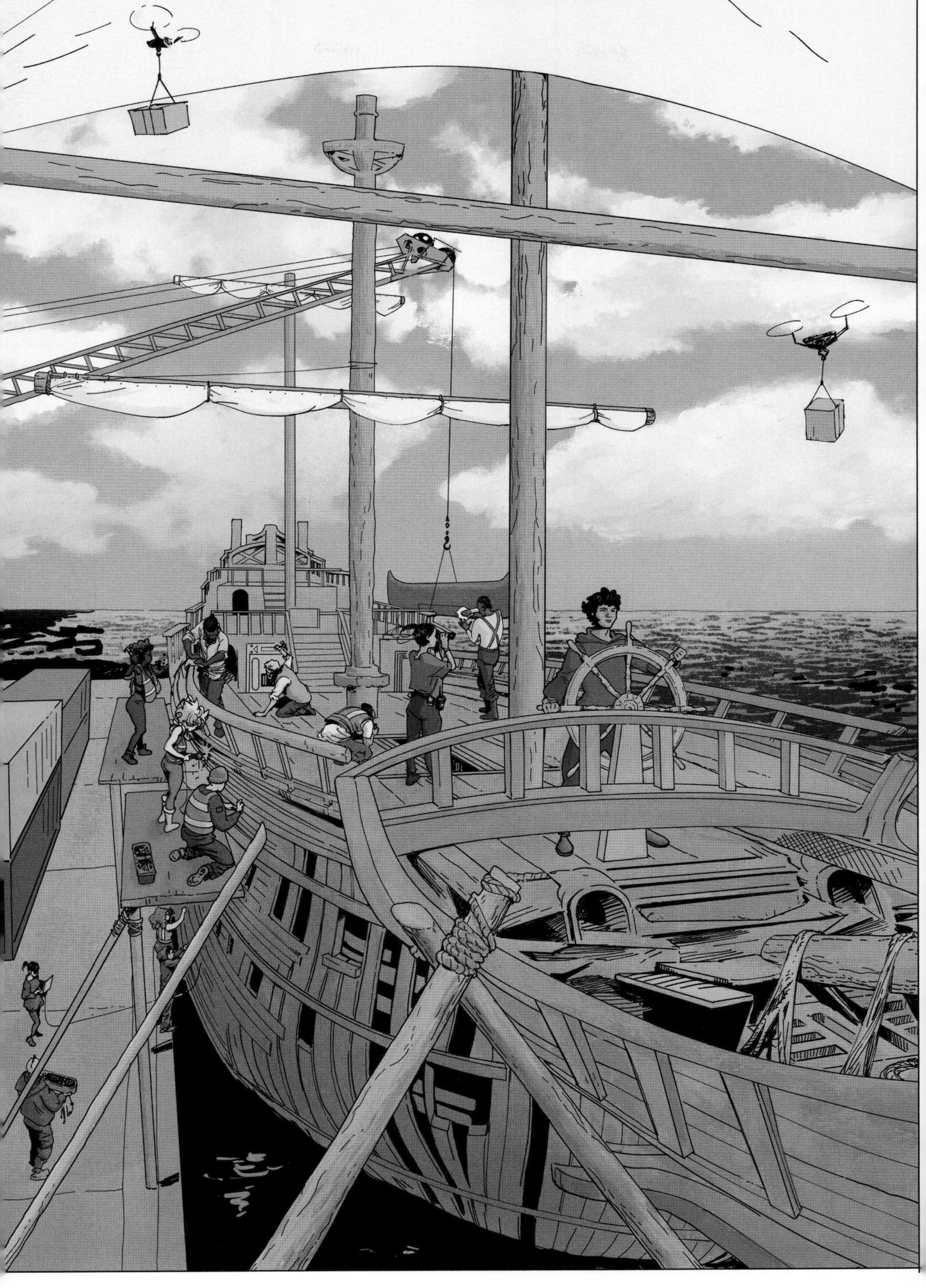

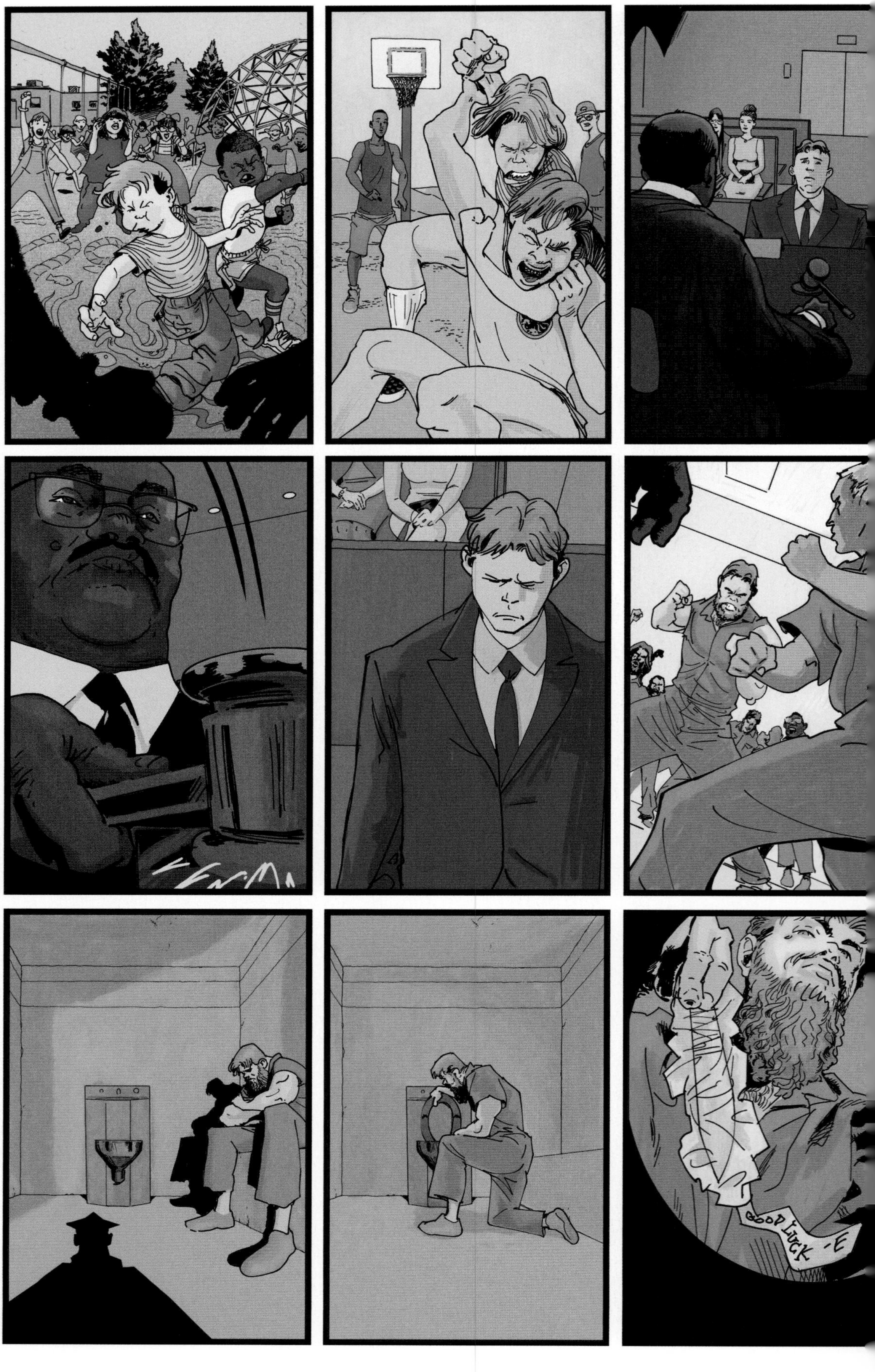
GOOD LUCK -E

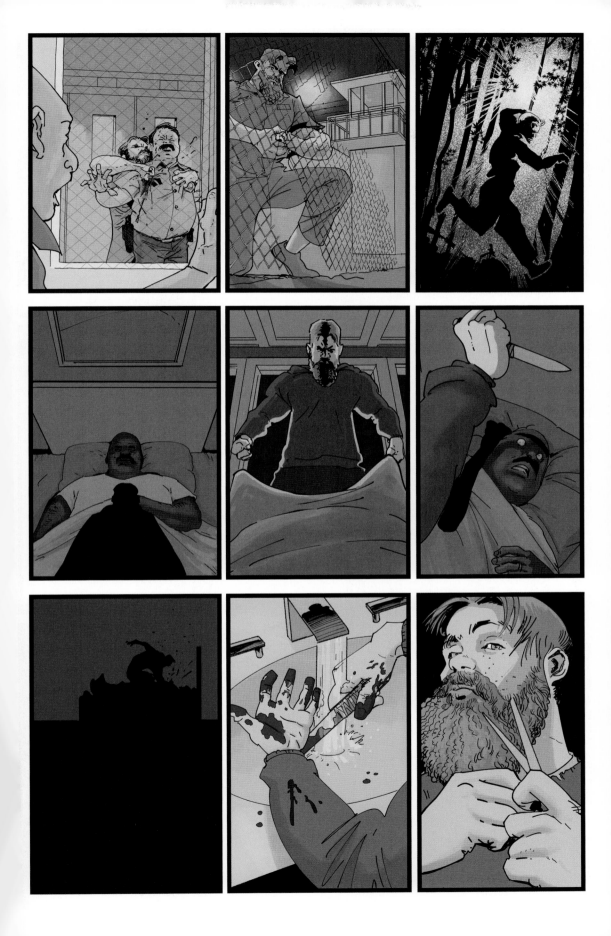

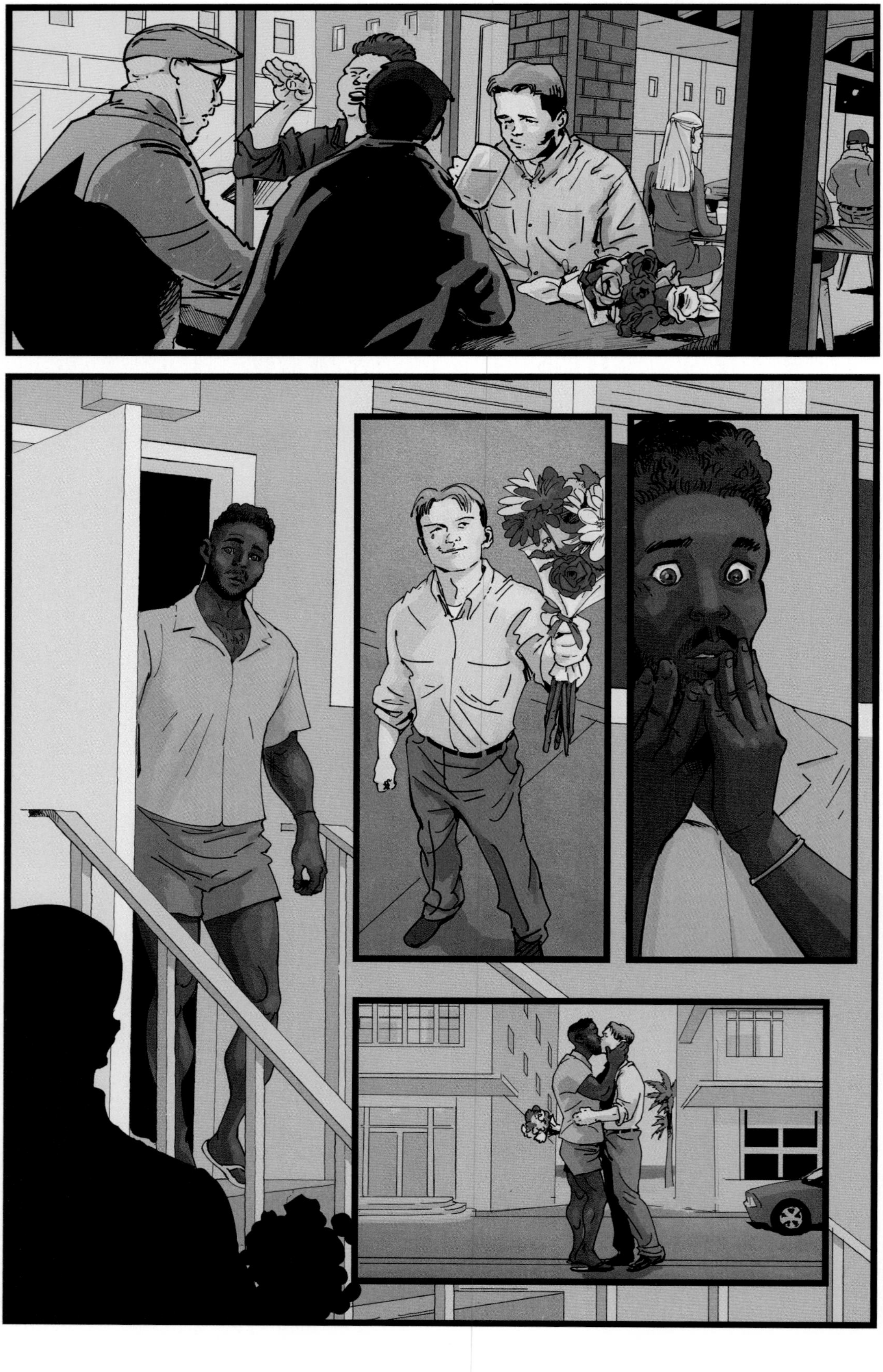

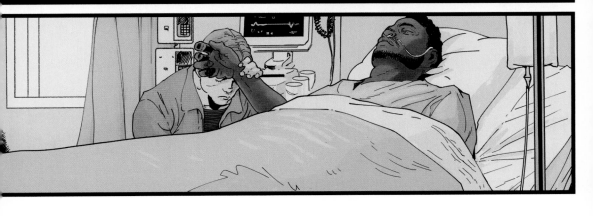

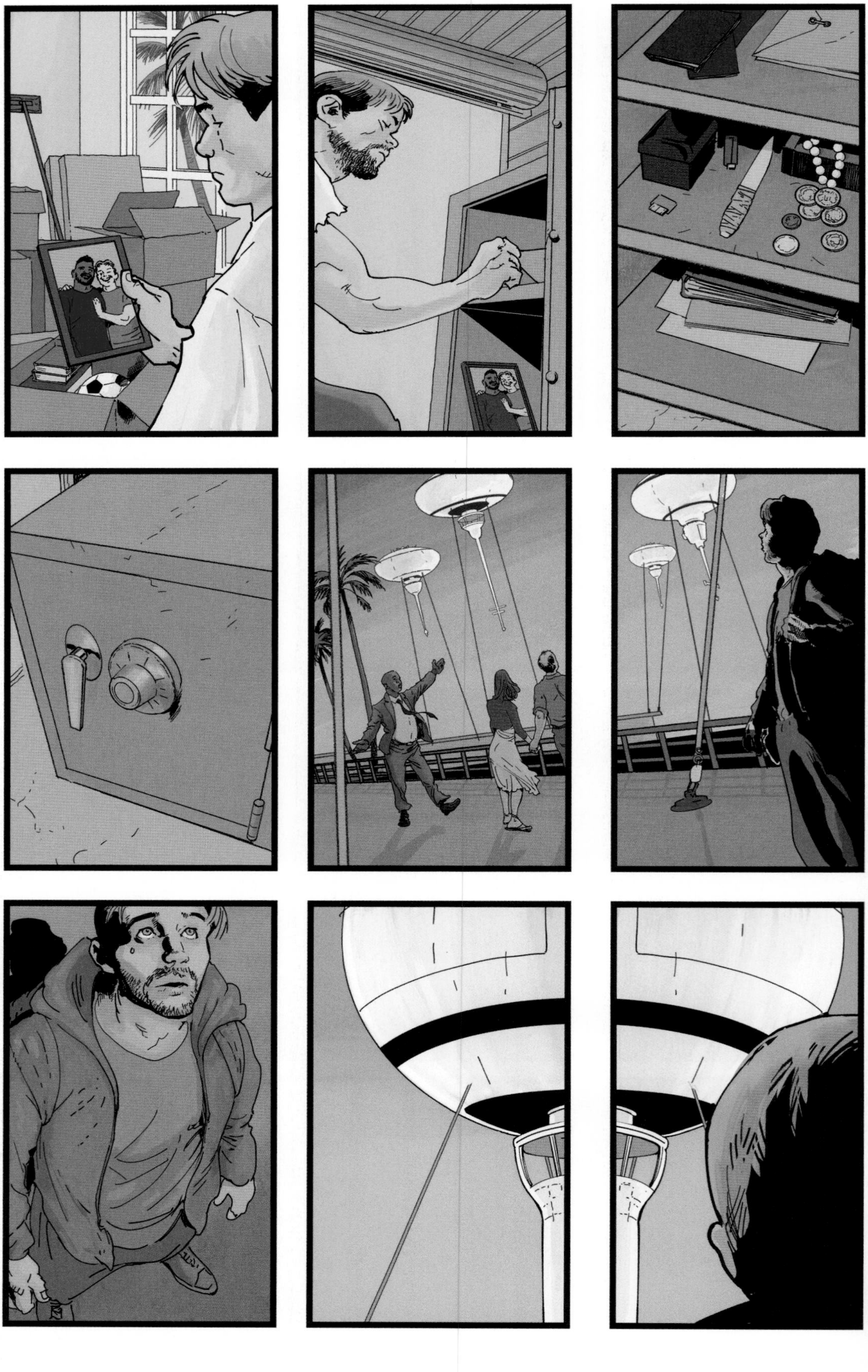

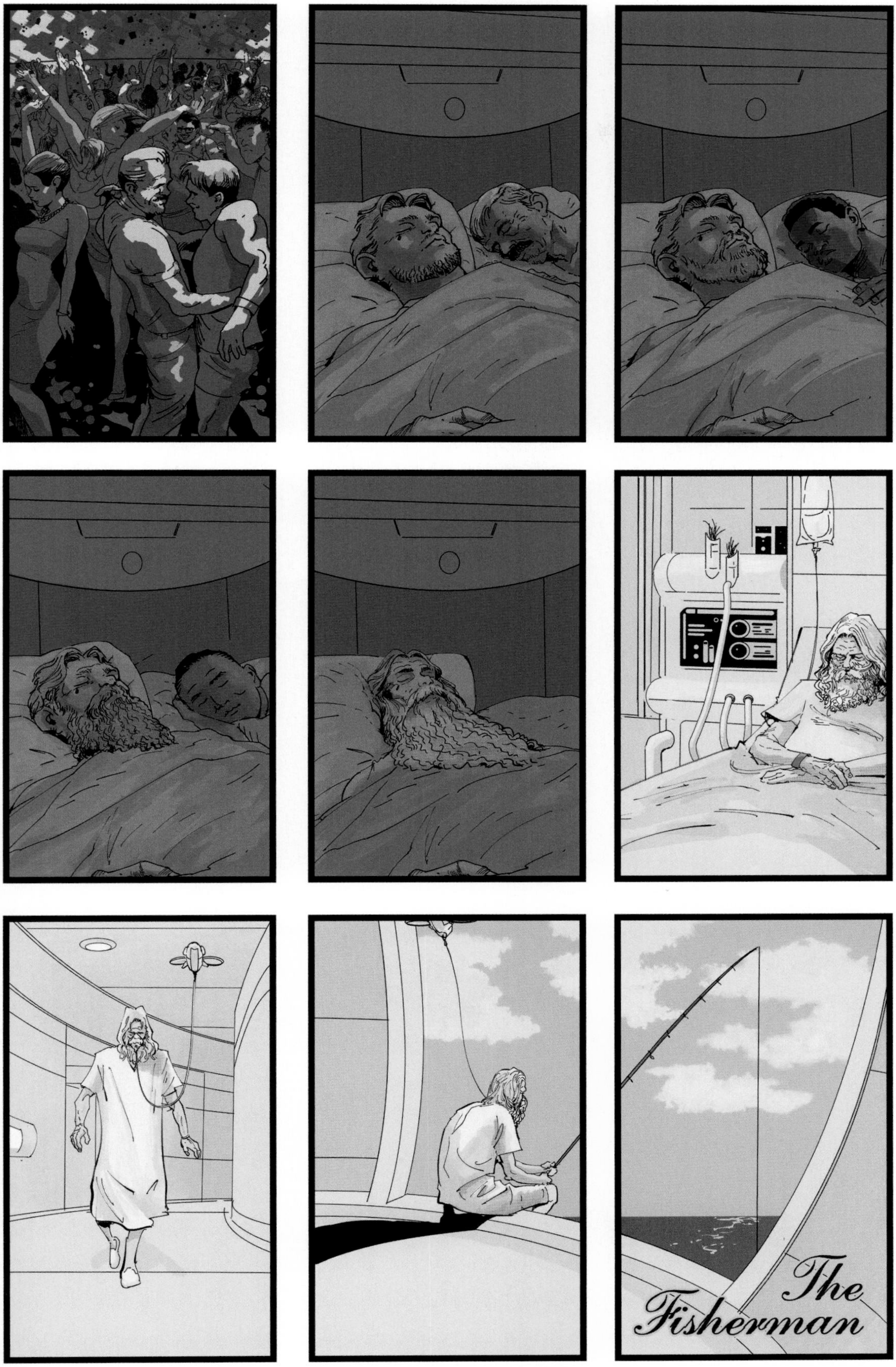
The Fisherman

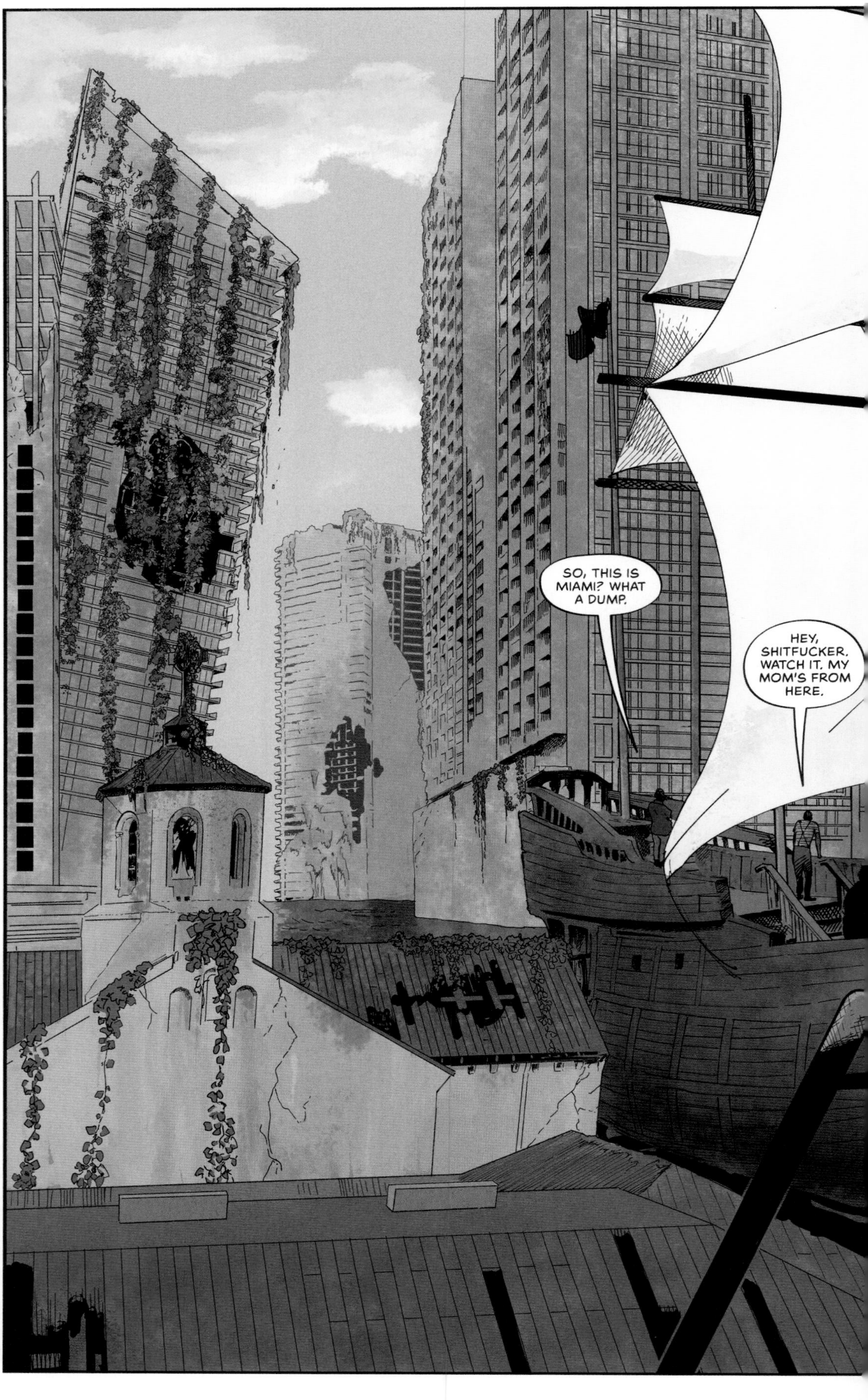
SO, THIS IS MIAMI? WHAT A DUMP.
HEY, SHITFUCKER. WATCH IT. MY MOM'S FROM HERE.

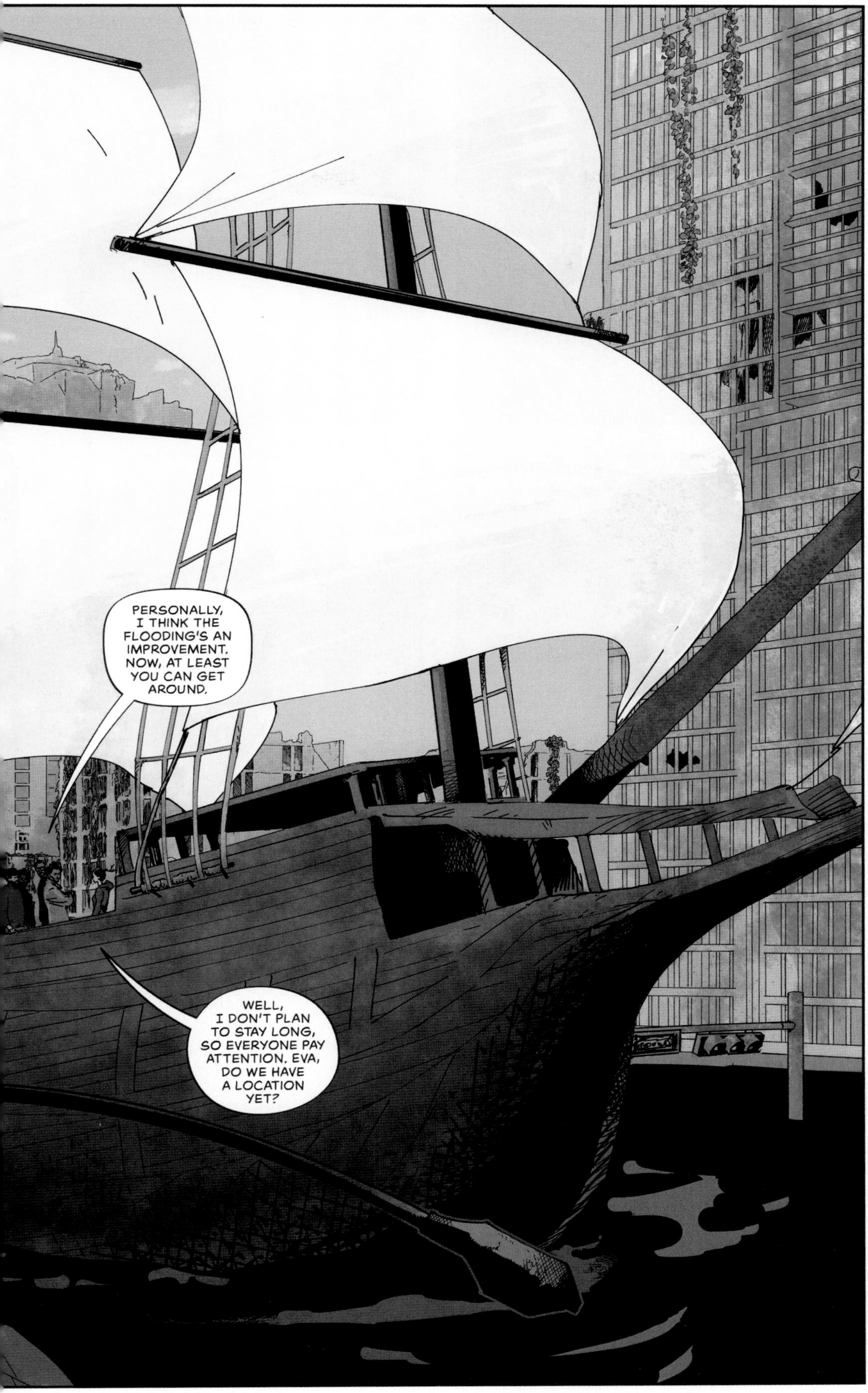
PERSONALLY, I THINK THE FLOODING'S AN IMPROVEMENT. NOW, AT LEAST YOU CAN GET AROUND.
WELL, I DON'T PLAN TO STAY LONG, SO EVERYONE PAY ATTENTION. EVA, DO WE HAVE A LOCATION YET?

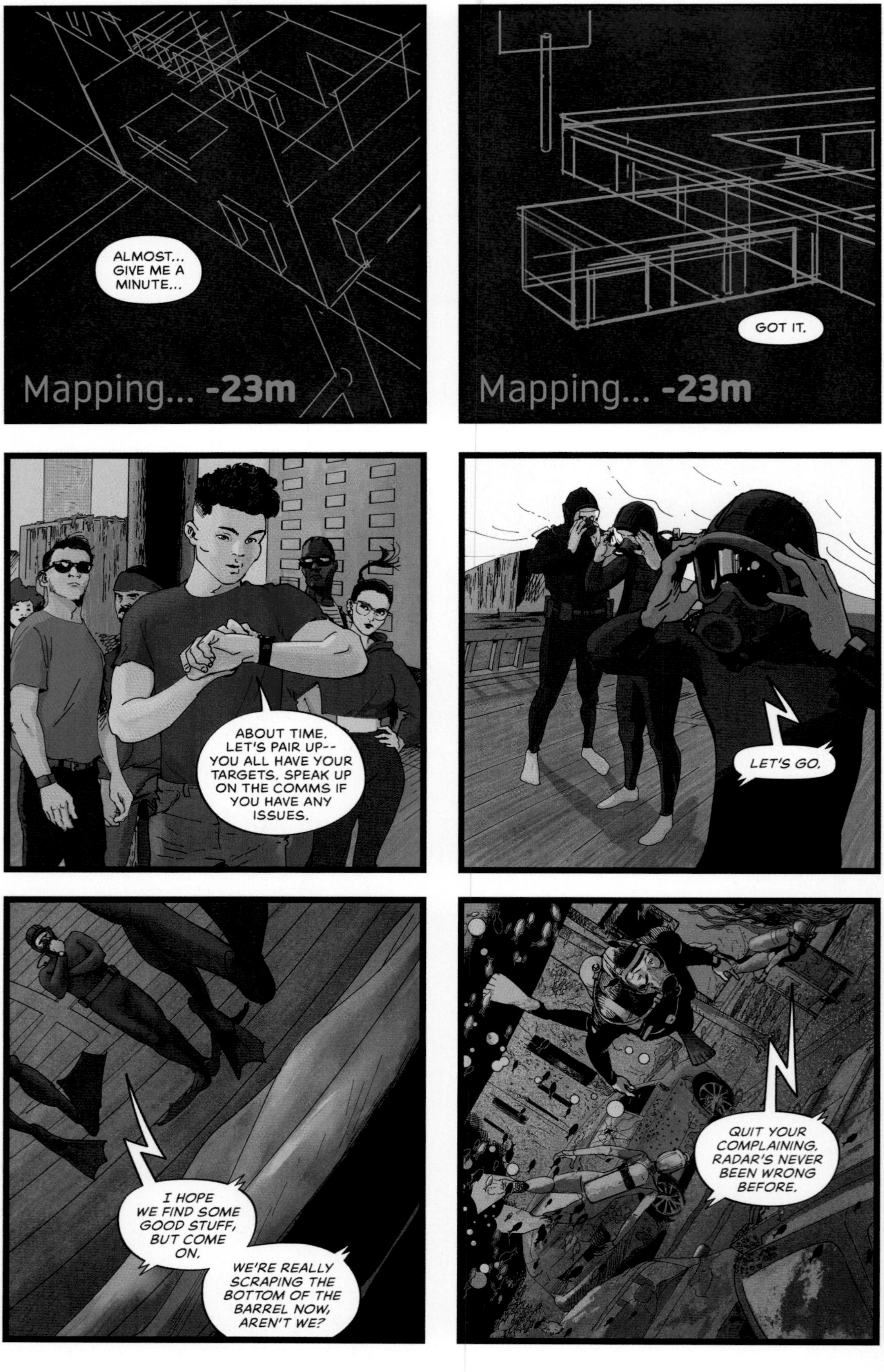
ALMOST... GIVE ME A MINUTE...
Mapping... -23m
GOT IT.
Mapping... -23m
ABOUT TIME. LET'S PAIR UP-- YOU ALL HAVE YOUR TARGETS. SPEAK UP ON THE COMMS IF YOU HAVE ANY ISSUES.
LET'S GO.
I HOPE WE FIND SOME GOOD STUFF, BUT COME ON.
WE'RE REALLY SCRAPING THE BOTTOM OF THE BARREL NOW, AREN'T WE?
QUIT YOUR COMPLAINING. RADAR'S NEVER BEEN WRONG BEFORE.

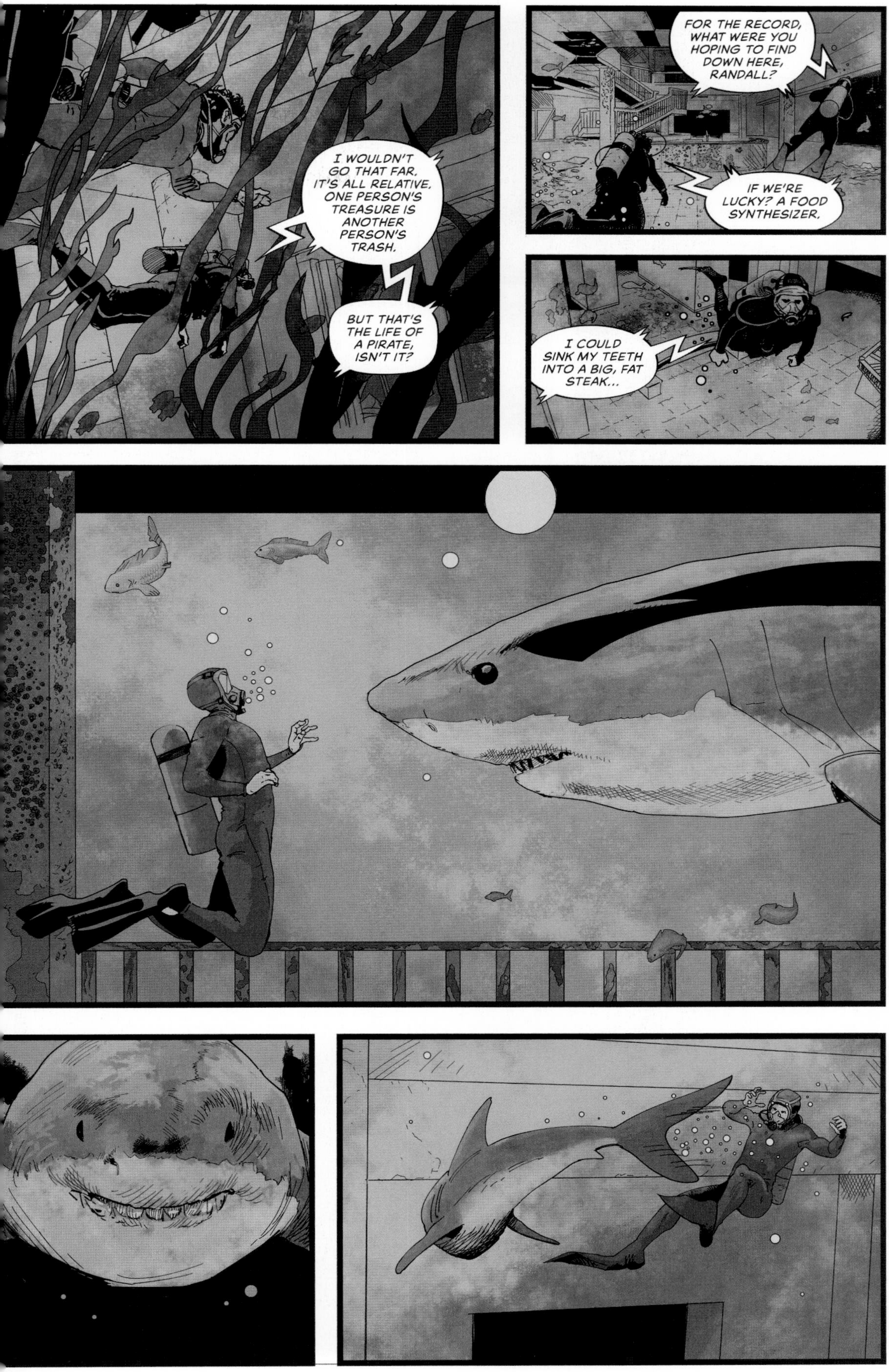
I WOULDN'T GO THAT FAR. IT'S ALL RELATIVE. ONE PERSON'S TREASURE IS ANOTHER PERSON'S TRASH.
BUT THAT'S THE LIFE OF A PIRATE, ISN'T IT?
FOR THE RECORD, WHAT WERE YOU HOPING TO FIND DOWN HERE, RANDALL?
IF WE'RE LUCKY? A FOOD SYNTHESIZER.
I COULD SINK MY TEETH INTO A BIG, FAT STEAK...

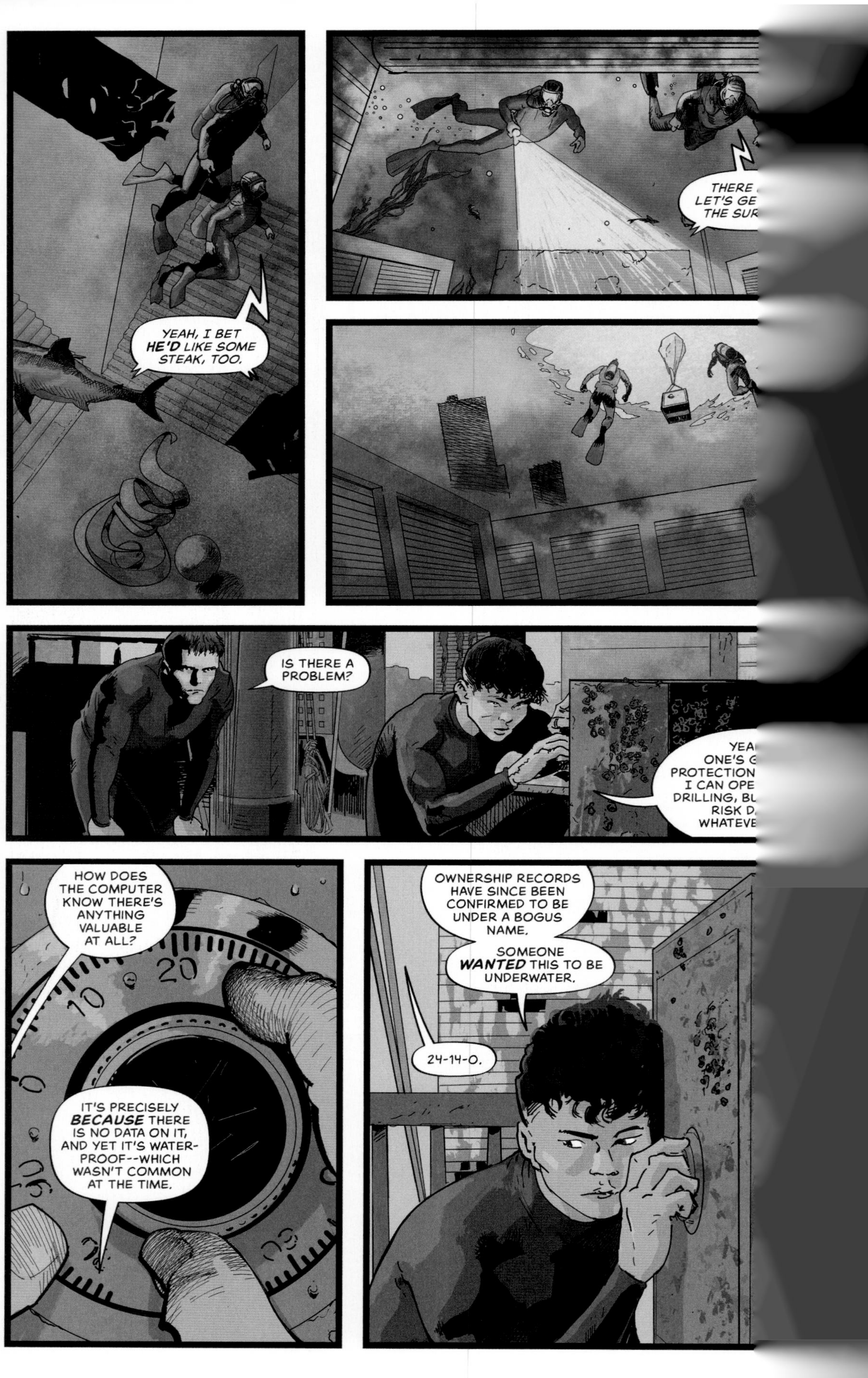
YEAH, I BET **HE'D** LIKE SOME STEAK, TOO.
THERE
LET'S GE
THE SUR
IS THERE A PROBLEM?
YEA
ONE'S G
PROTECTION
I CAN OPE
DRILLING, BU
RISK D
WHATEVE
HOW DOES THE COMPUTER KNOW THERE'S ANYTHING VALUABLE AT ALL?
IT'S PRECISELY **BECAUSE** THERE IS NO DATA ON IT, AND YET IT'S WATER-PROOF--WHICH WASN'T COMMON AT THE TIME.
OWNERSHIP RECORDS HAVE SINCE BEEN CONFIRMED TO BE UNDER A BOGUS NAME.
SOMEONE **WANTED** THIS TO BE UNDERWATER.
24-14-0.

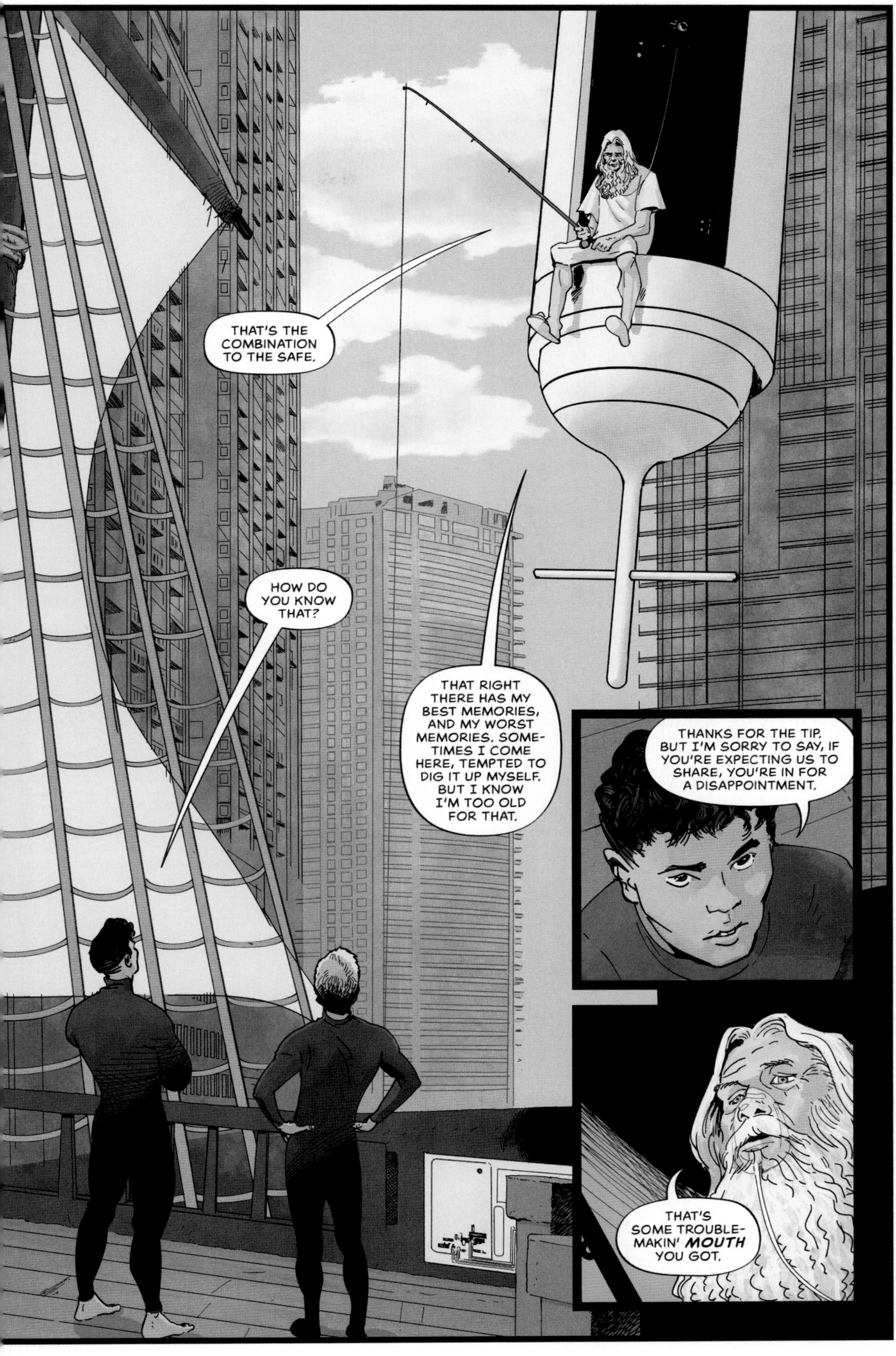
THAT'S THE COMBINATION TO THE SAFE.
HOW DO YOU KNOW THAT?
THAT RIGHT THERE HAS MY BEST MEMORIES, AND MY WORST MEMORIES. SOMETIMES I COME HERE, TEMPTED TO DIG IT UP MYSELF. BUT I KNOW I'M TOO OLD FOR THAT.
THANKS FOR THE TIP. BUT I'M SORRY TO SAY, IF YOU'RE EXPECTING US TO SHARE, YOU'RE IN FOR A DISAPPOINTMENT.
THAT'S SOME TROUBLE-MAKIN' MOUTH YOU GOT.

YOU REMIND ME OF *ME* WHEN I WAS YOUR AGE.

I HAVE A FEELING YOU AND I HAVE *NOTHING* IN COMMON.

I'M TIRED ENOUGH TO NOT WANT TO FIND OUT.

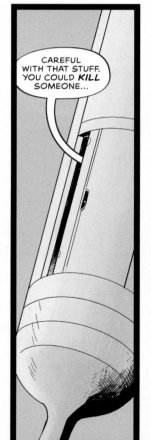

CAREFUL WITH THAT STUFF. YOU COULD *KILL* SOMEONE...

...OR STEAL THEIR *HEART.*

WHAT DO YOU THINK HE WAS TALKING ABOUT?

NOTHIN'. PROBABLY SPENT TOO MUCH TIME STARING AT THE SUN, AND NOW HIS BRAIN IS FRIED.

BUT LET'S GIVE IT A GO. 24...14...0.

KIK

NO WAY...
CHECK THIS OUT.
GUESS THAT COMPUTER WAS RIGHT, *HUH?* GOTTA BE WORTH AT ***LEAST*** A STEAK.
SURE.
MURDER WEAPON?
DEFINITELY.
GONNA SOLVE IT?
NOPE.
I THINK I'LL JUST KEEP IT.

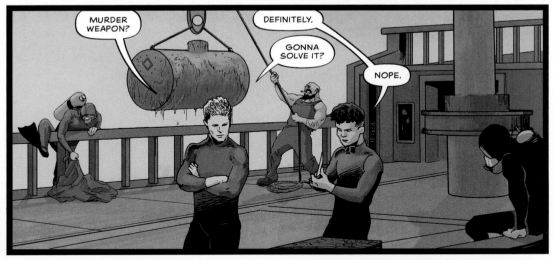

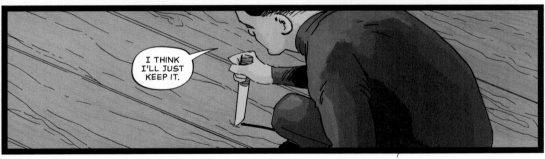

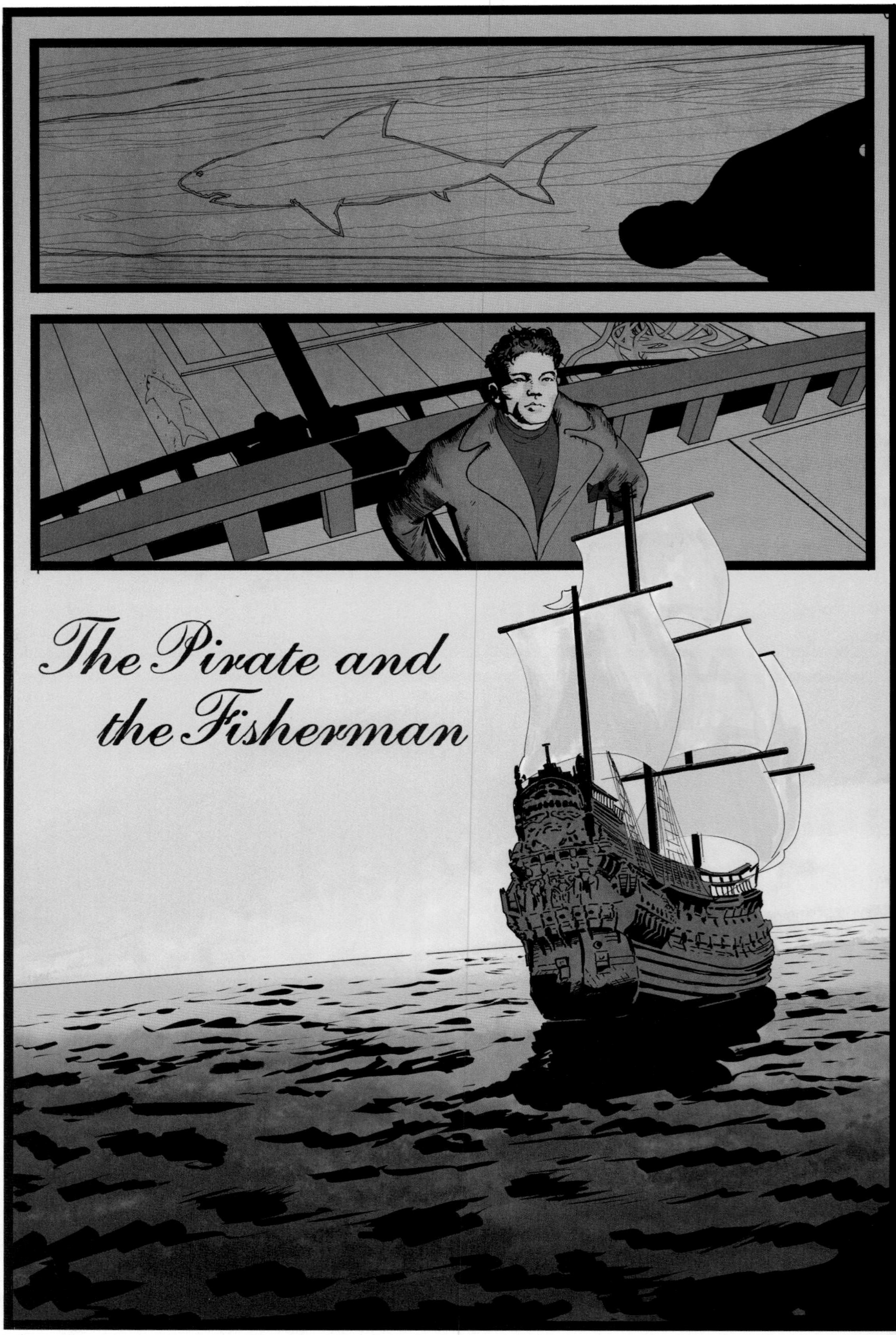
The Pirate and
the Fisherman

GROUNDED

ART

VANESA **DEL REY**

COLORS

JUHA **VELTTI**

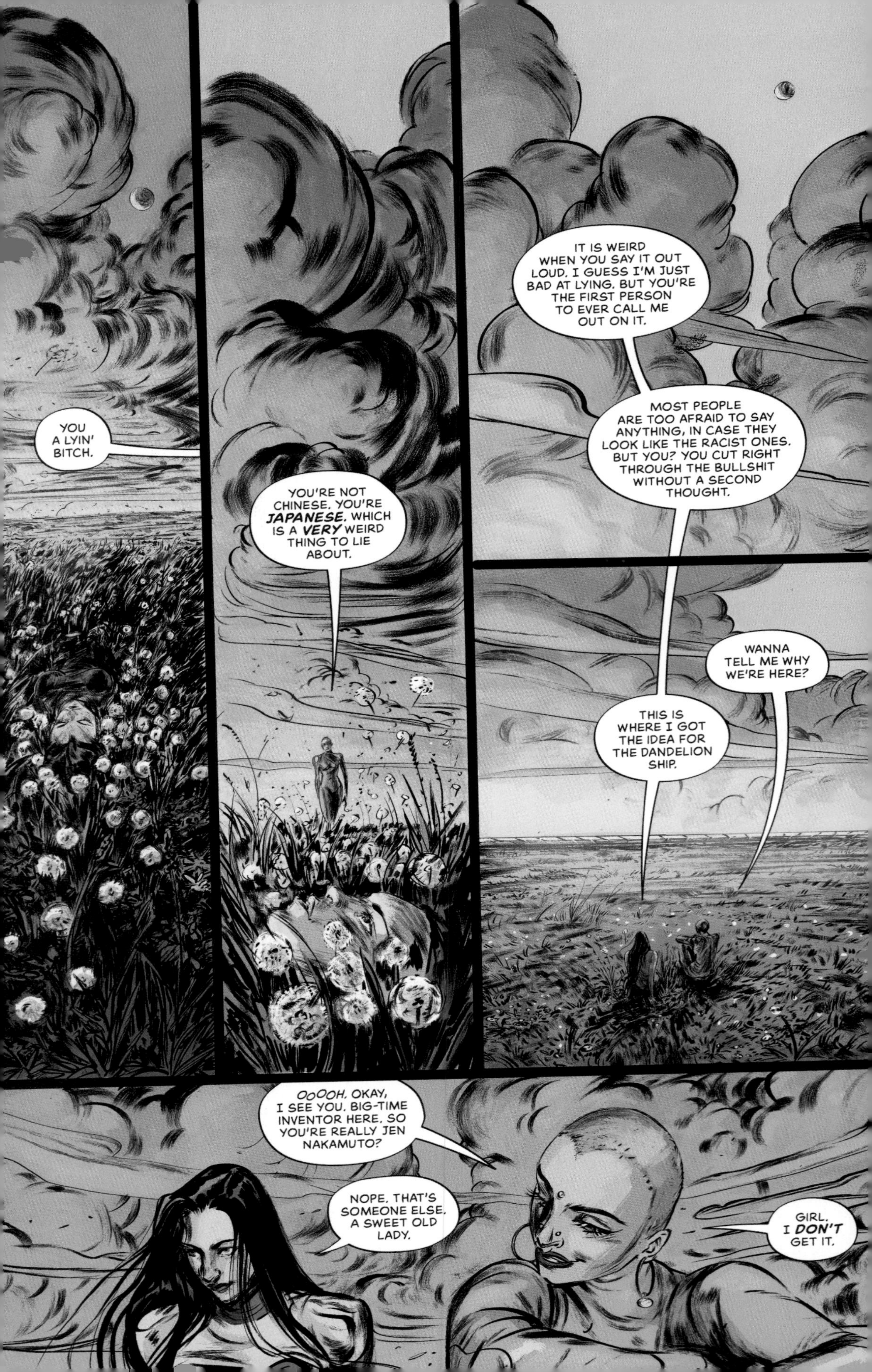
YOU A LYIN' BITCH.
YOU'RE NOT CHINESE. YOU'RE **JAPANESE.** WHICH IS A **VERY** WEIRD THING TO LIE ABOUT.
IT IS WEIRD WHEN YOU SAY IT OUT LOUD. I GUESS I'M JUST BAD AT LYING. BUT YOU'RE THE FIRST PERSON TO EVER CALL ME OUT ON IT.
MOST PEOPLE ARE TOO AFRAID TO SAY ANYTHING, IN CASE THEY LOOK LIKE THE RACIST ONES. BUT YOU? YOU CUT RIGHT THROUGH THE BULLSHIT WITHOUT A SECOND THOUGHT.
WANNA TELL ME WHY WE'RE HERE?
THIS IS WHERE I GOT THE IDEA FOR THE DANDELION SHIP.
OOOOH, OKAY, I SEE YOU, BIG-TIME INVENTOR HERE. SO YOU'RE REALLY JEN NAKAMUTO?
NOPE. THAT'S SOMEONE ELSE, A SWEET OLD LADY.
GIRL, I **DON'T** GET IT.

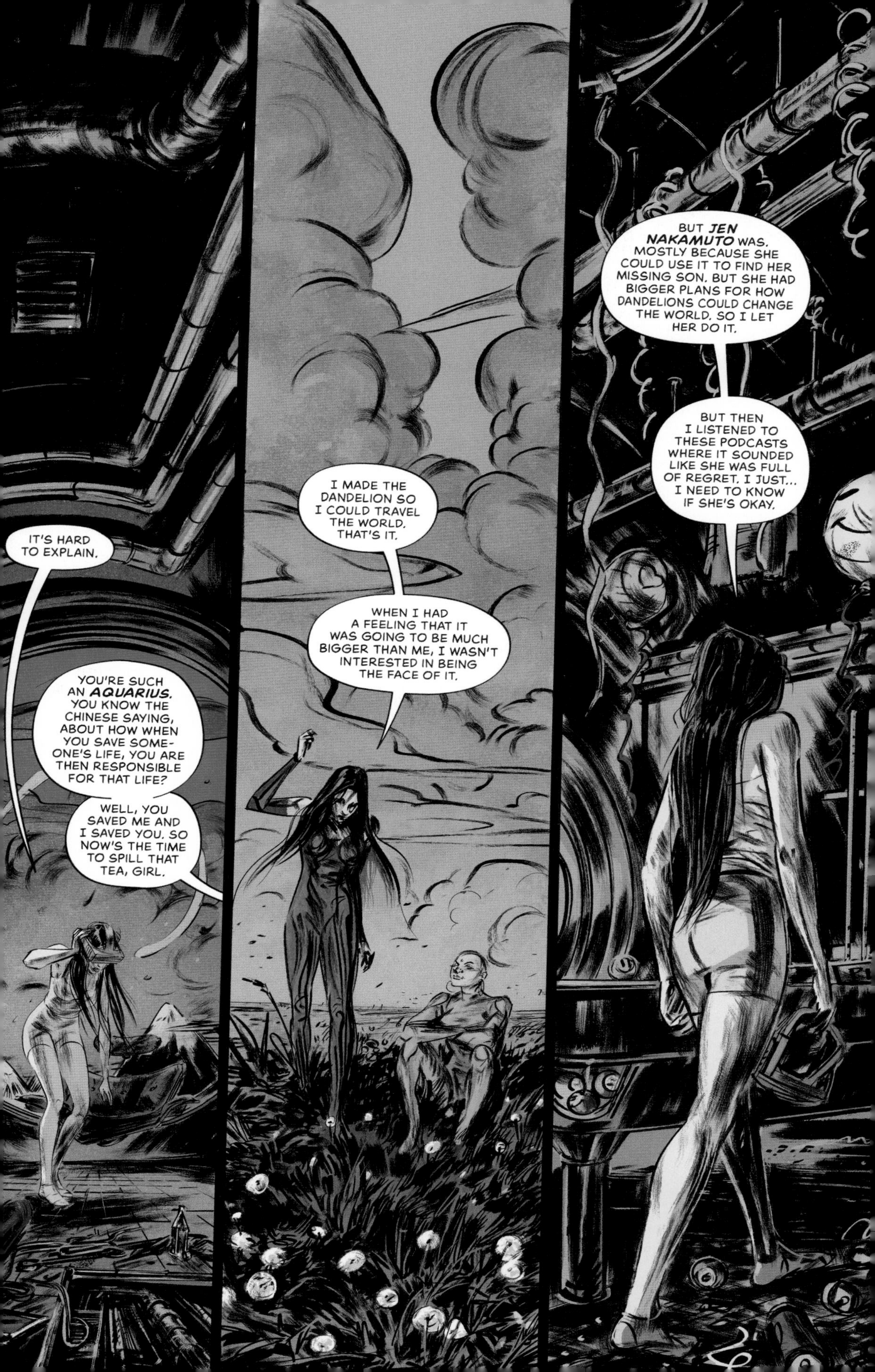
IT'S HARD TO EXPLAIN.
YOU'RE SUCH AN AQUARIUS. YOU KNOW THE CHINESE SAYING, ABOUT HOW WHEN YOU SAVE SOME-ONE'S LIFE, YOU ARE THEN RESPONSIBLE FOR THAT LIFE?
WELL, YOU SAVED ME AND I SAVED YOU, SO NOW'S THE TIME TO SPILL THAT TEA, GIRL.
I MADE THE DANDELION SO I COULD TRAVEL THE WORLD. THAT'S IT.
WHEN I HAD A FEELING THAT IT WAS GOING TO BE MUCH BIGGER THAN ME, I WASN'T INTERESTED IN BEING THE FACE OF IT.
BUT JEN NAKAMUTO WAS. MOSTLY BECAUSE SHE COULD USE IT TO FIND HER MISSING SON. BUT SHE HAD BIGGER PLANS FOR HOW DANDELIONS COULD CHANGE THE WORLD. SO I LET HER DO IT.
BUT THEN I LISTENED TO THESE PODCASTS WHERE IT SOUNDED LIKE SHE WAS FULL OF REGRET. I JUST... I NEED TO KNOW IF SHE'S OKAY.

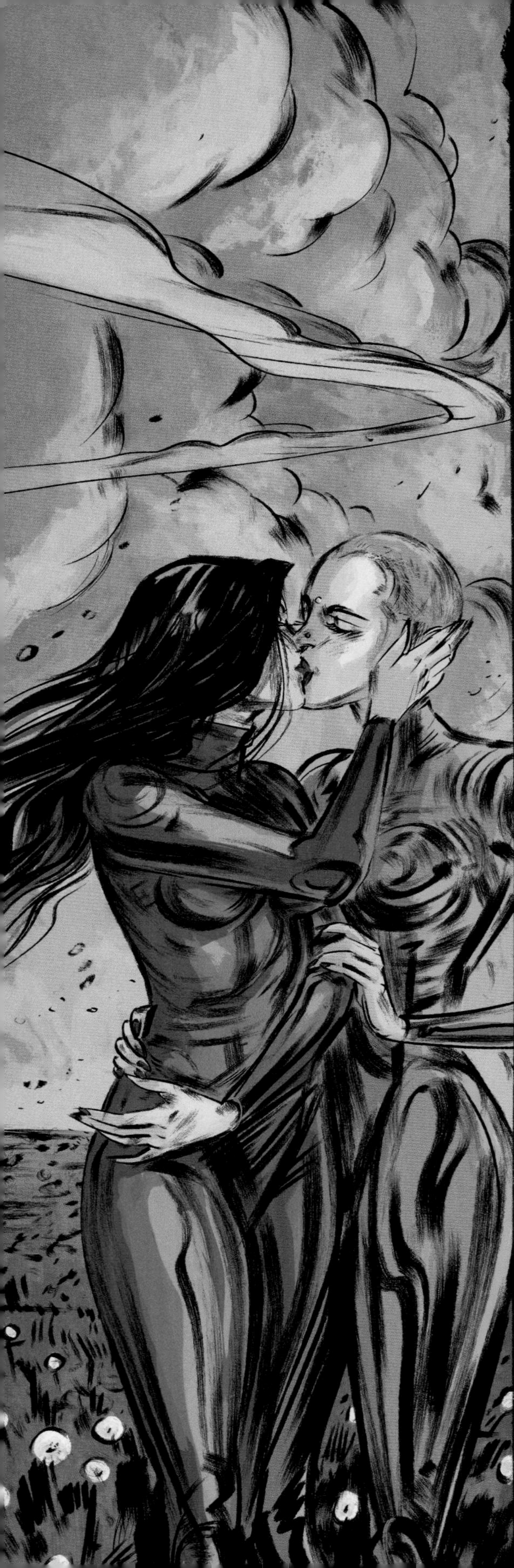

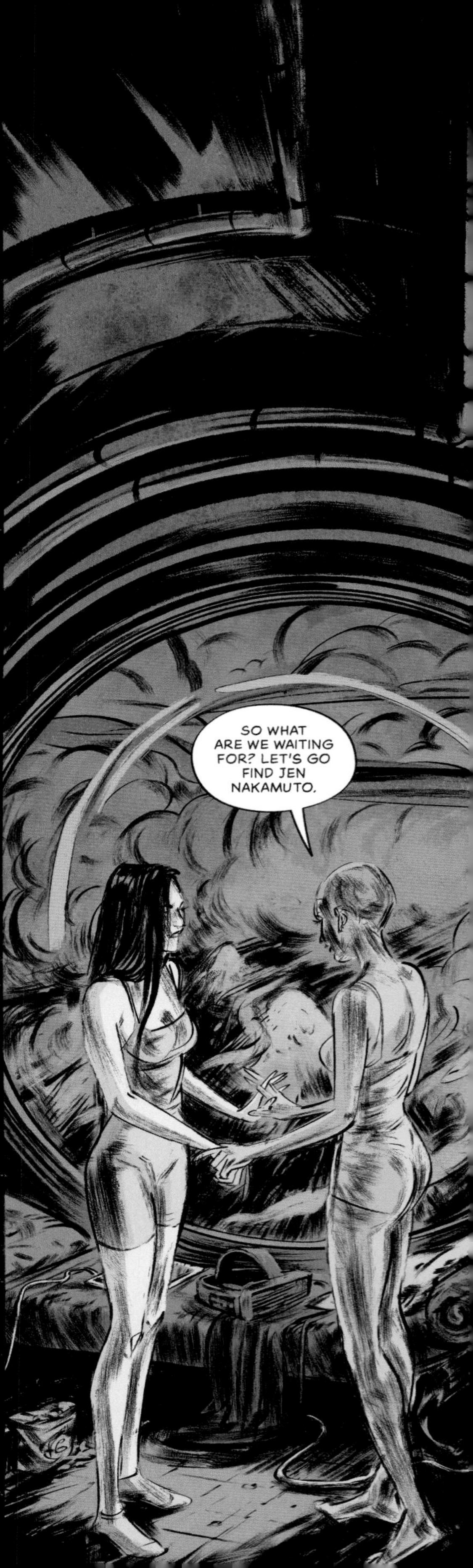
SO WHAT ARE WE WAITING FOR? LET'S GO FIND JEN NAKAMUTO.

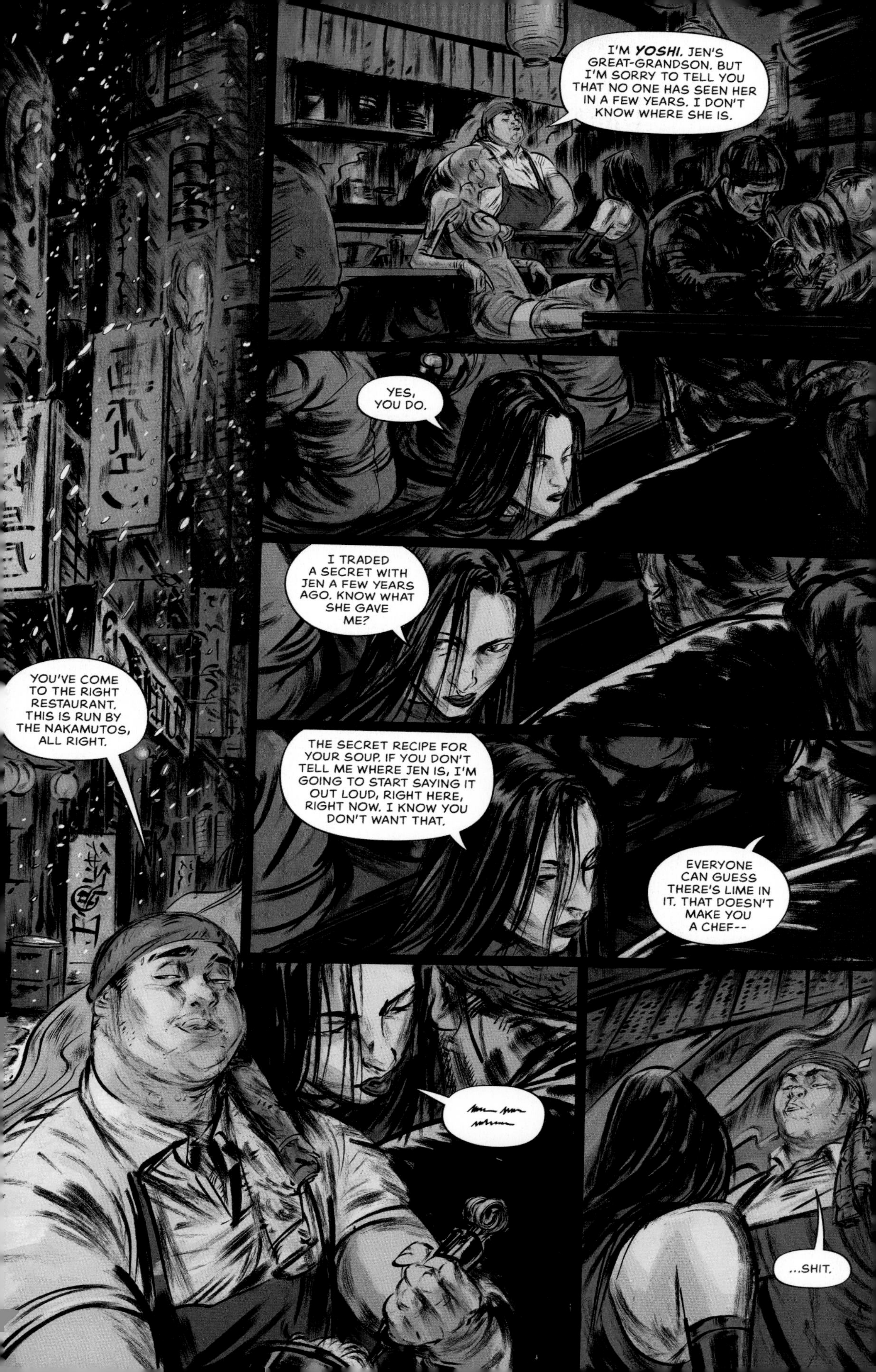
YOU'VE COME TO THE RIGHT RESTAURANT. THIS IS RUN BY THE NAKAMUTOS, ALL RIGHT.
I'M YOSHI. JEN'S GREAT-GRANDSON. BUT I'M SORRY TO TELL YOU THAT NO ONE HAS SEEN HER IN A FEW YEARS. I DON'T KNOW WHERE SHE IS.
YES, YOU DO.
I TRADED A SECRET WITH JEN A FEW YEARS AGO. KNOW WHAT SHE GAVE ME?
THE SECRET RECIPE FOR YOUR SOUP. IF YOU DON'T TELL ME WHERE JEN IS, I'M GOING TO START SAYING IT OUT LOUD, RIGHT HERE, RIGHT NOW. I KNOW YOU DON'T WANT THAT.
EVERYONE CAN GUESS THERE'S LIME IN IT. THAT DOESN'T MAKE YOU A CHEF--
...SHIT.

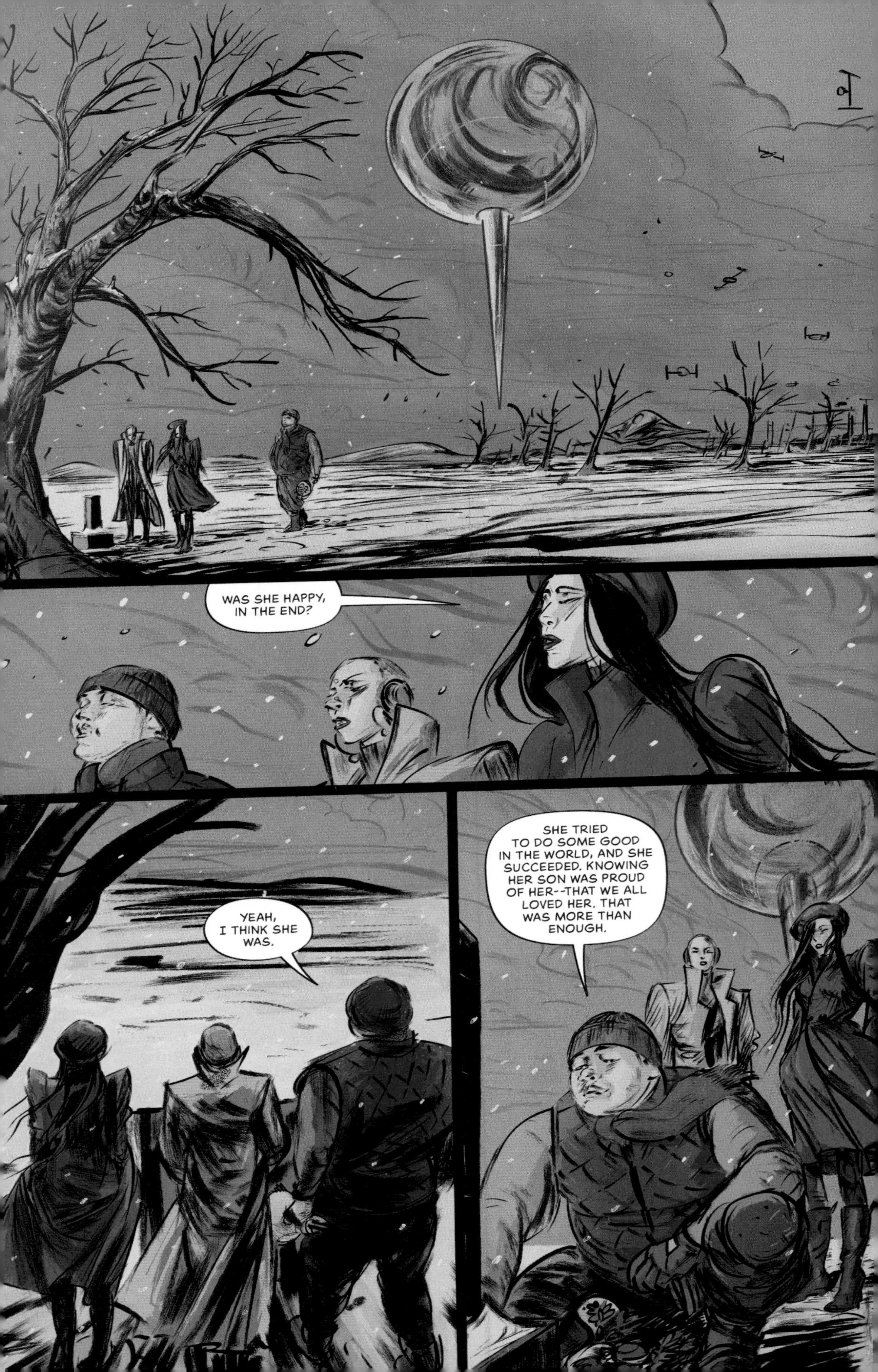
WAS SHE HAPPY, IN THE END?
YEAH, I THINK SHE WAS.
SHE TRIED TO DO SOME GOOD IN THE WORLD, AND SHE SUCCEEDED. KNOWING HER SON WAS PROUD OF HER--THAT WE ALL LOVED HER. THAT WAS MORE THAN ENOUGH.

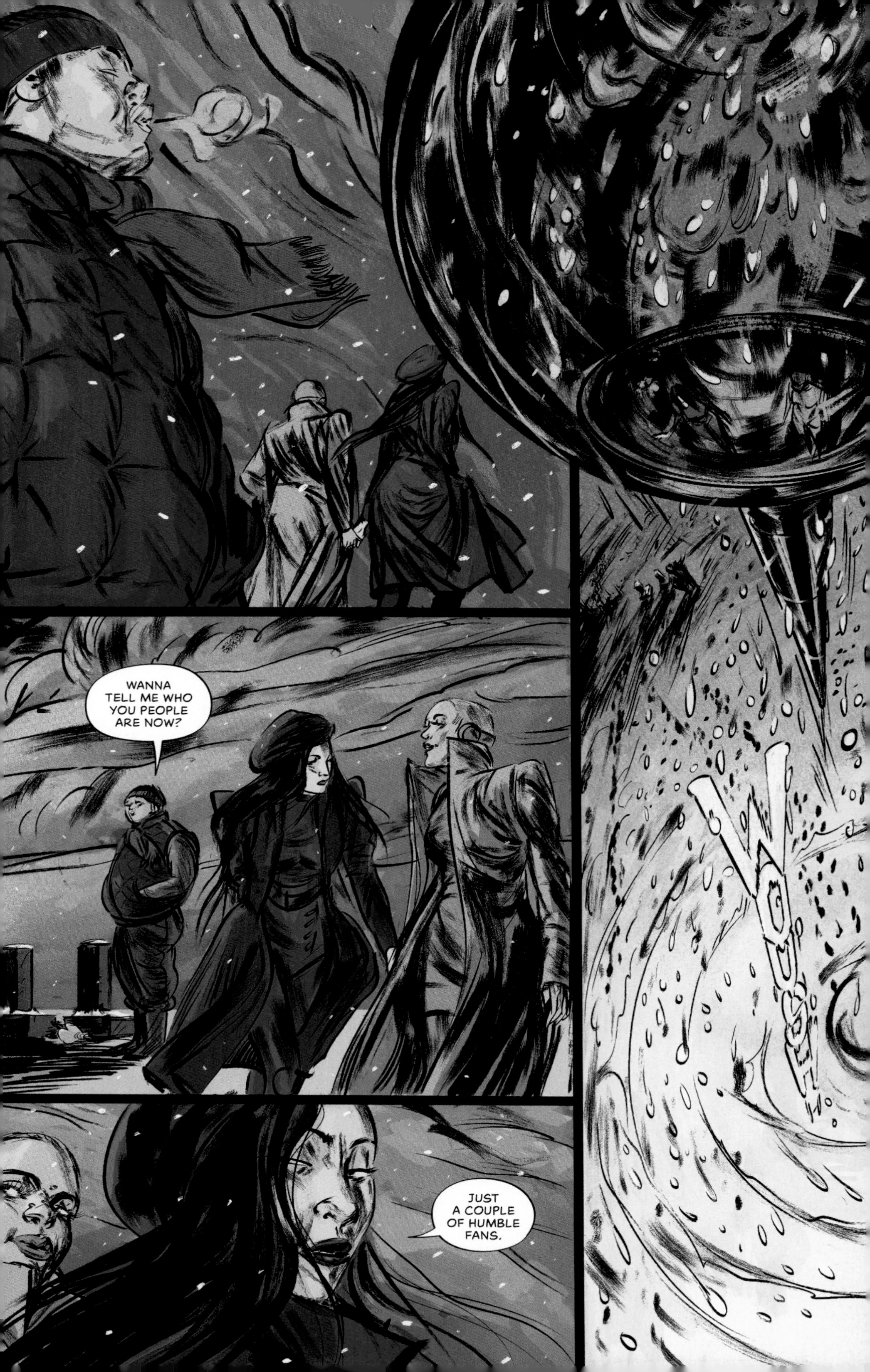
WANNA TELL ME WHO YOU PEOPLE ARE NOW?
JUST A COUPLE OF HUMBLE FANS.

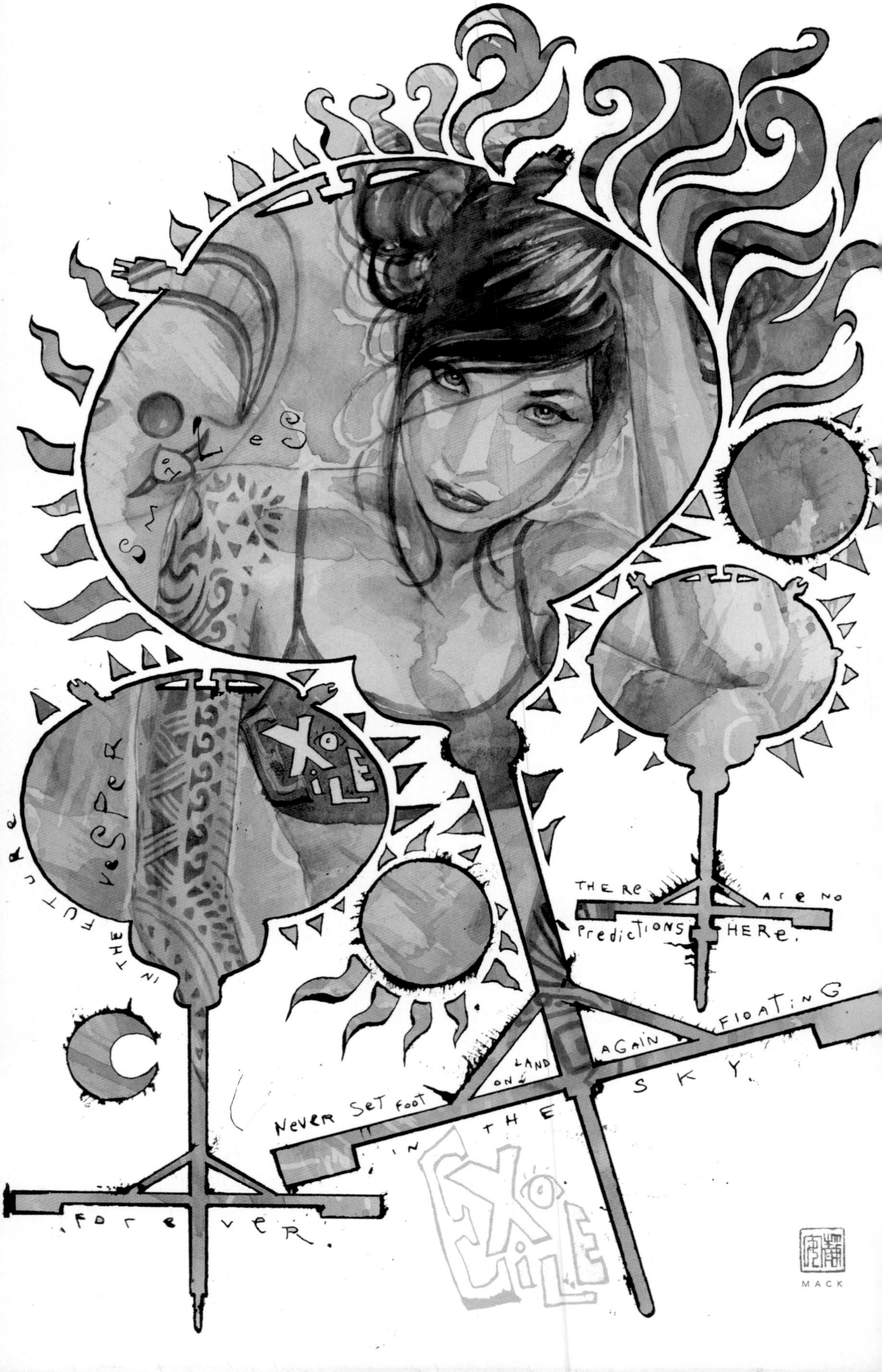

EXILE
IN THE FUTURE
VESPER
THERE ARE NO PREDICTIONS HERE.
NEVER SET FOOT ON LAND AGAIN FLOATING IN THE SKY.
FOREVER.
EXILE
MACK